SEAN O'CASEY: A BIBLIOGRAPHY OF CRITICISM

SEAN O'CASEY:
A BIBLIOGRAPHY OF
CRITICISM

by

E. H. MIKHAIL

With an introduction by
RONALD AYLING

University of Washington Press
Seattle

© E. H. Mikhail 1972

Published by the University of Washington Press 1972

Library of Congress Catalog Card Number 76-37007

International Standard Book Number 0-295-95167-2

Printed in Great Britain

Contents

v

Introduction

Serious students of Sean O'Casey's writings have long felt the need for three practical reference tools above all else: an edition of the playwright's correspondence, a detailed bibliography of his publications, and a really comprehensive checklist of critical literature concerning his life and work. It is pleasant to record that all three works are now well on the way to completion.

The *Collected Letters*, edited by Professor David Krause, are to appear in three volumes. This edition will assuredly be far more than a tool of reference. A monument to the life and thoughts of an extraordinary man, it will in my view also be a work of art in its own right. Naturally, the correspondence has considerable literary and theatrical value; far transcending this, however, is its realisation in many different moods and manners of a man who reveals deep compassion for the human condition and a great diversity of activities and interests. O'Casey's concern for all sorts and conditions of men, his receptivity to all aspects of human experience, and his inexhaustible comic spirit are manifest in letters (some to complete strangers) throughout a long and full life. Indeed, to my mind, among major contemporary authors only D. H. Lawrence can compare with O'Casey as a letter writer so far as breadth of human interest is concerned. The letters of Joyce, T. S. Eliot, Yeats, and even Shaw are anaemic in comparison.

A full-scale *Bibliography of O'Casey's Published Writings*, compiled by Michael J. Durkan and Ronald Ayling, is in the final stages of preparation. The volume will include a complete list of unpublished manuscripts and typescripts, together with details of major stage productions of O'Casey's plays. It should therefore serve to complement both the *Letters* and the present indispensable work of reference that you have before you.

It is obvious that a great deal of painstaking research has been put to intelligent use (a fact not always so apparent in critical checklists) in Professor Edward Mikhail's bibliography of O'Casey criticism. I have watched with growing admiration while the work has progressed from a relatively short checklist to its eventual breadth of scope, noting with approval the various practical improvements to its overall approach and structure made in the interests of readers with different bibliographical purposes in mind. It is now by far the most comprehensive bibliography on the subject and, what is perhaps just as important, it is admirably designed for speedy reference by students with a particular book, article or review in mind as well as for more detailed scholarly research. I am pleased to record my appreciation of an exacting task finely accomplished and to endorse the book's great usefulness for scholars and critics in an area of criticism that – as the bibliography itself demonstrates – is assuming greater proportions with each passing year.

RONALD AYLING

Edmonton, Canada
June 1971

Preface

Studies of Sean O'Casey have recently been on the increase. Some forty dissertations have so far been written on the Irish playwright. Hardly a month passes without a book or an article on him appearing. Professor William A. Armstrong is preparing a second edition of his bibliographical study for the British Council series. Dr Ronald Ayling is engaged on both a biography and, with Michael J. Durkan, a bibliography of the writings of the dramatist. Dr David Krause has almost completed his edition of O'Casey's letters. Mrs Eileen O'Casey's personal memoir of her husband, entitled *Sean*, is to be published at the end of this year.*

A bibliography of critical studies of Sean O'Casey is, therefore, overdue. Checklists and selected bibliographies have appeared separately or incorporated in books and periodicals. Otto Brandstädter's 'Eine O'Casey-Bibliographie', *Zeitschrift für Anglistik und Amerikanistik* (Berlin), II (1954) 204–54, was the most complete bibliography up to that year, but was weak on English material and contained several factual errors and many omissions. Charles A. Carpenter's 'Sean O'Casey Studies through 1964', *Modern Drama*, X 1 (May 1967) 17–23, which was reprinted in *The Sean O'Casey Reader*, ed. Brooks Atkinson (New York: St Martin's Press; London: Macmillan, 1968) pp. 993–9, was only selective and did not include anything after the playwright's death in 1964. I. M. Levidova and B. M. Parchevskaya's *Shon O'Keisi Biobibliograficheskii Ukazatel* (Moscow: Izdatel'stvo 'Kniga', 1964) is the fullest all-round bibliography to date, but it has many gaps in English and American coverage.

The present Bibliography, which comprises some 2500 entries, has entailed work for four years in more than twenty university and public libraries. This is not to draw attention to its completeness, but rather to ask pardon for any possible shortcomings. I have attempted to make it complete until the end of the year 1970, although some later studies have been included. The groundwork has been set up by systematically checking the general bibliographical aids listed at the end of this Preface.

I am indebted to the University of Lethbridge for granting me

---

* Since this Preface was written, the memoir has been published by Macmillan in September 1971.

sabbatical leave, which has made the completion of this work possible. I am also grateful to the Canada Council for awarding me research grants for four years in succession, which enabled me to travel and compile my material. Every help has been extended to me by the University of Lethbridge Library; the British Museum Library; the Newspaper Library at Colindale; the British Drama League Library; the Senate House Library; the National Library of Ireland; Trinity College Library; Leicester Public Library; Birmingham Public Library; Manchester Public Library; the Bodleian Library; and the New York Public Library.

It is physically impossible to list, or to recall, all those people who have assisted me in my work. A few persons, however, should be mentioned. From the very beginning Dr Ronald Ayling has been keenly interested in this Bibliography, which he has encouraged and criticised until it has taken its final shape. Mr John O'Riordan has graciously donated to me his valuable collection of reviews of O'Casey's plays which I have finally incorporated into my work. In addition, he has always been willing to answer any queries and to supply me with the necessary information during my stay in London. I have also received considerable help from Professor William A. Armstrong, Professor Bernard Benstock, Professor David Krause, Mr Richard Findlater, Dr Lila Maitra, Dr Carmela Moya and Dr Saros Cowasjee.

The following bibliographies have been used to form the basis of my work:

Abstracts of English Studies, 1958 to present (Boulder, Col.: National Council of Teachers of English).

Annual Bibliography of English Language and Literature, 1920 to present (London: Modern Humanities Research Association).

Cambridge Bibliography of English Literature, 5 vols (Cambridge: Cambridge University Press).

Cumulative Book Index, 1928 to present (New York: H. W. Wilson).

Dissertation Abstracts, 1938 to present (Ann Arbor, Mich.: University Microfilms).

Dissertations in English and American Literature: Theses Accepted by American, British and German Universities, 1865–1964, by Lawrence F. McNamee (New York and London: R. R. Bowker, 1968).

Doctoral Dissertations Accepted by American Universities, ed. Arnold H. Trotier and Marian Harman (New York: H. W. Wilson, 1933–55). Continued as *Index to American Doctoral Dissertations*, 1955 to present.

Dramatic Index, 1909–1949 (Boston: F. W. Faxon).

Essay and General Literature Index, 1900 to present (New York: H. W. Wilson).

Index to Little Magazines, 1943 to present (Denver: Alan Swallow).

Index to One-Act Plays, comp. by Hannah Logasa and Winifred Ver Nooy (Boston: F. W. Faxon, 1924); *Supplement, 1924–1931* (Boston: F. W. Faxon, 1932); *Second Supplement, 1932–1940* (Boston: F. W. Faxon, 1941); *Third Supplement, 1941–1948* (Boston: F. W. Faxon, 1950); *Fourth Supplement, 1948–1957* (Boston: F. W. Faxon, 1958).

Index to Plays 1800–1926, comp. by Ina Ten Eyck Firkins (New York: H. W. Wilson, 1927).

Index to Plays: Supplement, comp. by Ina Ten Eyck Firkins (New York: H. W. Wilson, 1935).

Index to Plays in Collections, ed. John H. Ottemiller (Washington: The Scarecrow Press, 1951).

Index to Theses Accepted for Higher Degrees in the Universities of Great Britain and Ireland, 1950 to present (London: ASLIB).

International Index to Periodicals, 1907 to present (New York: H. W. Wilson). From vol. xix (Apr. 1965–Mar. 1966) called *Social Sciences and Humanities Index*.

Masters Abstracts, 1962 to present (Ann Arbor, Mich.: University Microfilms).

New York Times Index.

PMLA Bibliography.

Play Index 1949–1952: An Index to 2626 Plays in 1138 Volumes, comp. by Dorothy Herbert West and Dorothy Margaret Peake (New York: H. W. Wilson, 1953).

Readers' Guide to Periodical Literature, 1900 to present (New York: H. W. Wilson).

Subject Index to Periodicals, 1915–61 (London: The Library Association). Continued as *British Humanities Index*, 1962 to present.

Theatre Dissertations, ed. Frederic M. Litto (Kent, Ohio: Kent State University Press, 1969).

The Times Index.

Year's Work in English Studies, 1919 to present (London: The English Association).

London
April 1971

E. H. MIKHAIL

Part I

BIBLIOGRAPHIES

BIBLIOGRAPHIES

ADELMAN, IRVING, and DWORKIN, RITA, 'Sean O'Casey', *Modern Drama: A Checklist of Critical Literature on 20th Century Plays* (Metuchen, N.J.: The Scarecrow Press, 1967) pp. 206–10.

ARMSTRONG, WILLIAM A., 'A Select Bibliography', *Sean O'Casey* (London: Longmans, 1967) pp. 35–9.

AYLING, RONALD (ed.), 'Select Bibliography', *Sean O'Casey* (London: Macmillan, 1969) pp. 261–9.

BLACK, H. M., 'A Check-List of First Editions of Works by Lord Dunsany and Sean O'Casey', *T.C.D. Annual Bulletin* (Dublin), (1957) 4–9.

BRANDSTÄDTER, OTTO, 'Eine O'Casey-Bibliographie', *Zeitschrift für Anglistik und Amerikanistik* (Berlin), II (1954) 240–54.

CARPENTER, CHARLES A., 'Sean O'Casey Studies through 1964', *Modern Drama*, X 1 (May 1967) 17–23. Reprinted in *The Sean O'Casey Reader*, ed. Brooks Atkinson (New York: St Martin's Press; London: Macmillan, 1968) pp. 993–9.

COLEMAN, ARTHUR, and TYLER, GARY R., 'Sean O'Casey', *Drama Criticism*, vol. I: *A Checklist of Interpretation since 1940 of English and American Plays* (Denver: Alan Swallow, 1966) pp. 154–6.

COWASJEE, SAROS, 'Bibliography', *Sean O'Casey: The Man Behind the Plays* (Edinburgh and London: Oliver & Boyd, 1963) pp. 256–61.
'Bibliography', *O'Casey* (Edinburgh and London: Oliver & Boyd, 1966) pp. 116–20.

EAGER, ALAN R., *A Guide to Irish Bibliographical Material: Being a Bibliography of Irish Bibliographies and Some Sources of Information* (London: The Library Association, 1964).

HARMON, MAURICE, *Modern Irish Literature, 1800–1967: A Reader's Guide* (Dublin: The Dolmen Press, 1967).

HOGAN, ROBERT, 'Bibliography: Sean O'Casey', *After the Irish Renaissance: A Critical History of the Irish Drama since 'The Plough and the Stars'* (Minneapolis: University of Minnesota Press, 1967; London, Macmillan, 1968) p. 271.

3

LEVIDOVA, I. M., and PARCHEVSKAYA, B. M., *Shon O'Keisi Biobibliograficheskii Ukazatel* (Moscow: Izdatel'stvo 'Kniga', 1964).

MACNAMARA, BRINSLEY (ed.), *Abbey Plays 1899–1948: Including the Productions of The Irish Literary Theatre* (Dublin: At the Sign of The Three Candles, n.d. [1949]). [Incorrect date for first production of *The Shadow of a Gunman*.]

MILLET, FRED B., *Contemporary British Literature: A Critical Survey and 232 Author-Bibliographies*, 3rd rev. and enl. edition, ed. John M. Manly and Edith Rickert (New York: Harcourt, Brace, 1944) p. 399.

PALMER, HELEN H., and DYSON, ANNA JANE (comps.), 'Sean O'Casey', *European Drama Criticism* (Hamden, Conn.: The Shoe String Press, 1968) pp. 300–5.

Part II

BOOKS BY SEAN O'CASEY
AND THEIR REVIEWS

(a) Collected Works

COLLECTED PLAYS, 4 vols (London and New York: Macmillan, 1949–51):

Vol. 1: *Juno and the Paycock. The Shadow of a Gunman. The Plough and the Stars. The End of the Beginning. A Pound on Demand* (1949)

Vol. 2: *The Silver Tassie. Within the Gates. The Star Turns Red* (1949)

Vol. 3: *Purple Dust. Red Roses for Me. Hall of Healing* (1951)

Vol. 4: *Oak Leaves and Lavender. Cock-a-Doodle Dandy. Bed-time Story. Time to Go* (1951).

Reviewed in *Times Literary Supplement* (London), (9 Dec 1949) p. 806 and (21 Sep 1951) p. 596; by G[erard] F[ay] in *Manchester Guardian* (28 Dec 1949) p. 5 and (14 Aug 1951) p. 4; by John Garrett in *Spectator* (London), CLXXXIV (24 Feb 1950), 248; by Clifford Odets in *New York Times Book Review* (5 Feb 1950) p. 5; by Brooks Atkinson in *New York Times* (16 Sep 1951) section 2, p. 1; by Francis Russell in *Christian Science Monitor* (Boston), (25 Feb 1950) p. 6; and by W. R. W. in *San Francisco Chronicle* (9 Apr 1950) p. 15.

MIRROR IN MY HOUSE: THE AUTOBIOGRAPHIES OF SEAN O'CASEY, 2 vols (New York: Macmillan, 1956). Reprinted as *Autobiographies*, 2 vols (London: Macmillan, 1963). Contains six volumes of autobiography:

Vol. 1: *I Knock at the Door*

Vol. 2: *Pictures in the Hallway*

Vol. 3: *Drums under the Windows*

Vol. 4: *Inishfallen, Fare Thee Well*

Vol. 5: *Rose and Crown*

Vol. 6: *Sunset and Evening Star.*

Reviewed by Granville Hicks in *New Republic* (N.Y.), CXXXV (22 Oct 1956) 17–18; in *New York Herald Tribune Book Review* (28 Oct 1956) p. 17; by David H. Greene in *Commonweal* (N.Y.), LXV (25 Jan 1957) 440–3; by John O'Shaughnessy in *Nation* (N.Y.), CLXXXIV (16 Mar 1957) 237–9; by Marvin Magalaner in *Sewanee Review*, LXV 1 (winter 1957) 170–4; in *Times* (London), (3 Oct 1963) p. 15; in *Times Literary Supplement* (London), (6 Sep 1963) p. 674; by Robert Nye in *Scotsman* (Edinburgh), (7 Sep 1963) p. 2; by

Valentin Iremonger in *Spectator* (London), CCXI (27 Sep 1963) 391; by John Wain in *Observer* (London), (11 Aug 1963) p. 16; by Padraic Fallon in *Irish Times* (Dublin), (17 Aug 1963) p. 6; and by J. Krehayen in *Neues Deutschland* (Berlin), (16 Nov 1963), p. 53.

(b) Separate works

SONGS OF THE WREN, 1st and 2nd series (Dublin and London: Maunsel, 1918).

MORE WREN SONGS (Dublin and London: Maunsel, 1918).

THE STORY OF THOMAS ASHE (Dublin and London: Maunsel, 1918).

THE SACRIFICE OF THOMAS ASHE (Dublin and London: Maunsel, 1918).

THE STORY OF THE IRISH CITIZEN ARMY (Dublin and London: Maunsel, 1919). Published under pseudonym 'P. O'Cathasaigh'.

Reviewed by E[imar] O'D[uffy] in *Irish Statesman* (Dublin), 1 3 (12 July 1919) 71.

TWO PLAYS (London and New York: Macmillan, 1925). Contains *Juno and the Paycock* and *The Shadow of a Gunman*.

Reviewed in *Times Literary Supplement* (London), (19 Feb 1925) p. 117; by Bonamy Dobree in *Nation and Athenaeum* (London), XXXVI (Mar 1925) 891; by C. E. Lawrence in *Bookman* (London), LXVIII (Apr 1925) 68–9; in *Spectator* (London), CXXXIV (14 Mar 1925) 415–16; in *New Statesman* (London), XXV 625 (18 Apr 1925) 20; by A. E. [George Russell] in *Irish Statesman* (Dublin), III 26 (7 Mar 1925) 822–3; in *Irish Book Lover* (Dublin), XV 1 (Jan 1925) 30; by W. D. in *Studies: An Irish Quarterly Review* (Dublin), XIV 55 (Sep 1925) 493–5; by Stark Young in *New York Times* (14 June 1925) section 8, p. 1; by Padraic Colum in *Theatre Arts Monthly* (N.Y.), IX (June 1925) 397–404; by Joseph Campbell in *Saturday Review of Literature* (N.Y.), II 5 (29 Aug 1925) 78–9; by Walter Prichard Eaton in *New York Herald Tribune Books* (29 Mar 1925) p. 9; by F. W. B. in *Boston Evening Transcript* (14 Mar 1925) Book Section, p. 5; by J. Ranken Towse in *New York Evening Post Literary Review* (21 Mar 1925) p. 5; in *New York Times Book*

Review (8 Mar 1925) p. 5; and in *Independent* (Boston), CXVII (18 Sep 1926) 332.

THE PLOUGH AND THE STARS (London and New York: Macmillan, 1926).

Reviewed in *Times Literary Supplement* (London), (15 Apr 1926) p. 280; by S. R. Littlewood in *Bookman* (London), LXX 416 (May 1926) 128–30; by Ivor Brown in *Saturday Review* (London), CXLI (10 Apr 1926) 473; in *Contemporary Review* (London), CXXX (July 1926) 123–5; by Walter Prichard Eaton in *New York Herald Tribune Books* (16 May 1926) pp. 9, 18; by Padraic Colum in *Saturday Review of Literature* (N.Y.), II (12 June 1926) 854; in *Independent* (Boston), XCVII (18 Sep 1926) 332; and in *Living Age* (Boston), CCCXXIX (22 May 1926) 432.

THE SILVER TASSIE (London and New York: Macmillan, 1928).

Reviewed in *Times Literary Supplement* (London), (5 July 1928) p. 501; by Paul Banks in *New English Weekly* (London), III 19 (24 Aug 1933) 446–7 [see reply by O'Casey, III 22 (14 Sep 1933) 520–1; counter-reply by Paul Banks, III 23 (21 Sep 1933) 541–2; and counter-counter-reply by O'Casey, III 26 (12 Oct 1933) 622–3]; by I. B. in *Manchester Guardian Weekly*, XVIII 25 (22 June 1928) 493; by Ivor Brown in *Saturday Review* (London), CXLV (23 June 1928) 801–2; by Y. O. [George Russell] in *Irish Statesman* (Dublin), X 20 (21 July 1928) 391–2 [see reply by O'Casey, X 22 (4 Aug 1928) 430–1; and counter-reply by Y. O., X 22 (4 Aug 1928) 431]; by A. E. M. in *Irish Book Lover* (Dublin), XVI 4–6 (July–Dec 1928) 109–11; in *Independent* (Boston), CXXI (18 Aug 1928) 165; by J. F. S. in *Boston Evening Transcript* (11 Aug 1928) Book Section, p. 2; and by Jane Dransfield in *Saturday Review of Literature* (N.Y.), V 21 (15 Dec 1928) 516.

WITHIN THE GATES London: Macmillan, 1933; New York: Macmillan, 1934).

Reviewed in *Times* (London), (28 Nov 1933) p. 12; in *Times Literary Supplement* (London), (7 Dec 1933) p. 872 and (24 Jan 1935) p. 37; by Osbert Burdett in *London Mercury*, XXX 175 (May 1934) 667–8; by A. G. Stock in *Socialist Review* (London), V 10 (Jan 1934) 46–9; by Hugh MacDiarmid in *Scots Observer* (Edinburgh), VIII 386 (17 Feb 1934) 7; by I. B. in *Manchester Guardian*

Weekly, XXIX 25 (22 Dec 1933) 495; by Brooks Atkinson in *New York Times* (31 Dec 1933) section 9, p. 1; by George Jean Nathan in *Vanity Fair* (N.Y.), XLI (Jan 1934) 42, 56; by Henry Ten Eyck Perry in *Yale Review*, XXIII 4 (summer 1934) 842–4; in *Saturday Review of Literature* (N.Y.), XI 16 (3 Nov 1934) 256; by Walter Prichard Eaton in *New York Herald Tribune Books* (28 Jan 1934) p. 17; by M[orton] D. Z[abel] in *Poetry* (Chicago), XLV (Dec 1934) 152–8; by V. Geddes in *New Masses* (N.Y.), no. 5 (30 Jan 1934) 25; and by A. Brulé in *Revue Anglo-Américaine* (Paris), année XI 5 (June 1934) 463–5.

WINDFALLS (London and New York: Macmillan, 1934). [Contains early poems, short stories and two plays, *The End of the Beginning* and *A Pound on Demand*.]

Reviewed in *Times Literary Supplement* (London), (8 Nov 1934) p. 770; by St John Ervine in *Observer* (London), (11 Nov 1934) p. 4; in *Spectator* (London) CLIII (16 Nov 1934) 772; by Desmond MacCarthy in *Sunday Times* (London), (28 Oct 1934) p. 8; by Samuel Beckett in *Bookman* (London), LXXXVI (Christmas 1934) 111; by Peter Monro Jack in *New York Times Book Review* (11 Nov 1934) p. 8; by Horace Gregory in *New York Herald Tribune Books* (25 Nov 1934) p. 16; and in *Theatre Arts Monthly* (N.Y.), XVIII (Dec 1934) 962–3.

THE FLYING WASP: A LAUGHING LOOK-OVER OF WHAT HAS BEEN SAID ABOUT THE THINGS OF THE THEATRE BY THE ENGLISH DRAMATIC CRITICS (London and New York: Macmillan, 1937).

Reviewed in *Times Literary Supplement* (London), (13 Mar 1937), p. 184; by D. Walker-Smith in *English Review* (London), LXIV (May 1937) 625–6; by Derek Verschoyle in *Spectator* (London), CLVIII (26 Mar 1937) 591–2; by James Agate in *Sunday Times* (London), (21 Mar 1937) p. 6 [see O'Casey's reply (28 Mar 1937) p. 5]; by J. S. Collis in *London Mercury*, XXXVI 211 (May 1937) 93; by James Agate in *John O'London's Weekly*, XXXVI (19 Mar 1937) 1000, 1026 [see replies by Hugh Ross Williamson, XXXVII (2 Apr 1937) 25–6, and O'Casey, XXXVII (9 Apr 1937) 39]; in *Dublin Magazine*, XII (July–Sep 1937) 86; by Peter Monro Jack in *New York Times Book Review* (13 June 1937) p. 6; by H. H. in *Christian Science Monitor Weekly Magazine* (Boston), XXIX 182 (30 June

1937) 11; by Walter Prichard Eaton in *New York Herald Tribune Books* (10 Oct 1937) p. 28; by B[arnard] H[ewitt] in *Quarterly Journal of Speech* (Chicago), XXIII (Dec 1937) 672; and by L. A. MacKay in *Canadian Forum* (Toronto), XVII (June 1937) 143.

I KNOCK AT THE DOOR: SWIFT GLANCES BACK AT THINGS THAT MADE ME (London and New York: Macmillan, 1939).

Reviewed in *Times* (London), (3 Mar 1939) p. 21; in *Times Literary Supplement* (London), (4 Mar 1939) p. 131; by Desmond MacCarthy in *Sunday Times* (London), (19 Mar 1939) p. 6 [reprinted in *Living Age* (Boston), CCCLVI (June 1939) 391–4]; by G. W. Stonier in *New Statesman and Nation* (London), XVII (11 Mar 1939) 396; by Howard Spring in *Evening Standard* (London), (16 Mar 1939) p. 17; by D. H. V. in *Spectator* (London), CLXII (3 Mar 1939) 362; by Seán O'Faoláin in *London Mercury*, XXXIX 233 (Mar 1939) 561–2; by Max Wood in *Fortnightly* (London), CXLV, n.s. (June 1939) 712–13; by Ivor Brown in *Manchester Guardian* (7 Mar 1939) p. 7; by Brooks Atkinson in *New York Times* (9 Apr 1939) section 10, p. 1; by Ralph Thompson in *New York Times* (18 July 1939), p. 17; by Horace Reynolds in *New York Times Book Review* (23 July 1939) pp. 4, 16; by V. S. Pritchett in *Christian Science Monitor Weekly Magazine*, XXXI 119 (15 Apr 1939) 10; by Ruth Page in *Boston Evening Transcript* (29 July 1939) 4, p. 1; by Shaemas O'Sheel in *New York Herald Tribune Books* (23 July 1939) p. 5; in *New Republic* (N.Y.), C (16 Aug 1939) 56; in *Time* (Chicago), XXXIV 4 (24 July 1939) 64; by Edith J. R. Isaacs in *Theatre Arts Monthly* (N.Y.), XXIII (Aug 1939) 611; by Padraic Colum in *Yale Review*, XXIX 1 (Sep 1939) 182–5; by Katherine Bregy in *Catholic World* (N.Y.), CL (Oct 1939) 114–15; by Ernest Boyd in *Saturday Review of Literature* (N.Y.), XX 14 (29 July 1939) 6; by J. Cambridge in *Sunday Worker* (N.Y.), (13 Aug 1939) p. 7; by Louis Kronenberger in *New Yorker* (N.Y.), XV (22 July 1939) 65–7; and by Eleanor Godfrey in *Canadian Forum* (Toronto), XIX (July 1939) 127.

THE STAR TURNS RED (London and New York: Macmillan, 1940).

Reviewed in *Times Literary Supplement* (London), (13 Apr 1940) pp. 182, 186; by D[erek] V[erschoyle] in *Spectator* (London),

CLXIV (15 Mar 1940) 388; by Benjamin Gilbert Brooks in *Nineteenth Century and After* (London), CXXVIII 762 (Aug 1940) 196–200; by Ivor Brown in *Manchester Guardian* (1 Mar 1940) p. 3; by J. J. H. in *Studies: An Irish Quarterly Review* (Dublin), XXIX (Mar 1940) 156–8; and by W. A. Darlington in *New York Times* (24 Mar 1940) section 9, p. 2.

PURPLE DUST: A WAYWARD COMEDY IN THREE ACTS (London and New York: Macmillan, 1940).

Reviewed in *Times Literary Supplement* (London), (23 Nov 1940) p. 594; by A. S. W. in *Manchester Guardian* (31 Dec 1940) p. 7; by Edward Farrer in *Life and Letters Today* (London), XXVIII 41 (Jan 1941) 88–90; by L. A. G. Strong in *Spectator* (London), CLXVI (17 Jan 1941) 70; by Denis Johnston in *Bell* (Dublin), I 4 (Jan 1941) 91–4; by J. J. H. in *Studies: An Irish Quarterly Review* (Dublin), XXX (Sep 1941) 463–4; in *Dublin Magazine*, XVI 1 (Jan– Mar 1941) 67; and by Walter Prichard Eaton in *New York Herald Tribune Books* (9 Feb 1941) p. 12.

RED ROSES FOR ME (London and New York: Macmillan, 1942).

Reviewed in *Times Literary Supplement* (London), (9 Jan 1943) p. 22; in *Spectator* (London), CLXIX (25 Dec 1942) 606; by G. W. Stonier in *New Statesman and Nation* (London), XXIV (14 Nov 1942) 324; by A. D. in *Manchester Guardian* (4 Dec 1942) p. 3; by M. R. K. in *Irish Press* (Dublin), (3 Dec 1942) p. 2; by Sean O'Faoláin in *Bell* (Dublin), VI 2 (May 1943) 112–21; by Horace Reynolds in *New York Times Book Review* (30 Jan 1944) p. 10; by Walter Prichard Eaton in *New York Herald Tribune Book Review* (30 Apr 1944) p. 17; by Edmund Wilson in *New Yorker* (N.Y.), XIX (5 Feb 1944) 73–4; by Eric Bentley in *Partisan Review* (N.Y.), XII 2 (spring 1945) 250; in *Christian Century* (Chicago), LXI 12 (22 Mar 1944) 370; in *Theatre Arts* (N.Y.), XXVIII 4 (Apr 1944) 256; by William P. Sears in *Churchman* (N.Y.), CLVIII (Mar 1944) 19; and by George Mayberry in *New Republic* (N.Y.), CX 7 (14 Feb 1944) 217–18.

PICTURES IN THE HALLWAY (London and New York: Macmillan, 1942).

Reviewed in *Times Literary Supplement* (London), (7 Mar 1942) p. 118; by Stephen Gwynn in *Time and Tide* (London), XXIII 13

(28 Mar 1942) 272–3 [see reply by O'Casey, XXIII 15 (11 Apr 1942) 306]; by Elizabeth Bowen in *Spectator* (London), CLXVIII (1 May 1942) 423; by G. W. Stonier in *New Statesman and Nation* (London), XXIII (28 Feb 1942) 147; by A. S. W. in *Manchester Guardian* (13 Mar 1942) p. 3; by Maurice Devane in *Dublin Magazine*, XVII 3 (July–Sep 1942) 44–5; by Robert Van Gelder in *New York Times* (7 Mar 1942) p. 15; by Brooks Atkinson in *New York Times* (5 Apr 1942) section 8, p. 1; by J. D. A. in *New York Times Book Review* (22 Mar 1942) p. 2; by Horace Reynolds in *New York Times Book Review* (22 Mar 1942) p. 5; by Jenny Ballou in *New York Herald Tribune Books* (22 Mar 1942) p. 4; in *New Yorker* (N.Y.), XVIII (11 Apr 1942) 87–8; by Ernest Boyd in *Saturday Review of Literature* (N.Y.), XXV (21 Mar 1942) 5; by Charles A. Brady in *America* (N.Y.), LXVII (11 Apr 1942) 20–21; by N. E[lizabeth] M[onroe] in *Catholic World* (N.Y.), CLV (May 1942) 244–5; by James Stern in *New Republic* (N.Y.), CVI 13 (30 Mar 1942) 434; and by S. Sillen in *New Masses* (N.Y.), (21 Apr 1942) 24–5.

DRUMS UNDER THE WINDOWS (London and New York: Macmillan, 1945).

Reviewed in *Times Literary Supplement* (London), (20 Oct 1945) p. 502 and (17 Nov 1945) p. 548; by G. W. Stonier in *New Statesman and Nation* (London), XXX (27 Oct 1945) 284; by George Orwell in *Observer* (London), (28 Oct 1945) p. 3; by N. N. in *Irish Independent* (Dublin), (12 Nov 1945) p. 4; in *Sunday Independent* (Dublin), (18 Nov 1945) p. 4; by Sean O'Faoláin in *Bell* (Dublin), XI 3 (Dec 1945) 815–21; by Orville Prescott in *New York Times* (8 May 1946) p. 23; by Brooks Atkinson in *New York Times* (22 Sep 1946) section 2, p. 1; by Richard Sullivan in *New York Times Book Review* (12 May 1946) p. 8; in *Time* (N.Y.), XLVII 19 (13 May 1946) 46; by Horace Reynolds in *New York Herald Tribune Weekly Book Review* (12 May 1946) p. 2; by Richard Watts in *New Republic* (N.Y.), CXIV (10 June 1946) 839–40; by Kathleen O'Brennan in *America* (N.Y.), LXXIV (2 Feb 1946) 494; by Robert B. Heilman in *Quarterly Review of Literature* (Annandale-on-Hudson), IV 1 (1947) 105–13; by Rolfe Humphries in *Nation* (N.Y.), CLXII (11 May 1946) 577–8; by William D'Arcy in *Catholic Historical Review*, XXXII (Jan 1947) 491–2; by Thomas Quinn Curtiss in *Theatre Arts* (N.Y.), XXX 8 (Aug 1946) 494; by Padraic

Colum in *Yale Review* (New Haven), XXXVI (autumn 1946) 154–6; by Patrick O'Donnell in *Catholic World* (N.Y.), CLXIII (July 1946) 375; in *Newsweek* (N.Y.), XXVII 19 (13 May 1946) 100–102; in *Saturday Review of Literature* (N.Y.), XXIX (11 May 1946) 7–8; by S. Finkelstein in *New Masses* (N.Y.), (11 June 1946) 21–2; and in *Story* (N.Y.), no. 119 (May–June 1946) 8.

OAK LEAVES AND LAVENDER: OR, A WORLD ON WALLPAPER (London and New York: Macmillan, 1946).

Reviewed in *Times Literary Supplement* (London), (4 May 1946) p. 215 and (11 May 1946) p. 224; by G. W. Stonier in *New Statesman and Nation* (London), XXX (25 May 1946) 380–1; by A. Farjeon in *Time and Tide* (London), XXVII 23 (8 June 1946) 544; by John Collier in *New Theatre* (London), III 2 (July 1946) 22; by Horace Reynolds in *New York Times Book Review* (11 May 1947) p. 18; by Walter Prichard Eaton in *New York Herald Tribune Weekly Book Review* (25 May 1947) p. 27; by P. S. in *San Francisco Chronicle* (11 May 1947) Magazine Section, p. 23; in *Christian Century* (N.Y.), LXIV 20 (14 May 1947) 626; and by George Freedley in *Library Journal* (N.Y.), LXXII 10 (15 May 1947) 811.

COCK-A-DOODLE DANDY (London and New York: Macmillan, 1949).

Reviewed in *Times Literary Supplement* (London), (27 May 1949) p. 340; by John Allen in *Drama* (London), no. 15 (winter 1949) 36; by G. F. in *Manchester Guardian* (13 May 1949) p. 4; by Robert Greacen in *Irish Writing* (Cork), no. 9 (Oct 1949) 69–70; by Horace Reynolds in *New York Times Book Review* (19 Feb 1950) p. 12; by W. R. W. in *San Francisco Chronicle* (9 Apr 1950) p. 15; by R. M. H. in *Christian Science Monitor Magazine* (Boston), XLII 78 (27 Feb 1950) 6; by Walter Prichard Eaton in *New York Herald Tribune Book Review* (9 Apr 1950) p. 15; and by Henry Hewes in *Saturday Review of Literature* (N.Y.), XXXVIII (1950) 9–10.

INISHFALLEN FARE THEE WELL (London and New York: Macmillan, 1949).

Reviewed in *Times Literary Supplement* (London), (19 Feb 1949) p. 115; by Desmond MacCarthy in *Sunday Times* (London), (30 Jan 1949) p. 3; by Louis MacNeice in *New Statesman and*

Nation (London), XXXVII (19 Feb 1949) 184–5; by Sean O'Faoláin in *John O'London's Weekly* (4 Feb 1949) 70–1; by Una Pope-Hennessy in *Spectator* (London), CLXXXII (Feb 1949) 160; by Bruce Bain [Richard Findlater] in *Tribune* (London), no. 630 (4 Feb 1949) 16; by G[erard] F[ay] in *Manchester Guardian* (1 Feb 1949) p. 3 [see O'Casey's reply (14 Feb 1949) p. 4]; by L. A. G. Strong in *Observer* (London), (30 Jan 1949) p. 3; by H. M. in *Drama* (London), no. 13 (summer 1949) 36; by Hayter Preston in *Cavalcade* (London), II (26 Feb 1949) 10; by W. Gallacher in *Labour Monthly* (London), XXXI 4 (Apr 1949) 126–7; by Annabel Farjeon in *Time and Tide* (London), XXX 6 (5 Feb 1949) 130; by Harold Nicolson in *Daily Telegraph* (London), (11 Feb 1949) p. 3; by Allen Hutt in *Daily Worker* (London), (3 Feb 1949) p. 2; by Anne Kelly in *Irish Democrat* (Dublin), (Apr 1949) p. 7; by Austin Clarke in *Irish Times* (Dublin), (29 Jan 1949) p. 9 [see O'Casey's reply (5 Feb 1949) p. 8]; by Robert Greacen in *Irish Writing* (Cork), no. 8 (July 1949) 88–9; by Orville Prescott in *New York Times* (22 Feb 1949) p. 21; by Brooks Atkinson in *New York Times* (27 Feb 1949) section 2, p. 1; by Joseph Wood Krutch in *New York Times Book Review* (27 Mar 1949) p. 30; by Horace Gregory in *New York Herald Tribune Weekly Book Review* (20 Feb 1949) p. 3; in *Catholic World* (N.Y.), CXCVI (May 1949) 152; by C. J. Rolo in *Atlantic* (Boston), CLXXXIII 4 (Apr 1949) 83–4; in *Time* (N.Y.), LIII 9 (28 Feb 1949) 56; by Charles Humboldt in *Masses and Mainstream* (N.Y.), II 4 (Apr 1949) 71–5; in *New Yorker*, XXV 1 (26 Feb 1949) 91; by Walter O'Hearn in *America* (N.Y.), LXXXI (11 June 1949) 342–3; in *Coronet* (Boulder, Col.), XXVII (Jan 1950) 14; by Horace Reynolds in *Saturday Review of Literature* (N.Y.), XXXII (5 Mar 1949) 18–19; by Horace Reynolds in *Yale Review*, XXXIX 1 (autumn 1949) 169–70; by William Sears in *Churchman* (N.Y.), CLXIII (June 1949) 15; by Marshall Wingfield in *Christian Century* (Chicago), LXVI 18 (4 May 1949) 563; in *American Mercury*, LXVIII (June 1949) 759; by R. M. H. in *Christian Science Monitor* (Boston), (24 Mar 1949) p. 11; and by Margaret Eliason in *Library Journal* (N.Y.), LXXIV 2 (15 Jan 1949) 125.

ROSE AND CROWN (London and New York: Macmillan, 1952).

Reviewed in *Times* (London), (9 July 1952) p. 8; in *Times Literary Supplement* (London), (1 Aug 1952) p. 502; in *New Statesman and*

Nation (London), XLIV (26 July 1952) 114; by Brian Inglis in *Spectator* (London), CLXXXIX (1 Aug 1952) 166; by Richard Findlater in *Theatre* (London), VII 156 (27 Sep 1952) 19; by Gerard Fay in *Manchester Guardian* (15 July 1952) p. 4; by Donagh MacDonagh in *Drama* (London), no. 27 (winter 1952) 37–8; by Austin Clarke in *John O'London's Weekly*, LXI (18 July 1952) 692; by Louis MacNeice in *Observer* (London), (13 July 1952) p. 7; by Peter Quennell in *Daily Mail* (London), (5 July 1952) p. 2; by T. A. Jackson in *Daily Worker* (London), (10 July 1952) p. 2; by N[iall] C[arroll] in *Irish Press* (Dublin), (23 Sep 1952) p. 6; by Robert Greacen in *Irish Writing* (Cork), nos. 20–21 (Nov 1952) 85–6; by Gabriel Fallon in *Irish Monthly* (Dublin), LXXX 951 (Nov 1952) 354–9; by Marie A. Updike White in *South Atlantic Quarterly*, LIII (1952) 156–7; by Walter Prichard Eaton in *New York Herald Tribune Book Review* (2 Nov 1952) p. 3; by Horace Reynolds in *New York Times Book Review* (2 Nov 1952) p. 5; by Brooks Atkinson in *New York Times* (14 Sep 1952) section 2, p. 1; by Maurice Valency in *Saturday Review of Literature* (N.Y.), XXXV (15 Nov 1952) 25; by Harold Hobson in *Christian Science Monitor* (Boston), (28 Aug 1952) p. 7; by Hugh Corbett in *Books Abroad* (Norman, Okl.), XXVII (spring 1953) 151–2; in *Daily Worker* (N.Y.), (13 Nov 1952) p. 7; by Stephen P. Ryan in *America* (N.Y.), LXXXVIII (20 Dec 1952) 330–2; by Charles J. Rolo in *Atlantic* (Boston), CXC 6 (Dec 1952) 99; in *New Yorker* (N.Y.), XXVIII (8 Nov 1952) 172–3; in *Time* (N.Y.), LX (10 Nov 1952) 86–7; by Charles Humboldt in *Masses and Mainstream* (N.Y.), VI 1 (Jan 1953) 58–60; by Joseph Carroll in *Theatre Arts* (N.Y.), XXXVI (8 Dec 1952) 6–8; by Frederick E. Faverty in *Chicago Sunday Tribune* (2 Nov 1952) pt 4, p. 4; and by Eric Bentley in *New Republic* (N.Y.), CXXVII (13 Oct 1952) 17–18.

SUNSET AND EVENING STAR (London and New York: Macmillan, 1954).

Reviewed in *Times* (London), (30 Oct 1954) p. 8; in *Times Literary Supplement* (London), (5 Nov 1954) p. 699; by T. C. Worsley in *New Statesman and Nation* (London), XLVIII (30 Oct 1954) 544 [see O'Casey's reply (6 Nov 1954) 582]; by J. C. Trewin in *Drama: The Quarterly Theatre Review* (London), XXXV (winter 1954) 34–8; by Austin Clarke in *Time and Tide* (London), XXXV 46 (13 Nov

1954) 1524; by Sean O'Herron in *British Weekly* (London), CXXXV (4 Nov 1954) 2; by E. D. O'Brien in *Illustrated London News*, CCXXVI (26 Feb 1955) 376; by Ivor Brown in *Observer* (London), (14 Nov 1954) p. 9; by Edith Shackleton in *Lady* (London), CXL (4 Nov 1954) 594; by Cicely Boas in *English* (London), X 58 (spring 1955) 151–2; by Eric Gillett in *National and English Review* (London), CXLIII (Dec 1954) 425; by Howard Spring in *Country Life* (London), CXVI (18 Nov 1954) 1787–89; by Richard Findlater in *Tribune* (London), (28 Jan 1955) p. 7; by Vernon Fane in *Sphere* (London), CCXIX (6 Nov 1954) 256; by Gerard Fay in *Manchester Guardian* (26 Nov 1954) p. 9; by W. A. Darlington in *Daily Telegraph* (London), (26 Nov 1954) p. 8; by Frederick Laws in *News Chronicle* (London), (5 Nov 1954) p. 2; by Philip Bolsover in *Daily Worker* (London), (4 Nov 1954) p. 2; by J. C. in *Belfast News-Letter* (20 Nov 1954) p. 2; by Austin Clarke in *Irish Times* (Dublin), (6 Nov 1954) p. 6; in *Sunday Independent* (Dublin) (31 Oct 1954) p. 1; by W. L. in *Irish Independent* (Dublin), (30 Oct 1954) p. 6; by John Jordan in *Irish Writing* (Cork), no. 29 (Dec 1954) 57–63; in *Standard* (Dublin), XXVII 163 (18 Feb 1955) 1; by Brooks Atkinson in *New York Times Book Review* (14 Nov 1954) pp. 1, 38; by V. S. Pritchett in *New Yorker* (N.Y.), XXXI (16 Apr 1955) 147–156; by Charles J. Rolo in *Atlantic* (Boston), CXCV 1 (Jan 1955) 83; by Marie A. Updike White in *South Atlantic Quarterly* (Durham), LV (1954) 242–3; by Hugh Corbett in *Books Abroad* (Norman, Okla.), XXIX 3 (summer 1955) 307; by Walter Prichard Eaton in *New York Herald Tribune Book Review* (14 Nov 1954) pt I, p. 5; by Horace Reynolds in *Christian Science Monitor* (Boston), (24 Nov 1954) p. 9; by George Freedley in *Library Journal* (N.Y.), LXXX 5 (1 Mar 1955) 577; in *College English* (Chicago), XVI 6 (Mar 1955) 391; by Granville Hicks in *New Leader* (N.Y.), (29 Nov 1954) p. 22; by Horace Gregory in *Saturday Review of Literature* (N.Y.), XXXVII (20 Nov 1954) 18–19; by Padraic Colum in *New Republic* (N.Y.), CXXXI (27 Dec 1954) 19; by Harold Clurman in *Nation* (N.Y.), CLXXIX (27 Nov 1954) 468; in *Time* (N.Y.), LXIV (15 Nov 1954) 102; by Donald A. Pitt in *San Francisco Chronicle* (5 Dec 1954) p. 22; by Gerald Weales in *Commentary* (N.Y.), XIX (Feb 1955) 201–2; by E. J. West in *Educational Theatre Journal* (Ann Arbor, Mich.), VII (Dec 1955) 354–6; and by Milton Howard in *Masses and Mainstream* (N.Y.), VIII (Jan 1955) 20–6.

THE BISHOP'S BONFIRE: A SAD PLAY WITHIN THE TUNE OF A POLKA (London and New York: Macmillan, 1955).

Reviewed in *Times Literary Supplement* (London), (8 July 1955) p. 378; and by Brooks Atkinson in *New York Times Book Review* (11 Sep 1955) p. 22.

THE GREEN CROW (New York: George Braziller, 1956; London: W. H. Allen, 1957.) [Contains parts of *The Flying Wasp*, four stories from *Windfalls*, and some new essays.]

Reviewed in *Times* (London), (14 Feb 1957) p. 11; in *Times Literary Supplement* (London), (15 Feb 1957) p. 99; by J. P. Henderson in *New Statesman and Nation* (London), LIII (23 Feb 1957) 252–3; in *Listener* (London), LVII (9 May 1957) 761, 763; by J. W. Lambert in *Sunday Times* (London), (24 Feb 1957) p. 9; by John Wain in *Observer* (London), (10 Feb 1957) p. 13; by Peter Green in *Time and Tide* (London), XXXVIII 14 (6 Apr 1957) 424–5; by J. MacC. in *Daily Worker* (London), (21 Feb 1957) p. 2; by Walter Prichard Eaton in *New York Herald Tribune Book Review* (6 May 1956) p. 8; by Brooks Atkinson in *New York Times Book Review* (18 Mar 1956) pp. 3, 22; by Frederick E. Faverty in *Chicago Sunday Tribune* (8 Apr 1956) p. 12; by E. J. West in *Educational Theatre Journal* (Ann Arbor, Mich.), IX (May 1957) 157–9; by Henry Popkin in *Kenyon Review*, XVIII (autumn 1956) 663–8; by W. Cross in *People's World Magazine* (San Francisco), (22 June 1956) p. 7; by William Hogan in *San Francisco Chronicle* (22 Mar 1956) p. 22; by Max Cosman in *Theatre Arts* (N.Y.), XL (July 1956) 8–9; in *Time* (N.Y.), LXVII (26 Mar 1956) 97–8; by R[aymond] Brugère in *Études anglaises* (Paris), XII (1957) 366–7; and by A[nne] Elistratova in *Problems of Literature* (Moscow), no. 8 (Nov 1957) 238–41 [in Russian].

THE DRUMS OF FATHER NED (London and New York: Macmillan, 1960).

Reviewed by G. Wilson Knight in *Stand* (London), IV 3 (summer 1960) 15–18; by Myke Myson in *Daily Worker* (London), (27 June 1960) p. 2; by Harold Clurman in *Saturday Review of Literature* (N.Y.), XLIII (5 Nov 1960) 31, 48; and by René Fréchet in *Études anglaises* (Paris), XV 3 (July–Sep 1962) 311.

BEHIND THE GREEN CURTAINS (London and New York: Macmillan, 1961.) [Contains the title-play, *Figuro in the Night*, and *The Moon Shines on Kylenamoe*.]

>Reviewed by Alan Simpson in *Sunday Times* (London), (23 July 1961) p. 26; by Myke Myson in *Daily Worker* (London), (19 June 1961) p. 2; by Gabriel Fallon in *Kilkenny Magazine*, no. 5 (autumn–winter 1961) 34–41 [see reply by Robert Hogan (spring 1962) 37–9; and counter-reply (spring 1962) 40–1]; by Brooks Atkinson in *New York Times* (14 July 1961) p. 20; and by Renée Saurel in *Temps modernes* (Paris), année XIX 207–8 (Aug–Sep 1963) 571–2.

FEATHERS FROM THE GREEN CROW: SEAN O'CASEY 1905–1925, ed. Robert Hogan (Columbia: University of Missouri Press, [1962]; London: Macmillan, 1963). [Contains two hitherto unpublished plays, *Cathleen Listens In* and *Nannie's Night Out*; some early newspaper articles; *The Sacrifice of Thomas Ashe*; and *The Story of the Irish Citizen Army*.]

>Reviewed in *Times* (London), (3 Oct 1963) p. 15; in *Times Literary Supplement* (London), (6 Sep 1963) p. 674; by John Wain in *Observer* (London), (11 Aug 1963) p. 16; by Valentin Iremonger in *Spectator* (London), CCXI (27 Sep 1963) 391; in *Time and Tide* (London), XLIV 34 (22–8 Aug 1963) 21; by Robert Nye in *Scotsman* (Edinburgh), (7 Sep 1963) p. 2; by Ronald Ayling in *Dubliner*, III 1 (spring 1964) 54–67; and by Gabriel Fallon in *Kilkenny Magazine*, no. 10 (autumn–winter 1963) 65–73.

UNDER A COLORED CAP: ARTICLES MERRY AND MOURNFUL WITH COMMENTS AND A SONG (London: Macmillan; New York: St Martin's Press, 1963).

>Reviewed in *Times* (London), (11 Apr 1963) p. 15; in *Times Literary Supplement* (London), (3 May 1963) p. 326; by Tim Pat Coogan in *Spectator* (London), CCX (3 May 1963) 580; by Louis MacNeice in *New Statesman* (London), LXV (3 May 1963) 678–9; by John Wain in *Observer* (London), (11 Aug 1963) p. 16; by Robert Robinson in *Sunday Times* (London), (14 Apr 1963) p. 25; in *Time and Tide* (London), XLIV 15 (11–17 Apr 1963) 28; by Gerard Fay in *Manchester Guardian* (26 Apr 1963) p. 6; by Tim Enright in *Daily Worker* (London), (11 Apr 1963) p. 2; by Eric Shorter in *Daily Telegraph* (London), (19 Apr 1963) p. 19; by Kenneth Allsop in *Daily Mail* (London), (11 Apr 1963) p. 8 [see

reply by Herbert Phillips (16 Apr 1963) p. 8]; by Gabriel Fallon in *Kilkenny Magazine*, no. 10 (autumn–winter 1963) 65–73; by Frank O'Connor in *Sunday Independent* (Dublin), (12 May 1963) p. 12; by Anne O'Neill-Barna in *New York Times Book Review* (23 June 1963) p. 7; by Sean Callery in *Saturday Review of Literature* (N.Y.), (29 June 1963) 32; and by Brooks Atkinson in *New York Times* (17 May 1963) p. 30.

BLASTS AND BENEDICTIONS: ARTICLES AND STORIES, ed. Ronald Ayling (London: Macmillan; New York: St Martin's Press, 1967).

Reviewed in *Times* (London), (19 Jan 1967) p. 14; in *Times Literary Supplement* (London), (26 Jan 1967) p. 65; in *Sunday Times* (London), (15 Jan 1967) p. 28; by Frederick Laws in *Daily Telegraph* (London), (30 Mar 1967) p. 20; by Elizabeth Coxhead in *Sunday Telegraph* (London), (15 Jan 1967) p. 14; by Irving Wardle in *Observer* (London), (22 Jan 1967) p. 27; by John Arden in *Manchester Guardian* (20 Jan 1967) p. 7; by Gerald Colgan in *Plays and Players* (London), XIV 10 (July 1967) 54; by Elizabeth Coxhead in *Lady* (London), CLXV (16 Feb 1967) 308; by Katharine J. Worth in *Shavian* (London), III, no. 7 (July 1967) 25–7; by Michael Foot in *Evening Standard* (London), (17 Jan 1967) p. 8; by Jack Sutherland in *Morning Star* (London), (12 Jan 1967) p. 4; by Elizabeth Jennings in *Catholic Herald* (London), (24 Feb 1967) p. 6; by John O'Riordan in *Tribune* (London), XXXI 22 (2 June 1967) 11; by Piers Brendon in *Books and Bookmen* (London), XII 5 (Feb 1967) 54–5 [see reply by John O'Riordan (Apr 1967) 8–9]; by G. W. B. in *New Theatre Magazine* (Bristol), VII 3 (summer 1967) 37–8; by C. S. in *Glasgow Herald* (14 Jan 1967) p. 9; by Mervyn Well in *Irish Times* (Dublin), (28 Jan 1967) p. 8; by John McCann in *Sunday Press* (Dublin), (19 Feb 1967) p. 21; in *Evening Herald* (Dublin), (13 Jan 1967) p. 4; by David Krause in *Modern Drama* (Lawrence, Kansas), XI (Dec 1967) 252–62; by Sam Wellbaum in *Independent Shavian* (N.Y.), V 3 (spring 1967) 46; in *New York Times Book Review* (23 Apr 1967) p. 30; by Sean Cronin in *Nation* (N.Y.), CCV (2 Oct 1967) 315–16; in *Independent Press Telegram* (Long Beach, Calif.), (8 July 1967); in *Booklist* (Chicago), (11 Jan 1967); in *Huntington Herald-Advertiser* (West Virginia), (5 May 1967) Book Page; in *Austell Enterprise* (8 June 1967); by M. J. Sidnell in *Canadian Forum* (Toronto), XLVII (Mar 1968) 288; and by G. Zlobin in *Voprosy Literatury* (Feb 1969).

Part III

CRITICISM ON SEAN O'CASEY

(a) Books

AGATE, JAMES, 'The Plough and the Stars: A play by Sean O'Casey, Fortune Theatre', The Contemporary Theatre, 1926 (London: Chapman and Hall, 1927) pp. 45–9.

My Theatre Talks (London: Arthur Barker, 1933) pp. 90, 150, 223.

'Beyond the Agates', First Nights (London: Ivor Nicholson & Watson, 1934) pp. 271–6 [on Within the Gates]

The Amazing Theatre (London: George G. Harrap, 1939).

Red Letter Nights (London: Jonathan Cape, 1944) [on Juno and the Paycock and The Plough and the Stars]

The Later Ego (New York: Crown 1951).

ALLEN, JOHN, 'Sean O'Casey', Masters of British Drama (London: Dennis Dobson, 1957) pp. 154–69.

ALLISON, ALEXANDER W., CARR, ARTHUR J., and EASTMAN, ARTHUR M. (eds), 'Sean O'Casey: Juno and the Paycock', Masterpieces of the Drama (New York: Macmillan, 1957) pp. 519–20.

ANDERSON, MAXWELL, Off Broadway: Essays about the Theater (New York: William Sloane Associates, 1947) pp. 49–50.

ARMSTRONG, WILLIAM A., 'The Irish Point of View: The Plays of Sean O'Casey, Brendan Behan, and Thomas Murphy', Experimental Drama (London: G. Bell, 1963) pp. 79–93.

(ed.), 'Introduction: The Irish Dramatic Movement', Classic Irish Drama (Harmondsworth: Penguin Books, 1964) pp. 7–15. [Contains Cock-a-Doodle-Dandy.]

Sean O'Casey (London: Longmans, for the British Council and the National Book League, 1967). Reviewed by Johannes Hedberg in Moderna Språk (Stockholm), LXI (1967) 394–6.

'Sean O'Casey', The Oxford Companion to the Theatre, ed. Phyllis Hartnoll (London: Oxford University Press, 1967) pp. 691–2.

'Sean O'Casey, W. B. Yeats and the Dance of Life', Sean O'Casey, ed. Ronald Ayling (London: Macmillan, 1969) pp. 131–42.

ATKINSON, BROOKS, *Broadway Scrapbook* (New York: Theatre Arts, 1947) pp. 13-16 [on *Within the Gates*], 147-51 [on *Juno and the Paycock*].

(ed.), 'Introduction', *The Sean O'Casey Reader: Plays, Autobiographies, Opinions* (London: Macmillan; New York: St Martin's Press, 1968). Reviewed in *New York Times Book Review* (15 Dec 1968) p. 1; in *Times Literary Supplement* (London), (17 July 1969) p. 771; in *Times Educational Supplement* (London), (16 May 1969) p. 1647; by John O'Riordan in *Tribune* (London), (18 Sep 1970) p. 11; by De Vere White in *Irish Times* (Dublin), (10 May 1969) p. 8 [see correspondence by Gabriel Fallon (14 May 1969); by L. Smith (15 May 1969); and by John O'Riordan (20 May 1969)]; by John Chapman in *San Francisco Chronicle* (15 Dec 1968); and by Robert Hogan in *Modern Drama* (Lawrence, Kansas), XII, no. 1 (May 1969), 107-8.

AYLING, RONALD (ed.), *Sean O'Casey*, Modern Judgements Series (London: Macmillan, 1969). Reviewed in *Times Literary Supplement* (London), (6 Mar 1969) p. 228; in *Economist* (London), (19 Apr 1969) pp. 79-80; by John O'Riordan in *Tribune* (London), XXXIII (26 Sep 1969) 14; by Seamus Treacy in *Irish Democrat* (London), (Sep 1969) p. 2; by Austin Clarke in *Irish Times* (Dublin), (12 July 1969) p. 8; by Brendan Kennelly in *Hibernia* (Dublin), (25 Apr-8 May 1969); by Saros Cowasjee in *Dublin Magazine*, VIII 4-5 (summer-autumn 1970) 121-3; and by Heinz Kosok in *Die Neueren Sprachen*, VIII (1969) 415-16.

(ed.), 'Preface', *Blasts and Benedictions* (London: Macmillan, 1967).

(ed.), 'Einleitung', *Wünsche und Verwünschungen* (Leipzig: Paul List Verlag, 1970).

'Sean O'Casey', *The Encyclopedia Americana*, vol. xx, International Edition (New York: American Corporation, 1969) pp. 606-7.

BALASHOV, PETER, 'O'Casey', *The Soviet History of English Literature* (Moscow, 1958) pp. 627-46.

BARNET, SYLVAN, BERMAN, MORTON, and BURTO, WILLIAM (eds), 'O'Casey: *Purple Dust*', *The Genius of the Irish Theatre* (New York: New American Library, 1960).

BARROWS, HERBERT, HEFFNER, HUBERT, CIARDI, JOHN, and DOUGLAS, WALLACE (eds), 'Sean O'Casey: *Juno and the Paycock*', *An Introduction to Literature* (Boston: Houghton Mifflin, 1959) pp. 615-16.

BECKERMAN, BERNARD, *Dynamics of Drama: Theory and Method of Analysis* (New York: Alfred A. Knopf, 1970).

BENTLEY, ERIC, *The Playwright as Thinker* (New York: Meridian Books, 1946). Reprinted as *The Modern Theatre: A Study of Dramatists and the Drama* (London: Robert Hale, 1948).

In Search of Theater (New York: Vintage Books, 1953) pp. 315–21. Reprinted from *Poetry* (Chicago), LXXIX (Jan 1952) 216–32.

'The Case of O'Casey', *The Dramatic Event: An American Chronicle* (Boston: Beacon Press, 1956) pp. 42–5. Reprinted from *New Republic* (N.Y.), CXXVII (13 Oct 1952) 17–18.

(ed.), '*Cock-a-Doodle Dandy* by Sean O'Casey', *The Modern Theatre*, vol. 5 (Garden City, N.Y.: Doubleday, 1957).

'The Politics of Sean O'Casey', *What Is Theatre?* (London: Dennis Dobson, 1957) pp. 107–11; (New York: Athenaeum, 1968) pp. 265–8. Reprinted from *New Republic* (N.Y.), CXXXIV (30 Jan 1956) 21 [on *Red Roses for Me*].

BERGHOLZ, HARRY, *Die Neugestaltung des Modernen Englischen Theaters 1870–1930* (Berlin: Karl Bergholz, 1933).

BISHOP, GEORGE W., *My Betters* (London: Heinemann, 1957) pp. 128–267.

BLACK, HESTER M., *The Theatre in Ireland: An Introductory Essay* (Dublin: Trinity College, 1957).

BLANSHARD, PAUL, *The Irish and Catholic Power* (London: Derek Verschoyle, 1954).

BLAU, HERBERT, *The Impossible Theater: A Manifesto* (New York: Macmillan, 1964) pp. 205–10.

BLOCK, HASKELL M., and SHEDD, ROBERT G. (eds), 'Sean O'Casey', *Masters of Modern Drama* (New York: Random House, 1962) pp. 433–4 [contains *Juno and the Paycock* and *Cock-a-Doodle Dandy*].

BLYTHE, ERNEST, *The Abbey Theatre* (Dublin: The National Theatre Society, n.d. [1963]).

BOAS, GUY (ed.), 'Introduction', '*Juno and the Paycock*' and '*The Plough and the Stars*' by Sean O'Casey (London: Macmillan, 1965).

BOYD, ALICE KATHARINE, *The Interchange of Plays between London and New York, 1910–1939: A Study in Relative Audience Response* (New York: King's Crown Press, 1948).

BRANDT, G. W., 'Realism and Parables (From Brecht to Arden)', *Contemporary Theatre*, ed. J. R. Brown and B. Harris, Stratford-upon-Avon Studies, IV (London: Edward Arnold, 1962) pp. 36–40 [on *The Silver Tassie*].

BROOK, DONALD, *The Romance of the English Theatre* (London: Rockliff, 1952) pp. 168–70.

BROWN, IVOR, 'Salute to Sean', *Theatre 1954–5* (London: Max Reinhardt, 1955) pp. 97–100.

BROWN, JOHN MASON, 'Without Mr O'Casey's Gates', *Two on the Aisle* (New York: W. W. Norton, 1938) pp. 126–30. Reprinted from *New York Evening Post* (23 Oct 1934) [on *Within the Gates*]. See O'Casey's reply, 'Within the Gates and Without', published in *Blasts and Benedictions*, ed. Ronald Ayling (London: Macmillan, 1967), pp. 118–23.

BRUSTEIN, ROBERT, *Seasons of Discontent: Dramatic Opinions 1959–1965* (London: Jonathan Cape, 1966).

BYRNE, DAWSON, 'Sean O'Casey', *The Story of Ireland's National Theatre, Dublin* (Dublin: Talbot Press, 1929) pp. 125–33.

CANFIELD, CURTIS (ed.), '*Juno and the Paycock*: Sean O'Casey', *Plays of the Irish Renaissance, 1880–1930* (New York: Ives Washburn, 1929) pp. 294–7.

(ed.), 'Preface', *Plays of Changing Ireland* (New York: Macmillan, 1936).

CHARQUES, R. D. (ed.), *Footnotes to the Theatre* (London: Peter Davies, 1938).

CHEW, SAMUEL C., 'The Irish Literary Renaissance', *A Literary History Of England*, ed. Albert C. Baugh (New York and London: Appleton-Century-Crofts, 1948) pp. 1507–15.

CLARK, WILLIAM SMITH, *Chief Patterns of World Drama* (New York: Houghton Mifflin, 1946) p. 889.

CLAYES, STANLEY A., and SPENCER, DAVID G. (eds.), 'Sean O'Casey: *Juno and the Paycock*', *Contemporary Drama: Thirteen Plays, American, English, European* (New York: Scribner's, 1962).

CLEEVE, BRIAN (comp.), *Dictionary of Irish Writers* (Cork: Mercier Press, 1970).

CLURMAN, HAROLD, '*Red Roses for Me*', *Lies Like Truth* (New York: Macmillan, 1958) pp. 122-4. Reprinted from *Nation* (N.Y.), CLXXXII (14 Jan 1956) 39-40.

COCHRAN, CHARLES B., *I Had Almost Forgotten* (London: Hutchinson, 1932).

Showman Looks On (London: J. M. Dent, 1946).

COLUM, PADRAIC, *The Road Round Ireland* (New York: Macmillan, 1926) pp. 262-71.

Arthur Griffith (Dublin: Browne & Nolan, 1959) p. 370.

'Sean O'Casey's Narratives', *Sean O'Casey*, ed. Ronald Ayling (London: Macmillan, 1969) pp. 220-7.

CORDELL, RICHARD ALBERT (ed.), 'Sean O'Casey', *Representative Modern Plays, British and American: From Robertson to O'Neill* (New York: Nelson, 1929) pp. 367-8 [contains *Juno and the Paycock*].

and MATSON, LOWELL (eds.), '*Purple Dust* by Sean O'Casey', *The Off-Broadway Theatre: Seven Plays* (New York: Random House, 1959) pp. 131-2.

CORRIGAN, ROBERT W. (ed.), 'The Irish Dramatic Flair', *Masterpieces of the Modern Irish Theatre* (New York: Collier Books, 1967) pp. 6-8 [contains *The Silver Tassie* and *Cock-a-Doodle Dandy*].

COWASJEE, SAROS, *Sean O'Casey: The Man Behind the Plays* (Edinburgh and London: Oliver & Boyd, 1963; New York: St Martin's Press, 1964; rev. paperback ed., Oliver & Boyd, 1965) [derives from a dissertation]. Reviewed in *Times Literary Supplement* (London), (21 Nov 1963) p. 943; by Denis Johnston in *Modern Drama*, VIII 3 (Dec 1965) 344-5; by Carmela Moya in *Études anglaises* (Paris), XX 2 (Apr-June 1967) 160-4; by Micheál OhAodha in *Irish Press* (Dublin), (23 Nov 1963) p. 12; by Ronald Ayling in *Kilkenny Magazine*, II (spring-summer 1964) 69-82, reprinted in *Drama Survey* (Minneapolis, Minn.), III 4 (Fall 1965) 582-91 [see reply by Cowasjee, 'Correspondence', IV 2 (summer 1965) 191-2]; by Gabriel Fallon in *Evening Press* (Dublin), (26 Oct 1963) p. 9; in *Plays and Players* (London), XI 3 (Dec 1963) 22; in *Current*

Literature (London), no. 657 (Jan 1964) 3; in *Kirkus Bulletin* (15 Feb 1964); and by Brooks Atkinson in *New York Times* (14 Apr 1964) p. 34.

O'Casey (Edinburgh and London: Oliver & Boyd, 1966; New York: Barnes & Noble, 1967). Reviewed in *Contemporary Review* (London), ccviii (June 1966) 335; in *Sunday Statesman* (Calcutta), (4 Sep 1966) p. 10; by Ronald Mason in *The Shavian* (London), iii 6 (winter 1966–7) 31; in *British Book News* (London), (Sep 1966) p. 696; by P. F. Byrne in *Evening Herald* (Dublin), (4 June 1966) p. 8; in *Times Literary Supplement* (London), (23 June 1966) p. 561; and by Ronald Ayling in *Dublin Magazine*, v 3–4 (autumn–winter 1966) 100.

COWELL, RAYMOND, 'O'Casey', *Twelve Modern Dramatists* (London and New York: Pergamon Press, 1967) [contains extract from *Juno and the Paycock*].

COXHEAD, ELIZABETH, 'Sean O'Casey', *Lady Gregory: A Literary Portrait* (London: Macmillan, 1961; rev. ed., Secker & Warburg, 1966; repr. 1970) chap. 13. Reviewed in *Times Literary Supplement* (London), (16 July 1970) 761–2.

CROFT-COOKE, RUPERT, *The Numbers Came* (London: Putnam, 1963) pp. 159–60.

CUBETA, PAUL M. (ed.), 'Sean O'Casey: *Juno and the Paycock*', *Modern Drama for Analysis*, rev. ed. (New York: Dryden Press, 1955) pp. 549–51, 617–22.

CUNLIFFE, JOHN W., 'Sean O'Casey', *Modern English Playwrights: A Short History of the English Drama from 1825* (London and New York: Harper, 1927) pp 231–50.

'Sean O'Casey', *English Literature in the Twentieth Century* (New York: Macmillan, 1933) pp. 114–21.

DAICHES, DAVID, *The Present Age after 1920* (London: The Cresset Press, 1958).

DARLINGTON, W. A., *I Do What I Like* (London: MacDonald, 1947) pp. 319–22.

Six Thousand and One Nights: Forty Years a Critic (London: George G. Harrap, 1960) p. 168.

CRITICISM ON SEAN O'CASEY

DAVISON, P. H., 'Contemporary Drama and Popular Dramatic Forms', *Aspects of Drama and the Theatre* (Sydney: Sydney University Press, 1962).

DE BLAGHD, EARNAN [Ernest Blythe], *Trasna Na Bóinne* [Across the Boyne] (Dublin: Sairséal Agus Dill, 1957) [autobiography].

DENSON, ALAN (ed.), *Letters from A.E.* (London and New York: Abelard-Schuman, 1961) pp. 167, 171.

DENT, ALAN, 'Red Roses for O'Casey', *Nocturnes and Rhapsodies* (London: Hamish Hamilton, 1950) pp. 100–1 [on *Red Roses for Me*].

DICKINSON, THOMAS H. (ed.), '*Juno and the Paycock*: Sean O'Casey', *Chief Contemporary Dramatists*, Third Series (Boston: Houghton Mifflin, 1958).

DOBRÉE, BONAMY, 'Sean O'Casey and the Irish Drama', *Sean O'Casey*, ed. Ronald Ayling (London: Macmillan, 1969) pp. 92–105.

DOWNER, ALAN S., *The British Drama: A Handbook and Brief Chronicle* (New York: Appleton-Century-Crofts, 1950) pp. 324–6.

DREW, ELIZABETH, *Discovering Drama* (New York: W. W. Norton; London: Jonathan Cape, 1937).

DRUZINA, M. V. *Shon O'Keisi – Dramaturg* (Moscow: Znanie, 1963). *Dramaturgia Shon O'Keisi* (Leningrad, 1965).

DUKES, ASHLEY, *The Scene Is Changed* (London: Macmillan, 1942). *Drama* (London: Oxford University Press, 1947) p. 98.

DURHAM, WILLARD HIGLEY, and DODDS, JOHN W. (eds.), 'Sean O'Casey', *British and American Plays 1830–1945* (New York: Oxford University Press, 1947) pp. 424–6 [contains *Juno and the Paycock*].

EATON, WALTER PRICHARD, *The Drama in English* (New York: Scribner's, 1930) pp. 290–1.

EGRI, LAJOS, *The Art of Dramatic Writing* (New York: Simon & Schuster, 1940) p. 5.

29

ELLIS-FERMOR, UNA, *The Irish Dramatic Movement* (London: Methuen, 1954) pp. 196–200. Reprinted in *Sean O'Casey*, ed. Ronald Ayling (London: Macmillan, 1969) pp. 106–9.

The Frontiers of Drama (London: Methuen, 1964).

FALLON, GABRIEL, *Sean O'Casey: The Man I Knew* (London: Routledge & Kegan Paul; Boston: Little, Brown, 1965). Reviewed in *Times* (London), (5 Aug 1965) p. 13; in *Times Literary Supplement* (London), (8 July 1965) p. 576; by Nigel Dennis in *Sunday Telegraph* (London), (6 June 1965) p. 16 [see reply by John O'Riordan, 'Could O'Casey Write' (13 June 1965) p. 7]; by Brendan Kennelly in *Spectator* (London), CCXV (2 July 1965) 18; by Robert Greacen in *Listener* (London), LXXIII (17 June 1965) 906–9; by Desmond MacNamara in *New Statesman* (London), LXX (23 July 1965) 129; by Hilary Pyle in *Review of English Studies*, XVII 66 (May 1966) 227–8; by Augustine Martin in *Irish Times* (Dublin), (19 June 1965) p. 8; by Francis MacManus in *Irish Press* (Dublin), (10 June 1965) p. 13; by Ronald Ayling in *Dublin Magazine*, IV 3–4 (autumn–winter 1965) 69–82 [see Fallon's reply (autumn–winter) 82]; by Ulick O'Connor in *Dublin Magazine*, IV 3–4 (autumn–winter 1965) 83–9; by Brian O'Doherty in *Book Week* (19 Sep 1965) p. 27; by Ronald Ayling in *Massachusetts Review*, VII 3 (summer 1966) 603–12; by Stephen P. Ryan in *America* (N.Y.), CXIII (16 Oct 1965) 444; by Robert Warnock in *Quarterly Journal of Speech*, LII (1965) 207–8; by Carmela Moya in *Études anglaises* (Paris), XX 2 (Apr–June 1967) 160–4; and by Walter Starkie in *New York Times Book Review* (24 Oct 1965) p. 10.

The Abbey and the Actor (Dublin: The National Theatre Society, 1969) pp. 22–3, 36–7.

FAY, GERARD, 'The Irish Theatre: A Decline and Perhaps, in the End, a Fall', *Theatre in Review*, ed. Frederick Lumley (Edinburgh: Richard Paterson, 1956) pp. 80–9.

The Abbey Theatre, Cradle of Genius (Dublin: Clonmore & Reynolds, 1958).

FECHTER, PAUL, *Das Europäische Drama*, vol. III (Mannheim: Bibliographisches Institut A.G., 1958) pp. 378–80 [on *The Bishop's Bonfire* and *Juno and the Paycock*].

FEHR, BERNHARD, *Die Englische Literatur der Gegenwart und die Kulturfragen Unserer Zeit*, Hefte zur Englandkunde, Heft 3 (Leipzig Verlag von Bernhard Tauchnitz, 1930).

FINDLATER, RICHARD, *The Unholy Trade* (London: Victor Gollancz, 1952) pp. 170–84. Reviewed by T. C. Worsley in *New Statesman and Nation* (London), XLIV (26 July 1952) 112.

FLANAGAN, HALLIE, *Shifting Scenes of the Modern European Theatre* (New York: Coward-McCann, 1928; London, Harrap, 1929).

FOX, R. M., *Green Banners: The Story of the Irish Struggle* (London: Secker & Warburg, 1938).

FRASER, G. S., *The Modern Writer and His World* (London: André Deutsch and Pelican Books, 1964).

FRÉCHET, RENÉ, 'Sean O'Casey: un épisode de la vie du Théatre irlandais', *Le Théatre Moderne: Hommes et Tendances*, ed. Jean Jacquot (Paris: Centre National de la Recherche Scientifique, 1958) pp. 321–36.

FREEDLEY, GEORGE, 'England and Ireland', *A History of Modern Drama*, ed. Barrett H. Clark and George Freedley (New York: Appleton-Century-Crofts, 1947) pp. 226–9.

FREEDMAN, MORRIS, 'The Modern Tragicomedy of Wilde and O'Casey', *The Moral Impulse: Modern Drama from Ibsen to the Present*, Preface by Harry T. Moore (Carbondale and Edwardsville: Southern Illinois University Press; London and Amsterdam: Feffer & Simons, 1967) pp. 63–73. Reprinted from *College English* (Chicago), XXV (Apr 1964) 518–22, 527.

FREIER, ROBERT, and LAZARUS, HERBERT (eds.), '*The End of the Beginning*': *Adventures in Modern Literature* (New York: Harcourt, Brace, 1956).

FRICKER, ROBERT, 'Sean O'Casey: *Juno and the Paycock*', *Das Moderne Englische Drama: Interpretationen*, ed. Horst Oppel (Berlin: Erich Schmidt Verlag, 1963) pp. 183–202.

GASCOIGNE, BAMBER, *Twentieth-Century Drama* (London: Hutchinson University Library, 1962).

GASSNER, JOHN (ed.), 'Sean O'Casey', *A Treasury of the Theatre, from Henrik Ibsen to Eugene Ionesco* (New York: Simon & Schuster, 1935) pp. 633–4 [contains *The Plough and the Stars*].

'The Second Coming: Sean O'Casey and Paul Vincent Carroll', *Masters of the Drama* (New York: Random House, 1940; 3rd rev. ed., 1954).

Producing the Play (New York: Holt, Rinehart & Winston, 1953) pp. 48, 448–9.

(ed.), 'Genius without Fetters', *Selected Plays of Sean O'Casey* (New York: George Braziller, 1954) pp. v–xxi. Reviewed by E. J. West in *Educational Theatre Journal*, VII (Dec 1955) 354–6; and by Horace Reynolds in *Christian Science Monitor* (Boston), (24 Nov 1954) p. 9.

'O'Casey: *Pictures in the Hallway*', *Theatre at the Crossroads* (New York: Holt, Rinehart & Winston, 1960) pp. 284–6.

'More "Readings": O'Casey and Dylan Thomas', *Theatre at the Crossroads* (New York: Holt, Rinehart & Winston, 1960) pp. 286–8.

Directions in Modern Theatre and Drama (New York: Holt, Rinehart & Winston, 1966).

GELB, ARTHUR, and GELB, BARBARA, *O'Neill* (London: Jonathan Cape, 1962) pp. 787–90.

GISH, LILLIAN, *The Movies, Mr Griffith, and Me* (London: W. H. Allen; Englewood Cliffs, N.J.: Prentice-Hall, 1969) pp. 322–3 [on *Within the Gates*].

GORELIK, MORDECAI, *New Theatres for Old* (New York: Samuel French, 1941) p. 373, n. 4 [on *The Plough and the Stars* film].

GRANVILLE-BARKER, HARLEY, *On Poetry in Drama* (London: Sidgwick & Jackson, 1937) pp. 25–6.

GRAVES, CHARLES, *The Cochran Story: A Biography of Sir Charles Blake Cochran, Kt.* (London: W. H. Allen, n.d.) pp. 163, 193.

GREGORY, ANNE, *Me and Nu: Childhood at Coole* (Gerrards Cross, Bucks: Colin Smythe, 1970) pp. 83–6.

GRIFFIN, GERALD, 'Sean O'Casey', *The Wild Geese: Pen Portraits of Famous Irish Exiles* (London: Jarrolds, n.d. [1938]) pp. 216–19.

GRIGSON, GEOFFREY (ed.), 'Sean O'Casey', *The Concise Encyclopaedia of Modern World Literature* (London: Hutchinson, 1963) pp. 318-19.

GUTHRIE, TYRONE, *A Life in the Theatre* (New York and London: McGraw-Hill, 1959) pp. 297-9.

GWYNN, STEPHEN, *Irish Literature and Drama in the English Language: A Short History* (London: Thomas Nelson, 1936) pp. 209-12.

HAGOPIAN, JOHN V., and DOLCH, MARTIN (eds.), 'Sean O'Casey: *The Shadow of a Gunman*', *Insight II: Analysis of Modern British Literature* (Frankfurt am Main: Hirschgraben-Verlag, 1965).

HATCHER, HARLAN (ed.), 'Sean O'Casey', *A Modern Repertory* (New York: Harcourt, Brace, 1953) pp. 71-5 [contains *Juno and the Paycock*].

HEFFNER, HUBERT (ed.), '*Juno and the Paycock*: Sean O'Casey', *The Nature of Drama* (Boston: Houghton Mifflin, 1959).

HENN, T. R., 'The Irish Tragedy (Synge, Yeats, O'Casey)', *The Harvest of Tragedy* (London: Methuen, 1956) pp 212-14.

HEPPNER, SAM, '*Cockie*' [C. B. Cochran], with a Foreword by Noel Coward (London: Leslie Frewin, 1969).

HOBSON, HAROLD, *Theatre* (London: Longmans, Green, 1948) pp. 83-5 [on *Oak Leaves and Lavender*].
Verdict at Midnight: Sixty Years of Dramatic Criticism (London and New York: Longmans, 1952) pp. 135-8 [on *Juno and the Paycock*].

HODSON, JAMES LANSDALE, 'Sean O'Casey', *No Phantoms Here* (London: Faber, 1932) pp. 147-56 [interview].

HOGAN, ROBERT, *The Experiments of Sean O'Casey* (New York: St Martin's Press, 1960). [Derives from a Ph.D. dissertation, University of Missouri, 1956]. Reviewed by Clayton Garrison in *Quarterly Journal of Speech* (Chicago), XLVII (1960) 312-13; by Kevin Sullivan in *Nation* (N.Y.), CXCII (29 Apr 1961) 375-6; by Harold Clurman in *Saturday Review of Literature* (N.Y.), XLIII (5 Nov 1960) 31, 48; and by Denis Johnston in *Modern Drama*, IV 3 (Dec 1961) 324-8.
After the Irish Renaissance: A Critical History of the Irish Drama since 'The Plough and the Stars' (Minneapolis: University of Minnesota Press, 1967; London: Macmillan, 1968).

and O'NEILL, MICHAEL J. (eds.), *Joseph Holloway's Abbey Theatre: A Selection from His Unpublished Journal 'Impressions of a Dublin Playgoer'*, with a Preface by Harry T. Moore (Carbondale and Edwardsville: Southern Illinois University Press, 1967).

and O'NEILL, MICHAEL J. (eds.), *Joseph Holloway's Irish Theatre*, 3 vols (Dixon, Calif.: Proscenium Press, 1968–70).

and MOLIN, SVEN ERIC (eds.), 'Discussion of *The Plough and the Stars*', *Drama: The Major Genres* (New York: Dodd, Mead, 1967).

HONE, JOSEPH, *W. B. Yeats, 1865–1939*, 2nd ed. (London and New York: Macmillan, 1962) pp. 387–9.

HOSKINS, KATHARINE BAIL, *Today the Struggle* (Austin, Texas: University of Texas Press, 1969).

HOWARTH, HERBERT, *The Irish Writers 1880–1940* (London: Rockcliff, 1958; New York: Hill & Wang, 1959).

HUDSON, LYNTON, *The Twentieth-Century Drama* (London: George G. Harrap, 1946) pp. 65–6.

HUGHES, GLENN, *A History of the American Theatre, 1700–1950* (New York and London: Samuel French, 1951) pp. 388–90, 432.

HUTCHINS, PATRICIA, 'Sean O'Casey and James Joyce', *James Joyce's World* (London: Methuen, 1957) pp. 235–6.

JACQUOT, JEAN, 'La Tragédie et l'Espoir', *Le Théatre Tragique* by Jean Jacquot *et al.* (Paris: Éditions du Centre National de la Recherche Scientifique, 1962) pp. 518–19 [on *Red Roses for Me* and *The Plough and the Stars*].

JOHN, AUGUSTUS, 'Sean O'Casey', *Finishing Touches*, ed. and introduced by Daniel George (London: Jonathan Cape, 1964) pp. 49–50.

JOHNSTON, DENIS, 'Sean O'Casey', *Living Writers: Being Critical Studies Broadcast in the B.B.C. Third Programme*, ed. Gilbert Phelps (London: Sylvan Press, 1947) pp. 28–38.

JONES, MARGO, '*Cock-a-Doodle Dandy*, by Sean O'Casey', *Theatre-in-the-Round* (New York and Toronto: Rinehart, 1951) pp. 181–2.

JORDAN, JOHN, 'The Irish Theatre: Retrospect and Premonition', *Contemporary Theatre*, ed. J. R. Brown and B. Harris (London: Edward Arnold, 1962) pp. 164–83.

'Illusion and Actuality in the Later O'Casey', *Sean O'Casey*, ed. Ronald Ayling (London: Macmillan, 1969) pp. 143–61 [based on a lecture delivered at Princeton University on 6 Jan 1966 under the auspices of the Committee of the Christian Gauss Seminars in Criticism].

KAIN, RICHARD M., *Dublin in the Age of William Butler Yeats and James Joyce* (Norman: University of Oklahoma Press, 1962).

KAVANAGH, PATRICK, *Collected Prose* (London: MacGibbon & Kee, 1967).

KAVANAGH, PETER, *The Irish Theatre: Being a History of the Drama in Ireland from the Earliest Period to the Present Day* (Tralee: Kerryman, 1946).

'Sean O'Casey', *The Story of the Abbey Theatre from its Origins in 1899 to the Present* (New York: Devin-Adair, 1950).

KENNELLY, BRENDAN, 'Sean O'Casey', *Encyclopaedia Britannica*, vol. XVI (London: William Benton, 1970) p. 835.

KERR, WALTER, *How Not to Write a Play* (Boston: The Writer, 1955) p. 66.

KITCHIN, LAURENCE, *Mid-Century Drama* (London: Faber & Faber, 1960; 2nd rev. ed., 1962).

'O'Casey', *Drama in the Sixties: Form and Interpretation* (London: Faber & Faber, 1966) pp. 103–6.

KNIGHT, GEORGE WILSON, *Christ and Nietzche: An Essay in Poetic Wisdom* (London: Staples Press, 1948).

The Golden Labyrinth: A Study of British Drama (London: Phoenix House, 1962) pp. 373–80.

The Christian Renaissance (London: Methuen, 1962) pp. 341–7. Reprinted from *Stand*, IV 3 (summer 1960) 15–18. Reprinted in *Sean O'Casey*, ed. Ronald Ayling (London: Macmillan, 1969) pp. 177–82.

KOSLOW, JULES, *The Green and the Red: Sean O'Casey, the Man and His Plays* (New York: Golden Griffin Books, 1950). Reprinted as *Sean O'Casey: The Man and His Plays* (New York: Citadel, 1966).

Reviewed by Harold Clurman in *New York Times Book Review* (10 Dec 1950) p. 5; and by Herbert Goldstone in *Wisconsin Studies in Contemporary Literature*, VIII 3 (summer 1967) 468–72.

KRAUSE, DAVID, *Sean O'Casey: The Man and His Work* (London: MacGibbon & Kee; New York: Macmillan, 1960; Collier Books, 1962; London, repr., 1967) [derives from a Ph.D. dissertation entitled 'Prometheus of Dublin', New York University, 1956]. Reviewed by V. S. Pritchett in *New Statesman* (London), LIX (16 Apr 1960) 560; by Micheál Mac Liammóir in *Sunday Times* (London), (27 Mar 1960) p. 26; by Louis MacNeice in *Observer* (London), (27 Mar 1960) 23; by Charles Hamblett in *Lilliput* (London), XLVI 6 (June 1960) 66; by Roy Walker in *Listener* (London), LXIII (14 Apr 1960), 672, 675; by Alan Brien in *Spectator* (London), CCIV (8 Apr 1960) 516–17; in *Times Literary Supplement* (London), (8 Apr 1960) p. 220; in *Times* (London), (30 Mar 1960) p. 13; by Gerard Fay in *Manchester Guardian* (8 Apr 1960) p. 15; by Laurence Thompson in *News Chronicle* (London), (30 Mar 1960) p. 6; by H. A. L. Craig in *Irish Times* (Dublin), (30 Mar 1960) p. 8; by Robert W. Caswell in *Studies* (Dublin), XLIX 194 (summer 1960) 212–14; in *Newsweek* (N.Y.), LVI (8 Aug 1960) 77; by Alan Pryce-Jones in *New York Herald Tribune Book Review* (7 Aug 1960) p. 3; by Brooks Atkinson in *New York Times Book Review* (7 Aug 1960) p. 1; by Vivian Mercier in *Hudson Review*, (winter 1960) 631–6; by Kevin Sullivan in *Nation* (N.Y.), CXCII (29 Apr 1961) 375–6; by Harold Clurman in *Saturday Review of Literature* (N.Y.), XLIII (5 Nov 1960) 31, 48; by Denis Johnston in *Modern Drama*, IV, 3 (Dec 1961) 324–8; by John O'Riordan in *Books and Bookmen* (London), V 8 (May 1960) 26; by John O'Riordan in *Tribune* (London), XXXI 22 (2 June 1967) 11; and by Ernst Schoen in *Theater der Zeit*, n.s. III (1960).

'The Theatre of Dion Boucicault', *The Dolmen Boucicault* (Dublin: The Dolmen Press, 1964).

A Self-Portrait of the Artist as a Man: Sean O'Casey's Letters (Dublin: The Dolmen Press; London: Oxford University Press, 1968). Reprinted in *Sean O'Casey*, ed. Ronald Ayling (London: Macmillan, 1969) pp. 235–51. Reviewed in *Times Literary Supplement* (London), (28 Nov 1968) p. 1333. See 'Sean O'Casey' by Phiannon Gooding (12 Dec 1968) p. 1409 [letter to the Editor].

'Sean O'Casey', *The Reader's Encyclopaedia of World Drama*, ed. John Gassner and Edward Quinn (New York: Crowell, 1969; London: Methuen, 1970).

KRONENBERGER, LOUIS (ed.), '*Juno and the Paycock* by Sean O'Casey', *Cavalcade of Comedy: 21 Brilliant Comedies from Jonson and Wycherley to Thurber and Coward* (New York: Simon & Schuster, 1953) pp. 532–3.

(ed.), *The Best Plays of 1955–1956* (New York: Dodd, Mead, 1956).

(ed.), *The Best Plays of 1956–1957* (New York: Dodd, Mead, 1957).

KRUTCH, JOSEPH WOOD, '*Modernism' in Modern Drama: A Definition and an Estimate* (Ithaca, N.Y.: Cornell University Press, 1953).

KUNITZ, STANLEY J., 'Sean O'Casey', *Living Authors: A Book of Biographies*, ed. Dilly Tante (New York: H. W. Wilson, 1931).

and HAYCRAFT, HOWARD (eds.), 'Sean O'Casey', *Twentieth Century Authors: A Biographical Dictionary of Modern Literature* (New York: H. W. Wilson, 1942).

and HAYCRAFT, HOWARD (eds.), 'Sean O'Casey', *Twentieth Century Authors*, First Supplement (New York: H. W. Wilson, 1955).

LAWSON, JOHN HOWARD, *Theory and Technique of Playwrighting* (New York: G. P. Putnam's, 1936; Hill & Wang, 1960) pp. xxiii–xxiv.

LEECH, CLIFFORD, *Tragedy* (London: Methuen, 1969) pp. 26, 37, 40.

LEGG, L. G. WICKHAM (ed.), *Dictionary of National Biography: Supplement 1931–1940* (Oxford: Oxford University Press, 1949).

LEWIS, ALLAN, 'Irish Romantic Realism – Sean O'Casey: *Red Roses for Me*', *The Contemporary Theatre: The Significant Playwrights of Our Time* (New York: Crown Publishers, 1962) pp. 169–91.

LINDSAY, JACK, 'Sean O'Casey as a Socialist Artist', *Sean O'Casey*, ed. Ronald Ayling (London: Macmillan, 1969) pp. 192–203.

LUMLEY, FREDERICK, *Trends in 20th Century Drama: A Survey since Ibsen and Shaw* (London: Barrie & Rockcliff, 1960) pp. 223–5. Reprinted under the title *New Trends in 20th Century Drama: A Survey since Ibsen and Shaw* (London: Barrie & Rockliff, 1967) pp. 294–6.

McCann, Sean (ed.), *The World of Sean O'Casey*, Four Square Books (London: The New English Library, 1966). Reviewed by Hugh Leonard in *Plays and Players* (London), xiv, 10 (July 1967) 55–6; by Ronald Ayling in *Tribune* (London), xxx 51 (23 Dec 1966) 16 [see Anthony Butler's reply (6 Jan 1967) p. 8, and Ayling's counter-reply (20 Jan 1967) p. 8; also letter to the Editor by John O'Riordan (20 Jan 1967) p. 8]; and by Mary Bergh in *Irish Democrat* (Dublin), (Jan 1967) p. 7.

(ed.), *The Story of the Abbey Theatre* (London: The New English Library, 1967).

MacCarthy, Desmond, 'Hyde Park (*Within the Gates*)', *Drama* (London and New York: Putnam, 1940). Reprinted from *New Statesman and Nation* (London), vii (17 Feb 1934) 226–7.

MacDiarmid, Hugh [Christopher Murray Grieve], 'Sean O'Casey', *The Company I've Kept: Essays in Autobiography* (London: Hutchinson, 1966) pp. 161–9. Reviewed with adverse comments on O'Casey by Bernard Maher in *Irish Times* (Dublin), (19 Nov 1966) p. 9. See reply by Ronald Ayling (29 Nov 1966) p. 7 [letter to the Editor].

'Slàinte Chùramach, Seán', *Sean O'Casey*, ed. Ronald Ayling (London: Macmillan, 1969) pp. 252–60.

Mac Liammóir, Micheál, 'Problem Plays', *The Irish Theatre*, ed. Lennox Robinson (London: Macmillan, 1939) pp. 199–227.

All for Hecuba: An Irish Theatrical Autobiography (London: Methuen, 1946).

Theatre in Ireland (Dublin: Published for the Cultural Relations Committee of Ireland by Colm O'Lochlainn, At the Sign of the Three Candles, 1950; reprinted with Sequel, 1964).

Macmillan, Harold, *Winds of Change, 1914–1939* (London: Macmillan, 1966) p. 187.

MacNamara, Brinsley (ed.), *Abbey Plays 1899–1948: Including the Productions of the Irish Literary Theatre* (Dublin: At the Sign of the Three Candles, n.d. [1949]).

Magill, Frank N. (ed.), 'Sean O'Casey', *Cyclopedia of World Authors* (New York: Harper, 1958) pp. 797–9.

MALONE, ANDREW E., *The Irish Drama, 1896–1928* (London: Constable, 1929; New York: Benjamin Blom, 1965) pp. 209–19. Reprinted in *Sean O'Casey*, ed. Ronald Ayling (London: Macmillan, 1969) pp. 68–75.

MALONE, MAUREEN, *The Plays of Sean O'Casey*, with a Preface by Harry T. Moore (Carbondale and Edwardsville: Southern Illinois University Press; London and Amsterdam: Feffer & Simons, 1969). Reviewed by David Krause in *Modern Drama* (Lawrence, Kansas), XIII no. 3 (Dec 1970) 336–40.

MANTLE, BURNS (ed.), *The Best Plays of 1927–28 and the Year Book of the Drama in America* (New York: Dodd, Mead, 1928) [contains *The Plough and the Stars*, abridged].

MARGULIES, MARTIN B., *The Early Life of Sean O'Casey* (Dublin: Dolmen Press, 1970). Reviewed by John O'Riordan in *Tribune* (London), (9 July 1971); by R. B. Marriott in *Stage and Television Today* (London), (12 Aug 1971) p. 8; and by Sean McMahon in *Irish Press* (Dublin), (15 May 1971).

MARRIOTT, J. W., *Modern Drama* (London: Thomas Nelson, n.d. [1934]) pp. 200–2.

MELCHINGER, SIEGFRIED, *Concise Encyclopedia of Modern Drama* (London: Vision Press, 1970).

MERCHANT, FRANCIS, *A.E.: An Irish Promethean* (Columbia, S.C.: Benedict College Press, 1954) pp. 205–7, 238–9 [includes an O'Casey letter].

MERCIER, VIVIAN, *The Irish Comic Tradition* (Oxford: Oxford University Press, 1962).

and GREENE, DAVID H. (eds.), '*The Shadow of a Gunman*: Sean O'Casey', *1000 Years of Irish Prose: The Literary Revival* (New York: Grosset & Dunlap, 1961).

METSCHER, THOMAS, *Sean O'Caseys Dramatisher Stil* (Braunschweig: Georg Westermann Verlag, 1967). Reviewed by Elisabeth Freundlich in *Das Argument 61*, XII (9–10 Dec 1970) 755–7.

MILLER, ANNA IRENE, *The Independent Theatre in Europe, 1887 to the Present* (New York: Ray Long & Richard R. Smith, 1931; Benjamin Blom, 1966) pp. 289–91, 309–10.

MORGAN, CHARLES, 'On Sean O'Casey's *The Silver Tassie*', *The English Dramatic Critics: An Anthology, 1660–1932*, ed. James Agate (London: Arthur Barker, 1932; New York: Hill & Wang, n.d. [1958]) pp. 347–9. Reprinted from *Times* (London), (12 Oct 1929) p. 8. Reprinted in *Sean O'Casey*, ed. Ronald Ayling (London: Macmillan, 1969) pp. 88–90.

MORITZ, CHARLES (ed.), 'Sean O'Casey', *Current Biography Yearbook 1962* (New York: H. W. Wilson, 1962) pp. 324–7.

(ed.) 'Sean O'Casey', *Current Biography Yearbook 1964* (New York: H. W. Wilson, 1964) p. 326.

MUIR, KENNETH, 'Verse and Prose', *Contemporary Theatre*, Stratford-upon-Avon Studies 4, ed. John Russell Brown and Bernard Harris (London: Edward Arnold, 1962) pp. 100–2.

NATHAN, GEORGE JEAN, 'O'Casey', *Art of the Night* (New York: Alfred A. Knopf, 1928) pp. 185–93. Reprinted in *The Magic Mirror: Selected Writings on the Theatre*, ed. Thomas Quinn Curtiss (New York: Alfred A. Knopf, 1960) pp. 180–5.

Encyclopaedia of the Theatre (New York: Alfred A. Knopf, 1940).

(ed.), 'Foreword', *Five Great Modern Irish Plays* (New York: The Modern Library, 1941) [contains *Juno and the Paycock*].

(ed.), '*The Plough and the Stars* by Sean O'Casey', *World's Great Plays* (Cleveland, Ohio: World Publishing Company, 1944; New York: Grosset's Universal Library, 1961).

The Theatre Book of the Year 1946–1947: A Record and an Interpretation (New York: Alfred A. Knopf, 1947) pp. 231–9.

The Theatre in the Fifties (New York: Alfred A. Knopf, 1953).

et al. (eds.), *American Spectator Yearbook* (New York, 1941) pp. 251–6.

NEWMAN, EVELYN, *The International Note in Contemporary Drama* (New York: Kingsland Press, 1931) pp. 36–43 [on *The Silver Tassie*].

NICHOLS, BEVERLEY, 'Sean O'Casey, or A Rough Diamond', *Are They the Same at Home? Being a Series of Bouquets Differently Distributed* (New York: George H. Doran, 1927) pp. 235–8 [interview].

NICHOLSON, HUBERT, 'The O'Casey Horn of Plenty', *A Voyage to Wonderland and Other Essays* (London: Heinemann, 1947) pp. 36–54. Reprinted in *Sean O'Casey*, ed. Ronald Ayling (London: Macmillan, 1969) pp. 207–19 [on O'Casey's autobiographies].

NICOLL, ALLARDYCE, *World Drama, from Aeschylus to Anouilh* (London: George G. Harrap, 1949) pp. 807–10.

British Drama: An Historical Survey from the Beginnings to the Present Time (London: Harrap, 1958).

'Sean O'Casey', *Chambers's Encyclopaedia*. New revised edition, vol. x (Oxford: Pergamon Press, 1966) pp. 166–7.

NOWELL-SMITH, SIMON (ed.), *Letters to Macmillan* (London: Macmillan; New York: St Martin's Press, 1967).

O'CASEY, EILEEN, *Sean*, ed. with an introduction by J. C. Trewin (London: Macmillan, 1971).

O'CASEY, SEAN, 'On Playwrighting', *Selected Plays of Sean O'Casey*, ed. John Gassner (New York: George Braziller, 1954) pp. xxiii–xxiv.

'Before Curtain-Rise', *Selected Plays of Sean O'Casey*, ed. John Gassner (New York: George Braziller, 1954) pp. xxv–xxviii.

'*Cock-a-Doodle Dandy* (1958)', *Playwrights on Playwrighting*, ed. Toby Cole (New York: Hill & Wang, 1960) pp. 247–9. Reprinted from *New York Times* (9 Nov 1958) section 2, pp. 1, 3.

O'CONNOR, FRANK, 'The Abbey Theatre', *My Father's Son* (London: Macmillan, 1968).

A Short History of Irish Literature: A Backward Look (London: Macmillan; New York: Capricorn Books, 1968) pp. 216–21.

O'CONNOR, ULICK, *Brendan Behan* (London: Hamish Hamilton, 1970).

OHAODHA, MICHEÁL, 'Sean O'Casey', *The Abbey – Then and Now* (Dublin: The Abbey Theatre, 1969) pp. 60–1 [extract from a broadcast tribute on the occasion of O'Casey's death].

PASCAL, ROY, *Design and Truth in Autobiography* (London: Routledge & Kegan Paul; Cambridge, Mass.: Harvard University Press, 1960) pp. 151–5.

PEACOCK, RONALD, *The Poet in the Theatre* (London: Routledge, 1946), p. 6.

PEARSON, HESKETH, *Bernard Shaw: His Life and Personality* (London: Methuen, 1961) pp. 282–3.

PELLIZZI, CAMILLO, *English Drama: The Last Great Phase*, trans. Rowan Williams (London: Macmillan, 1935) pp. 236–40.

POWER, PATRICK C., *A Literary History of Ireland* (Cork: Mercier Press, 1969) pp. 174 ff.

PRESCOTT, JOSEPH (ed.), 'Sean O'Casey Concerning James Joyce', *Irish Renaissance: A Gathering of Essays, Memoirs, and Letters from 'The Massachusetts Review'*, ed. Robin Skelton and David R. Clark (Dublin: Dolmen Press, 1965). Reprinted from *The Massachusetts Review* (Amherst, Mass.), v 2 (winter 1964) 335–6.

PRIOR, MOODY E., *The Language of Tragedy* (New York: Columbia University Press, 1947).

PRITCHETT, V. S., *Dublin: A Portrait* (London: The Bodley Head, 1967) pp. 10–11, 14–16.

RAINE, KATHLEEN (ed.), *Letters on Poetry from W. B. Yeats to Dorothy Wellesley* (London: Oxford University Press, 1964) pp. 1, 22.

REYNOLDS, ERNEST, *Modern English Drama: A Survey of the Theatre from 1900* (London: George G. Harrap, 1949) pp. 155–6.

RIVOALLAN, A[NATOLE], 'La littérature irlandaise', *L'Irlande* (Paris: Librairie Armand Colin, 1934).

Littérature Irlandaise Contemporaine (Paris, 1939).

ROBINSON, LENNOX, *Curtain Up: An Autobiography* (London: Michael Joseph, 1942).

Towards an Appreciation of the Theatre (Dublin: Metropolitan Publishing Co., 1945) pp. 16–19.

(ed.), *Lady Gregory's Journals 1916–1930* (London: Putnam, 1946; New York: Macmillan, 1947) [contains important background material about the early plays].

Pictures in a Theatre: A Conversation Piece (Dublin: The Abbey Theatre, n.d. [1947]).

Ireland's Abbey Theatre: A History, 1899–1951 (London: Sidgwick & Jackson, 1951).

RUDIN, SEYMOUR, 'Playwright to Critic: Sean O'Casey's Letters to George Jean Nathan', *Irish Renaissance*, ed. R. Skelton and D. R. Clark (Dublin: Dolmen Press, 1965). Reprinted from *Massachusetts Review* (Amherst, Mass.), v 2 (winter 1964) 326–34.

RUSSELL, CARO MAE GREEN, 'Sean O'Casey, Portrayer of Slum Life', *Modern Plays and Playwrights* (Chapel Hill, N.C.: University of North Carolina Press, 1936).

RYAN, DESMOND, *Remembering Sion: A Chronicle of Storm and Quiet* (London: Arthur Barker, 1934) pp. 81–4.

SAHAL, N., 'Sean O'Casey', *Sixty Years of Realistic Irish Drama* (Bombay: Macmillan, 1971) chap. 7, pp. 90–119.

SARUXANJAN, A., *Tvorčestvo Šona O'Kejsi* (Moscow: Nauka, 1965).

SHANK, THEODORE J. (ed.), *A Digest of 500 Plays: Plot Outlines and Production Notes* (New York: Collier Books, 1963) pp. 412–16.

SHIPLEY, JOSEPH T., *Guide to Great Plays* (Washington, D.C.: Public Affairs Press, 1956) pp. 461–5 [on *Juno and the Paycock*, *The Plough and the Stars* and *The Silver Tassie*].

SHORT, ERNEST, *Theatrical Cavalcade* (London: Eyre & Spottiswoode, 1942) pp. 208–10.
Sixty Years of Theatre (London: Eyre & Spottiswoode, 1951) pp. 376–8.

SKELTON, ROBIN, and CLARK, DAVID R. (eds.), *Irish Renaissance: A Gathering of Essays, Memoirs, and Letters from 'The Massachusetts Review'* (Dublin: Dolmen Press, 1965).

SNOWDEN, J. A., 'Sean O'Casey and Naturalism', *Essays and Studies 1971*, ed. Bernard Harris (London: John Murray, 1971) pp. 56–68.

SNYDER, FRANKLYN BLISS and MARTIN, ROBERT GRANT (eds.), 'Sean O'Casey', *A Book of English Literature*, vol. 2 (New York: Macmillan, 1943) pp. 1142–4 [contains *Juno and the Paycock*].

SOBEL, BERNARD (ed.), *The Theatre Handbook and Digest of Plays* (New York: Crown Publishers, 1940).

SPEAIGHT, ROBERT, 'Sean O'Casey', *Drama since 1939* (London: Published for the British Council by Longmans Green, 1947) pp. 25–7.

SPINNER, KASPAR, *Die Alte Dame Sagt: Nein! Drei Irische Dramatiker: Lennox Robinson – Sean O'Casey – Denis Johnston*, Swiss Studies in English (Berne: Francke Verlag, 1961).

STARKIE, WALTER, 'Sean O'Casey', *The Irish Theatre: Lectures Delivered during the Abbey Theatre Festival Held in Dublin in August 1938*, ed. Lennox Robinson (London: Macmillan, 1939) pp. 149–76.

STAUFFER, RUTH MATILDA, CUNNINGHAM, WILLIAM H., and SULLIVAN, CATHERINE J. (eds.) 'Sean O'Casey: *The End of the Beginning*', *Adventures in Modern Literature*, 3rd ed. (New York: Harcourt, Brace, 1951) pp. 607–8.

STOCK, A. G., 'The Heroic Image: *Red Roses for Me*', *Sean O'Casey*, ed. Ronald Ayling (London: Macmillan, 1969) pp. 126–30.

STYAN, J. L., *The Elements of Drama* (Cambridge: Cambridge University Press, 1960) pp. 189–95.

The Dramatic Experience: A Guide to the Reading of Plays (Cambridge: Cambridge University Press, 1965).

The Dark Comedy (Cambridge: Cambridge University Press, 1968).

SWAFFER, HANNEN, 'Sean O'Casey', *Hannen Swaffer's Who's Who* (London: Hutchinson, n.d. [1929]) pp. 17–18.

THOMPSON, DAVID (ed.), '*Hall of Healing*: Sean O'Casey', *Theatre Today*, The Heritage of Literature Series (London: Longmans, 1965).

TINDALL, WILLIAM YORK, *Forces in Modern British Literature, 1885–1956* (New York: Random House, 1956).

TORCHIANA, DONALD, *W. B. Yeats and Georgian Ireland* (Evanston, Ill.: Northwestern University Press, 1966).

TREWIN, J. C., *The English Theatre* (London: Paul Elek, 1948) pp. 65–9.

The Theatre since 1900 (London: Andrew Dakers, 1951).

A Play Tonight (London: Elek Books, 1952) pp. 89, 122, 147.

'Dubliner (Sean O'Casey, 1880–   )', *Dramatists of Today* (London and New York: Staples Press, 1953) pp. 56–66.

'Introduction', *Three More Plays by Sean O'Casey* (London: Macmillan; New York: St Martin's Press, 1965) [contains *The Silver Tassie, Purple Dust* and *Red Roses for Me*].

TUCKER, S. MARION and DOWNER, ALAN S. (eds.), 'Sean O'Casey and His Plays', *Twenty-Five Modern Plays* (New York: Harper & Row, 1953) pp. 723–4 [contains *The Plough and the Stars*].

TYNAN, KENNETH, '*The Bishop's Bonfire* by Sean O'Casey, at the Gaiety, Dublin', *Curtains* (London: Longmans; New York: Atheneum, 1961) pp. 83–5. Reprinted from *Observer* (London), (6 Mar 1955) p. 11.

'*The Shadow of a Gunman* by Sean O'Casey, at the Bijou', *Curtains* (London: Longmans; New York: Atheneum, 1961) pp. 285–8. Reprinted from *New Yorker* (N.Y.), XXXIV (6 Dec 1958) 112.

ULANOV, BARRY (ed.), 'Sean O'Casey: *Purple Dust*', *Makers of the Modern Theater* (New York: McGraw-Hill, 1961).

VAN DOREN, MARK, 'Considering the Source', *Private Reader* (New York: Holt, 1942) pp. 351–2 [on *The Plough and the Stars*]. Partially reprinted from *Nation* (N.Y.), CXLIV 7 (13 Feb 1937) 194.

VAN DOREN, CARL and VAN DOREN, MARK, *American and British Literature since 1890* (New York: Appleton-Century-Crofts, 1953) pp. 338–40.

VEITCH, NORMAN, *The People's: Being a History of The People's Theatre Newcastle upon Tyne 1911–1939* (Gateshead: Northumberland Press, 1950) pp. 177, 183.

VÖLKER, KLAUS, *Irisches Theater II: Sean O'Casey* (Hanover: Fredrich Verlag, 1968).

WADE, ALLAN (ed.), *The Letters of W. B. Yeats* (London: Rupert Hart-Davis, 1954).

WARD, A. C., *The Nineteen-Twenties: Literature and Ideas in the Post-war Decade* (London: Methuen, 1930) pp. 73–5 [on *The Silver Tassie*].

Twentieth-Century English Literature, 1901–1960 (London: Methuen, 1966).

WARNOCK, ROBERT (ed.), 'Sean O'Casey: *Juno and the Paycock*', *Representative Modern Plays: British* (Chicago: Scott, Foresman, 1953) pp. 357–65.

WATSON, E. BRADLEE, and PRESSEY, BENFIELD (eds.), 'Juno and
the Paycock by Sean O'Casey', Contemporary Drama: European,
English and Irish, American Plays (New York: Scribner's, 1931)
pp. 799–800.

and PRESSEY, BENFIELD (eds.), 'Purple Dust by Sean O'Casey',
Contemporary Drama: Fifteen Plays, American, English and Irish,
European (New York: Scribner's, 1959) pp. 379–80.

WHITE, J. R., Misfit: An Autobiography (London: Jonathan Cape,
1930).

WHITE, TERENCE DE VERE (ed.), A Leaf from The Yellow Book: The
Correspondence of George Egerton (London: Richards Press, 1958)
pp. 108, 152, 166.

WHITING, FRANK M., An Introduction to the Theatre (New York and
Evanston, Ill.: Harper & Row, 1961) pp. 84–5.

WHITMAN, CHARLES HUNTINGTON (ed.), 'Sean O'Casey: Juno and
the Paycock', Representative Modern Dramas (New York: Macmillan,
1936) pp. 785–8.

WIECZOREK, HUBERT, Irische Lebenshaltung im Neuen Irischen Drama
(Breslau: Priebatsch's Buchhandlung, 1937).

WILLIAMS, RAYMOND, 'The Colour of Sean O'Casey', Drama from
Ibsen to Eliot (London: Chatto & Windus, 1952; rev. ed., 1964)
pp. 169–74 [contains a hostile criticism]. Considerably revised
essay on O'Casey in Drama from Ibsen to Brecht (London: Chatto &
Windus, 1968) pp. 147–53.

WILLIAMSON, AUDREY, Theatre of Two Decades (London: Rockliff,
1951) pp. 186–9.
'From Paris to Dublin: The Bishop's Bonfire', Contemporary Theatre,
1953–1956 (London: Rockliff, 1956).

WILSON, A. E., Post-war Theatre (London: Home & Van Thal, n.d.
[1949] pp. 39, 103.

WITTIG, KURT, Sean O'Casey als Dramatiker: Ein Beitrag zum
Nachkriegsdrama Irlands (Leipzig: Fritz Scharf, 1937) [published
dissertation submitted to Marburg University]. Reviewed by A.B.
in Archiv für d. Studium d. neueren Sprachen (Herrig), CLXXIII (1937)
267; and by Karl Arns in Anglia Beiblatt, XLIX (1937) 273–4.

YEATS, W. B., *Pages from a Diary Written in Nineteen Hundred and Thirty* (Dublin: Cuala Press, 1944) pp. 57–8.

ZASLAWSKI, HEINZ, *Die Werke Sean O'Caseys, unter Besonderer Berücksichtigung Seiner Zweiten Periode* (Wien, 1949) [published dissertation].

(b) Periodicals

'The Abbey Directors and Mr Sean O'Casey', *Irish Statesman* (Dublin), X 14 (9 June 1928) 268–72 [contains letters from O'Casey, Yeats, Lennox Robinson and Walter Starkie on *The Silver Tassie*].

'Abbey's New Policy: Famous Theater at Dublin to Import Plays from Continent', *Literary Digest* (N.Y.), CXIX 22 (1 June 1935) 24.

ABIRACHED, ROBERT, 'Deux pièces de Sean O'Casey', *Études* (Paris), CCIX (June 1961) 382–7.

ADAMOV, ARTHUR, '*Roses Rouges Pour Moi*', *L'Humanité* (Paris), (5 Sep 1960) p. 2.

ALLDRIDGE, JOHN, 'What's Wrong with the Abbey?', *Irish Digest* (Dublin), XXIX 4 (Feb 1948) 17–19 [condensed from *Manchester Evening News*].

ALLEN, RALPH, 'Pvt Saroyan and the War', *New York Times Magazine* (4 June 1944) p. 46 [William Saroyan on Sean O'Casey].

ALSOP, JOSEPH, Jr, 'Sean O'Casey, Irish Patriot', *Vanity Fair* (N.Y.), XLIII (Dec 1934) 35, 76.

ANDERSON, MAXWELL, 'Prelude to Dramatic Poetry', *New York Times* (6 Oct 1935) section 11, pp. 1, 3.

ARMSTRONG, WILLIAM A., 'History, Autobiography, and *The Shadow of a Gunman*', *Modern Drama*, II 4 (Feb 1960) 417–24.

'The Sources and Themes of *The Plough and the Stars*', *Modern Drama*, IV 3 (Dec 1961) 234–42.

'As It Happens', *Times* (London), (15 Mar 1967), p. 12 [on Shivaun O'Casey].

ATKINSON, BROOKS, 'Paradox of O'Casey: He Is One of the Great Modern Writers But His Plays Are Seldom Offered', *New York Times* (2 Apr 1950) section 2, p. 1.

'Art and Dollars: Thousands for Rubbish But Not for O'Casey', *New York Times* (11 Jan 1953) section 2, p. 1.

'O'Casey's Communism Is Really a Dream of a Better Life for Mankind', *New York Times* (13 Sep 1960) p. 34.

'Visit with Sean O'Casey: Despite Infirmities, Green Crow Is Still in Good Form', *New York Times* (31 Dec 1962) p. 5 [interview].

'Sean O'Casey, Nearly Blind, Still Thunders But Always with Fondest Greetings', *New York Times* (14 Apr 1964) p. 34.

'Critic Recalls the Dramatist as "A Darlin' Man" ', *New York Times* (19 Sep 1964) pp. 1, 12 [obituary].

'In 84 Years of Unselfish Life, O'Casey Had His Heart Fail Him Only Once', *New York Times* (22 Sep 1964) p. 36.

'Sean Sean Fare Thee Well', *Idea and Image* (N.Y.), Charter Issue (1967) pp. 11–13.

'Au Revoir to the Abbey Theatre', *Sunday Times* (London), (25 Jan 1959) p. 9.

'The Author of *Juno*: A Talk with Mr O'Casey', *Observer* (London), (22 Nov 1925) p. 9 [interview].

AYLING, RONALD, 'Rowdelum Randy: A Postscript on O'Casey and His Critics', *Enquiry* (Nottingham), I 1 (Mar 1958) 48–54; I 2 (June 1958) 36.

'The Poetic Drama of T. S. Eliot', *English Studies in Africa*, II 2 (Sep 1959) 247–50 [on O'Casey's possible influence on Eliot's technique].

'O'Casey at 80', *Irish Times* (Dublin), (16 May 1960) p. 9.

'*Nannie's Night Out*', *Modern Drama*, V 2 (Sep 1962) 154–63.

'Feathers Flying: Politics in the Early Life and Thought of Sean O'Casey', *Dubliner*, III 1 (spring 1964) 54–67.

'Sean O'Casey: The Writer Behind His Critics', *Kilkenny Magazine*, II (spring–summer 1964) 69–92. Reprinted in *Drama Survey* (Minneapolis), III 4 (fall 1965) 582–91. Cf. Saros Cowasjee, ibid., IV (summer 1966) 191–2.

'Feathers Finely Aflutther', *Modern Drama*, VII 2 (Sep 1964) 135–47.

'Sean O'Casey: Fact and Fancy', *Dublin Magazine*, IV 3-4 (autumn-winter 1965) 69-82. Reprinted [revised] in *Massachusetts Review*, VII 3 (summer 1966) 603-12.

'W. B. Yeats on Plays and Players', *Modern Drama*, IX 1 (May 1966) 1-10.

'O'Casey's Words Live On', *New World Review* (N.Y.), XXXIV 10 (Nov 1966) 52-9.

'Sean O'Casey and His Critics', *New Theatre Magazine* (Bristol), VIII 1 (autumn 1968) 5-19.

'A Note on Sean O'Casey's Manuscripts and His Working Methods', *Bulletin of the New York Public Library*, LXXIII 6 (June 1969) 359-67. [Originally written in June 1965 as an introduction to a list, prepared by Ronald Ayling, of the papers then in the possession of the O'Casey Trustees and since acquired by the Berg Collection of English and American Literature in the New York Public Library.]

'The Autobiographies of Sean O'Casey', *Research Studies* (Pullman, Wash.), XXXVII 2 (June 1969) 122-9.

'Character Control and "Alienation" in *The Plough and the Stars*', *James Joyce Quarterly* (Tulsa, Okla.), VIII 1 (fall 1970) 29-47.

BACHMANN, C. H., 'Das Spiel als Zuflucht: Notizen zu Stücken von Schéhadé, Jeffers, O'Casey und Barrie', *Anregung* (Köln), XII (1960) 246-7.

'Back to the Egyptians', *Times* (London), (13 Apr 1968) p. 10 [on Breon O'Casey].

BAGGETT, PATRICIA, 'Sean O'Casey's Development of a Basic Theme', *Dublin Magazine*, XXXI 4 (Oct-Dec 1956) 25-34.

'Ban on Plays for Eire Radio: Mr O'Casey's Decision', *Times* (London), (29 July 1958) p. 2.

BARZUN, JACQUES, 'O'Casey at Your Bedside', *Griffin Magazine* (London), III (Oct 1954) 4-9. Reprinted in *Tulane Drama Review* (New Orleans), II 2 (Feb 1958) 57-61; and in *Sean O'Casey*, ed. Ronald Ayling (London: Macmillan, 1969) pp. 120-5.

SEAN O'CASEY: A BIBLIOGRAPHY OF CRITICISM

BECKETT, SAMUEL, 'Gratitude and Homage', *Irish Times* (Dublin), (30 Mar 1960) p. 8.

BEHAN, BRENDAN, 'O'Casey', *Irish Times* (Dublin), (29 Aug 1961) p. 5 [letter to the Editor].

BELLAK, GEORGE, 'Tea with Sean', *Theatre Arts* (N.Y.), XXXVII (Sep 1953) 70–1, 91–2 [interview].

BENSTOCK, BERNARD, 'A Covey of Clerics in Joyce and O'Casey', *James Joyce Quarterly* (Tulsa, Okla.), II 1 (fall 1964) 18–32.
'The Mother-Madonna-Matriarch in Sean O'Casey', *Southern Review* (Baton Rouge, La.), VI, n.s., 3 (summer 1970) 603–23.
'Kelly, Burke and Shea', *James Joyce Quarterly* (Tulsa, Okla.), VIII 1 (fall 1970) 124–6.

BENTLEY, ERIC, 'The Drama at Ebb', *Kenyon Review*, VII 2 (spring 1945) 169–84.
'World Theatre: 1900–1950', *Theatre Arts* (N.Y.), XXXIII (Dec 1949) 22–7.
'Discovering a Play', *Theatre Arts* (N.Y.), XXXIV (Oct 1950) 40–3, 94–5.
'Irish Theatre: Splendeurs et Misères', *Poetry* (Chicago), LXXIX 4 (Jan 1952) 216–32. Reprinted in *In Search of Theater* (New York: Vintage Books, 1953) pp. 315–21.
'The Case of O'Casey', *New Republic* (N.Y.), CXXVII (13 Oct 1952) 17–18. Reprinted in *The Dramatic Event: An American Chronicle* (Boston: Beacon Press, 1956) pp. 42–5.
'The Drama: An Extinct Species?', *Partisan Review* (N.Y.), XXI 4 (July–Aug 1954) 411–17.

BERGHOLZ, HARRY, 'Sean O'Casey', *Englische Studien* (Leipzig), LXV 1 (1930) 49–67.

BISHOP, G. W., 'Sean O'Casey: Poet-Playwright', *Theatre Guild Magazine*, VII (Feb 1930) 11–14, 55.

BOAS, GUY, 'The Drama of Sean O'Casey', *College English* (Chicago), X 2 (Nov 1948) 80–6.

BRERETON-BARRY, R., 'The Need for a State Theatre', *Irish Statesman* (Dublin), III 7 (25 Oct 1924) 210–12. [See correspondence (1 Nov 1924) p. 238; (8 Nov 1924) p. 270; and (15 Nov 1924) p. 301.]

BRIEN, ALAN, 'O'Casey – Child of Slums', *Sunday Telegraph* (London), (20 Sep 1964) p. 6 [obituary].

'Broadway Pays Tribute to O'Casey', *Irish Times* (Dublin), (13 Oct 1964) p. 5.

BROMAGE, MARY COGAN, 'Literature of Ireland Today', *South Atlantic Quarterly* (Durham, N.C.), XLII 1 (Jan 1943) 27–37.

'The Yeats–O'Casey Quarrel', *Michigan Quarterly Review*, LXIV 14 (winter 1958) 135–44.

BROWNE, MAURICE, 'Playwright and Box Office', *Listener* (London), XX 495 (7 July 1938) 10–11 [discussion with O'Casey]. Reprinted in *Blasts and Benedictions*, ed. Ronald Ayling (London: Macmillan, 1967) pp. 3–8.

BRUGÈRE, RAYMOND, 'Sean O'Casey et le Théâtre irlandais', *Revue Anglo-Américaine* (Paris), III (Feb 1926) 206–21.

BRULE, A., 'Sean O'Casey et le Théâtre moderne', *Revue Anglo-Américaine* (Paris), VI (Oct 1928) 53–7.

BURROWES, WESLEY, 'Writers Are Not Encouraged', *Irish Times* (Dublin), (18 Mar 1968) p. 10.

BURTON, PHILIP, 'Something to Crow About: An Approach to *Cock-a-Doodle Dandy*', *Theatre Arts* (N.Y.), XLII (Nov 1958) 22–4.

CANDIDA, 'An Irishwoman's Diary', *Irish Times* (Dublin), (8 Aug 1966) p. 7 [interview with Eileen O'Casey].

'An Irishwoman's Diary: O'Casey Papers', *Irish Times* (Dublin), (20 Oct 1969) p. 9.

CARENS, JAMES F., 'Four Letters: Sean O'Casey to Oliver St John Gogarty', *James Joyce Quarterly* (Tulsa, Okla.), VIII 1 (fall 1970) 111–18.

CAROLL, PAUL VINCENT, 'Can the Abbey Theatre Be Restored?', *Theatre Arts* (N.Y.), XXXVI 1 (Jan 1952) 18–19, 79.

'Cathedral Sermon Praises O'Casey', *Irish Times* (Dublin), (16 Nov 1964) p. 11.

GOLGAN, GERALD, 'Threadbare Harlequin', *Plays and Players* (London), X 5 (Feb 1963) 20–2.

COAKLEY, JAMES, and FELHEIM, MARVIN, 'Some Suggestions about the Relationships between O'Casey and Classical Comedy', *Modern Drama* (Lawrence, Kansas), IV, no. 4 (Winter 1970-1) 265-71.

COLUM, PADRAIC, 'Sean O'Casey', *Theatre Arts Monthly* (N.Y.), IX (June 1925) 397-404.

'The Narrative Writings of Sean O'Casey', *Irish Writing: The Magazine of Contemporary Irish Literature* (Cork), no. 6 (Nov 1948) 60-9. See also O'Casey's reply, a letter dated Nov 1948, no. 7 (Feb 1949) 87.

'Ibsen in Irish Writing', *Irish Writing* (Cork), no. 7 (Feb 1949) 66-70 [O'Casey not influenced by Ibsen].

'Come-Back in Erin', *Sunday Times* (London), (6 Mar 1955) p. 3.

C[ONACHER], W. M., '*The Plough and the Stars* by Sean O'Casey', *Queen's Quarterly*, XXXIV (Apr-June 1927) 420-9.

COSTON, HERBERT H., 'Sean O'Casey: Prelude to Playwrighting', *Tulane Drama Review* (New Orleans), V 1 (Sep 1960) 102-12. Reprinted in *Sean O'Casey*, ed. Ronald Ayling (London: Macmillan, 1969) pp. 47-59.

COWASJEE, SAROS, 'An Evening with Sean O'Casey', *Illustrated Weekly of India* (17 May 1959) 43. Also in *Irish Times* (Dublin), (25 July 1959) p. 8.

'O'Casey Seen through Holloway's Diary', *Review of English Literature* (Leeds), VI 3 (July 1965) 58-69.

'The Juxtaposition of Tragedy and Comedy in the Plays of Sean O'Casey', *Wascana Review*, II 1 (1966) 75-89.

COXHEAD, ELIZABETH, 'Mr Sean O'Casey', *Times* (London), (22 Sep 1964) p. 15.

CRAIG, H. A. L., 'A Burning Man', *Irish Times* (Dublin), (30 Mar 1960) p. 8.

CROWTHER, BOSLEY, 'Who Is Then the Gentleman? A Few Notes on Sean O'Casey, the Irish Dramatist, Who Is Here with His Play *Within the Gates*', *New York Times* (14 Oct 1934) section 10, p. 1 [interview].

D., O. G., 'Radio Review: O'Casey Season', *Evening Herald* (Dublin), (10 Mar 1955) p. 5.

DANIEL, WALTER C., 'Patterns of Greek Comedy in O'Casey's *Purple Dust*', *Bulletin of the New York Public Library*, LXVI 9 (Nov 1962) 603-12.

DARLINGTON, W. A., 'London Economics: West End Managers Complain of Tax Burden in Slumping Market', *New York Times* (8 June 1947) section 2, p. 1 [on difficulties in presenting O'Casey's plays].

'Stormy Genius', *Daily Telegraph* (London), (28 Sep 1964) p. 17 [obituary].

'Death of One of the Great Irish Dramatists: Mr Sean O'Casey', *Illustrated London News*, CCXLV (26 Sep 1964) 475.

'Death of Sean O'Casey', *Manchester Guardian* (19 Sep 1964), p. 1.

DE BAUN, VINCENT, 'Sean O'Casey and the Road to Expressionism', *Modern Drama*, IV 3 (Dec 1961) 254-9.

DESMOND, SHAW, 'The Irish Renaissance', *Outlook* (N.Y.), (15 Oct 1924) pp. 247-9.

'De Valera as Play Censor', *Manchester Guardian Weekly*, XXX 15 (13 Apr 1934) 296.

DRUMMOND, ANGUS, 'O'Casey Says', *Courier* (London), XLII 4 (Apr 1964) 40-1.

DRUZINA, M. V., 'O Scenicnosti Dramaturgii Shona O'Kejsi', *Teatr* (Moscow), XXIII 11 (Nov 1962) 180-4.

'A Dublin Tempest', *Literary Digest* (N.Y.), XCVIII 5 (4 Aug 1928) 24-5 [by William P. Sears, on the quarrel over *The Silver Tassie*].

DUFFUS, R. L., 'Dublin – story of Two Cities', *New York Times Magazine* (17 Mar 1957) pp. 28, 39, 41.

DURANTEAU, JOSANE, 'Notes sur le Théâtre de Sean O'Casey', *Critique* (Paris), XVI 162 (Nov 1960) 935-40.

EARP, T. W., 'Irish and English', *New Statesman* (London), XXXV (5 July 1930) 409.

EDWARDS, A. C., 'The Lady Gregory Letters to Sean O'Casey', *Modern Drama*, VIII 1 (May 1965) 95-111.

EDWARDS, OWEN DUDLEY, 'American Image of Ireland', *Irish Times* (Dublin), (11 Jan 1963) p. 8.

ELISTRATOVA, A[NNE], 'Sean O'Casey', *Soviet Literature* (Moscow), no. 11 (Nov 1952) 164–9. Reprinted in *Neues Deutschland*, xxx (June 1953).

ESSLINGER, PAT[RICIA] M., 'Sean O'Casey and the Lockout of 1913: *Materia Poetica* of the Two Red Plays', *Modern Drama*, VI 1 (May 1963) 53–63.

'The Irish Alienation of O'Casey', *Eire–Ireland: A Journal of Irish Studies* (St Paul, Minn.), 1 1 (spring 1965–6) 18–25.

FALLON, GABRIEL, 'A Child among Them', *Bonaventura* (Dublin), 1 2 (autumn 1937) 74–80.

'The Ageing Abbey', *Irish Monthly* (Dublin), LXVI 778 (Apr 1938) 265–72; LXVI 779 (May 1938) 339–44.

'My Friend Sean O'Casey', *Irish Digest* (Dublin), XXVI 1 (Nov 1946) 33–6 [condensed from *Feature Magazine*].

'Pathway of a Dramatist', *Theatre Arts* (N.Y.), XXXIV (Jan 1950) 36–9.

'Juno and Joxer and Fluther: They Were All Born in the House with the Sycamore Tree', *Sunday Independent* (Dublin), (24 Dec 1950) p. 6.

'The Abbey and Sean O'Casey', *Theatre* (London), VII 158 (25 Oct 1952) 15.

'Ashes of Exile', *Irish Monthly* (Dublin), LXXX 951 (Nov 1952) 354–9.

'Why is There No Irish Claudel or Mauriac?', *Evening Press* (Dublin), (5 Feb 1955) p. 5.

'O'Casey, the Dramatist in Search of an Author', *Evening Press* (Dublin), (12 Feb 1955) p. 5.

'Fighting Genius of O'Casey', *Irish Times* (Dublin), (19 Feb 1959) p. 5 [lecture at the Town Hall, Rathmines, Dublin].

'An Irishman's Diary: Speculation', *Irish Times* (Dublin), (29 Mar 1960) p. 6.

'The House on the North Circular Road: Fragments from a Biography', *Modern Drama*, IV 3 (Dec 1961) 223–33.

'Dublin's Fourth Theatre Festival', *Modern Drama*, V 1 (May 1962) 21–6 [on *The Drums of Father Ned*].

'Sean O'Casey', *Catholic Standard* (Dublin), II 65 (2 Oct 1964) 1, 4 [obituary].

'Profiles of a Poet', *Modern Drama*, VII (Dec 1964) 329–44.

FARRAGHER, BERNARD, 'Brendan Behan's Unarranged Realism', *Drama Critique* (N.Y.), IV (Feb 1961) 38–9 [*The Hostage* apparently exploits O'Casey's method].

FIELDING, HENRY, 'Truth about Sean', *Daily Herald* (London), (27 Apr 1964) p. 6.

FITZGERALD, JOHN J., 'Sean O'Casey's Dramatic Slums', *Descant* (Texas), X (fall 1965) 26–34.

FITZ-SIMON, CHRISTOPHER, 'The Theatre in Dublin', *Modern Drama*, II 3 (Dec 1959) 289–94.

FOLEY, DONAL, 'O'Casey Out to Make Them Laugh', *Irish Press* (Dublin), (18 Sep 1957) p. 6 [interview].

'London Diary: Nobel Prize?', *Sunday Review* (Dublin), VII (5 May 1963) 6.

'Forsaking Ireland: Sean O'Casey Makes Permanent Home in London', *Daily Sketch* (London), (7 July 1926) p. 2.

FOX, R. M. 'The Machine Drama', *New Statesman* (London), XXVI (9 Jan 1926) 383–4. Reprinted in *Living Age* (Boston), CCCXXVIII (20 Feb 1926) 421–4 [on *Juno and the Paycock*].

'Sean O'Casey: A Worker Dramatist', *New Statesman* (London), XXVI (10 Apr 1926) 805–6.

'Drama of the Dregs', *New Statesman* (London), XXVII (21 Aug 1926) 525–6.

'Realism in Irish Drama', *Irish Statesman* (Dublin), X (23 June 1928) 310–12.

'Modern Irish Drama', *Theatre Arts* (N.Y.), XXIV (Nov 1940) 22–5.

'Irish Drama Knocks at the Door', *Life and Letters* (London), LXI 140 (Apr 1949) 16–21.

'Sean O'Casey's Dublin', *Irish Times* (Dublin), (2 May 1960) p. 8.

'Sean O'Casey and the Soul of Man', *Aryan Path* (Bombay), XXXIV 8 (Aug 1963) 366–9.

'Portrait of O'Casey as a Young Man', *Irish Times* (Dublin), (1 Dec 1964) p. 8.

FREEDMAN, MORRIS, 'The Modern Tragicomedy of Wilde and O'Casey', *College English* (Chicago), xxv (Apr 1964) 518–22, 527. Reprinted in *The Moral Impulse* (Carbondale and Edwardsville: Southern Illinois University Press, 1967) pp. 63–73.

'Freedom of Dublin for O'Casey?', *Irish Times* (Dublin), (26 Apr 1960) p. 4.

FREUNDLICH, ELISABETH, 'Dramatiker Sean O'Casey', *Theater und Zeit* (Berlin), III (July 1955) 181–3.

'From Starvation to Success: The Dramatic Career of Sean O'Casey', *John O'London's Weekly*, XVIII (19 Nov 1927) 200.

FUNKE, LEWIS, 'News and Gossip of the Rialto: Interview', *New York Times* (27 Mar 1960) section 2, p. 1.

GARDNER, PAUL, '1,400 Pay Tribute to O'Casey Artistry', *New York Times* (12 Oct 1964) p. 35.

GASSNER, JOHN, 'The Prodigality of Sean O'Casey', *Theatre Arts* (N.Y.), xxxv (June 1951) 52–3; (July 1951) 54–5; (Aug 1951) 48–9. Reprinted in *The Theatre in Our Times: A Survey of the Men, Materials and Movements in the Modern Theatre* (New York: Crown, 1954) pp. 240–8; and in *Sean O'Casey*, ed. Ronald Ayling (London: Macmillan, 1969) pp. 110–19.

'The Winter of Our Discontent', *Theatre Arts* (N.Y.), XXXIX 8 (Aug 1955) 22–4, 86.

'The Possibilities and Perils of Modern Tragedy', *Tulane Drama Review*, I 3 (June 1957) 3–14.

GOLDSTONE, HERBERT, 'The Unevenness of O'Casey: A Study of *Within the Gates*', *Forum* (Houston), IV 6 (winter–spring 1965) 37–42.

GOOD, J. W., 'A New Irish Dramatist', *New Statesman* (London), XXII (29 Mar 1924) 731.

GRAY, KEN, 'Edna O'Brien States Case', *Irish Times* (Dublin), (17 Nov 1966) p. 10. See reply by John O'Riordan, 'O'Casey, Letter-Writer' (23 Nov 1966) p. 9 [letter to the Editor].

GREANY, HELEN T., 'Some Interesting Parallels: Pope and the Paycock', *Notes and Queries* (London), CIII 5 (June 1958) 253.

'Great Love for Ireland', *Newsweek* (N.Y.), LXIV (28 Sep 1964) 91 [obituary].

GREGORY, LADY, 'How Great Plays Are Born: The Coming of Mr O'Casey', *Daily News* (London), (27 Mar 1926), p. 6.

GUIDI, AUGUSTO, 'Le rose rossi di S. O'Casey', *L'Italia che scrive* (Rome), L 2–3 (Feb–Mar 1967) 27.

GUNN, JOHN, 'Telly? Count Me Out, Says O'Casey', *Sunday Review* (Dublin), V (13 Aug 1961) 28.

GUTHRIE, TYRONE, 'Closeup of Ireland's Basic Problem', *New York Times Magazine* (19 Jan 1964) pp. 22, 24, 26.

HABART, MICHEL, 'Sean O'Casey', *L'Avant-Scène* (Paris), no. 230 (Nov 1960) 34–5 [on *Bedtime Story*].

HARMAN, BILL J., and ROLLINS, RONALD G., 'Mythical Dimensions in O'Casey's *Within the Gates*', *West Virginia University Philological Papers*, XVI (1967) 72–8.

HARVEY, ANTHONY E., 'Letters from Sean O'Casey to a Randolph-Macon Senior', *Randolph-Macon Bulletin*, XXVI (Sep 1954) 7–9, 23–6.

HARVEY, FRANCIS, 'O'Casey', *Irish Times* (Dublin), (2 Apr 1960) p. 9 [letter to the Editor].

HAWKINS, A. DESMOND, 'The Poet in the Theatre', *Criterion: A Literary Review* (London), XIV (October 1934) 29–39.

'Hawthornden Prize Awarded: Lord Oxford's Tribute to Mr Sean O'Casey', *Times* (London), (24 Mar 1926) p. 11.

H[AYES], J. J., 'On Foreign Stages', *New York Times* (15 Nov 1925) section 8, p. 2. See O'Casey's reply, 'To the Dramatic Editor' (27 Dec 1925) section 7, p. 2.

HAYES, J. J., 'O'Casey of Dublin', *Boston Evening Transcript* (13 Feb 1926) pt 3, pp. 4, 5, 7.

HENNIGAN, AIDAN, 'O'Casey Plays Not for TV', *Irish Press* (Dublin), (9 May 1961) p. 3.

'O'Casey Rejects Plea', *Irish Press* (Dublin), (20 Mar 1962) p. 3.

HETHMON, ROBERT, 'Great Hatred, Little Room', *Tulane Drama Review* (New Orleans), v 4 (June 1961) 51–5 [on *Cathleen Listens In*].

HEWES, HENRY, 'Mirror in the Hallway', *Saturday Review of Literature* (N.Y.), XXXIX (22 Sep 1956) 30 [interview].

'High Tribute Paid to O'Casey's Memory', *Irish Independent* (Dublin), (21 Sep 1964) p. 6.

HODSON, J. L., 'The Strange Mystery of Sean O'Casey', *News Chronicle* (London), (21 Dec 1931) p. 6 [interview].

HOGAN, ROBERT, 'The Experiments of Sean O'Casey', *Dublin Magazine*, XXXIII 1 (Jan–Mar 1958), 4–12. Cf. 'Riches Scorned', *Times Literary Supplement* (London), (31 Jan 1958) p. 61; Robert Hogan, ibid. (21 Mar 1958) p. 153.

'O'Casey's Dramatic Apprenticeship', *Modern Drama*, IV 3 (Dec 1961) 243–53.

'In Sean O'Casey's Golden Days', *Dublin Magazine*, v 3–4 (autumn–winter 1966) 80–93. Reprinted in *After the Irish Renaissance* (London: Macmillan, 1967) pp. 235–52; revised version reprinted in *Sean O'Casey*, ed. Ronald Ayling (London: Macmillan, 1969) pp. 162–76.

'The Haunted Inkbottle: A Preliminary Study of Rhetorical Devices in the Late Plays of Sean O'Casey', *James Joyce Quarterly* (Tulsa, Okla.), VIII 1 (fall 1970) 76–95.

HONE, J. M., 'A Letter from Ireland', *London Mercury*, XIV 79 (June 1926) 189–91.

'Honour for O'Casey Next?', *Times Pictorial* (Dublin), LXXII (30 Mar 1946) 4.

HOWARD, MILTON, 'Orwell or O'Casey?', *Masses and Mainstream* (N.Y.), VIII 1 (Jan 1955) 20–6.

HYNES, MALACHY, 'A Burrow of Culture: The Two Jims', *Irish Times* (Dublin), (6 May 1959) p. 10.

'I Won't Write for Abbey – O'Casey', *Sunday Press* (Dublin), (4 Mar 1962) p. 5 [interview].

IGOE, W. J., 'Sean O'Casey, Tragic Jester', *Critic* (Chicago), XIX (June–July 1961) 15–16, 67–9.

'Sean O'Casey: At Home Only with People', *Catholic Herald* (Dublin), (25 Sep 1964) p. 10. See reply by John O'Riordan (2 Oct 1964) p. 5 [letter to the Editor].

INGALLS, LEONARD, 'Drive on Censor Gains in Britain: Butler Tells Commons Close Attention Will Be Given to Stage Reform Bid', *New York Times* (9 May 1958) p. 19 [O'Casey member of Theatre Censorship Reform Committee].

'Invalids', *Times* (London), (26 Apr 1947) p. 4; (27 Feb 1956) p. 8; (1 Mar 1956) p. 8; (20 Mar 1956) p. 10.

'Ireland's New Playwright', *Literary Digest* (N.Y.), LXXXIX (17 Apr 1926) 27–8.

'Irish Academy of Letters: Names of the First Members', *Times* (London), (20 Sep 1932) p. 10.

'Irish Literary Shillalahs', *New York Times* (6 Feb 1930) p. 22 [editorial on dispute between O'Casey and George Russell over art]. Provoked letter to the Editor from O'Casey (20 Mar 1930).

J., W., 'Wonderful London Yesterday', *Daily Graphic* (London), (24 Mar 1926) p. 5.

JOHNSTON, DENIS, 'Sean O'Casey: An Appreciation', *Daily Telegraph* (London), (11 Mar 1926) p. 15. Reprinted in *Living Age* (Boston), CCCXXIX (17 Apr 1926) 161–3; and in *Sean O'Casey*, ed. Ronald Ayling (London: Macmillan, 1969) pp. 82–5.

'Joxer in Totnes: A Study in Sean O'Casey', *Irish Writing* (Cork), no. 13 (Dec 1950) 50–3.

'Humor – Hibernian Style', *New York Times* (5 Feb 1961) Drama Section, p. 3.

'Sean O'Casey: A Biography and an Appraisal', *Modern Drama*, IV 3 (Dec 1961) 324–8.

'Sean O'Casey', *Nation* (N.Y.), CXCIX (5 Oct 1964) 198 [obituary].

JORDAN, JOHN, 'A World in Chassis', *University Review* (Dublin), I 4 (spring 1955) 21–8.

K[IRWIN], H. N., 'Evolution of a Playwright; Mr Sean O'Casey's Works and His Outlook', *Freeman's Journal* (Dublin), (15 Mar 1924) p. 5.

KAUFMAN, MICHAEL W., 'The Position of *The Plough and the Stars* in O'Casey's Dublin Trilogy', *James Joyce Quarterly* (Tulsa, Okla.), VIII I (fall 1970) 48–63.

KELLY, SEAMUS, 'Dublin', *Holiday* (Philadelphia, Pa.), XIX I (Jan 1956) 38–43.
'Greatest Playwright in a Half-Century', *Irish Times* (Dublin), (19 Sep 1964) p. 5.

KENNELLY, BRENDAN, 'The Two Irelands of Synge and O'Casey', *New Knowledge* (London), VI I (1966) 961–5.

KERR, WALTER, 'Where O'Casey's Career Went Wrong', *New York Times* (2 Feb 1969) pp. I, II. See 'They Crow for Sean O'Casey' (2 Mar 1969) pp. 15, 40 [letters to the Editor].

KIRWAN, H. N., 'Sean O'Casey, the Man and the Dramatist', *Crystal* (Dublin), I (Feb 1926) 5, 20.

KNIGHT, G. WILSON, 'Ever a Fighter: On Sean O'Casey's *The Drums of Father Ned*', *Stand*, IV 3 (summer 1960) 15–18. Reprinted as appendix to *The Christian Renaissance* (London: Metheun, 1962) pp. 341–7; and in *Sean O'Casey*, ed. Ronald Ayling (London: Macmillan, 1969) pp. 177–82.

KOLOZSVÁRI, EMIL, 'Sean O'Casey', *Nagyvilág* (Budapest), XIII I (Jan 1968) 112–18.

KORNILOVA, E[LENA], 'Vsegda s Irlandiej, Vsegda s Narodom', *Teatr* (Moscow), XX 5 (May 1959) 167–78.

KOSOK, VON HEINZ, 'Sean O'Casey: 1880–1964', *Die Neueren Sprachen*, XIII (Oct 1964) 453–68.
'Sean O'Casey's *Hall of Healing*', *Die Neueren Sprachen* (Apr 1970) 168–79.

KRAJEWSKA, WANDA, 'Sean O'Casey i Ekspresjonizm', *Kwartalnik Neofilologiczny* (Warsaw), XLI 4 (1965) 363–79.

KRAUSE, DAVID, 'The Playwright's Not for Burning', *Virginia Quarterly Review*, XXXIV I (winter 1958) 60–76 [on *The Silver Tassie*].
'"The Rageous Ossean": Patron-Hero of Synge and O'Casey', *Modern Drama*, IV 3 (Dec 1961) 268–91.

'Sean O'Casey', *Spectator* (London), CCIX (28 Sep 1962) 435 [letter to the Editor on 'Letters of Sean O'Casey'].

'Sean O'Casey: 1880–1964', *Massachusetts Review* (Amherst), VI 2 (winter–spring 1965) 233–51. Reprinted in *Irish Renaissance*, ed. Robin Skelton and David R. Clark (Dublin: Dolmen Press, 1965) and in *The World of Sean O'Casey*, ed. Sean McCann (London: The New English Library, 1966).

'O'Casey and Yeats and the Druid', *Modern Drama*, XI (Dec 1968) 252–62.

'The Principle of Comic Disintegration', *James Joyce Quarterly* Tulsa, Okla.), VIII 1 (fall 1970) 3–12.

LARSON, GERALD A., 'An Interview with Mrs Sean O'Casey', *Educational Theatre Journal* (Columbia, S.C.), XVII 3 (fall 1965) 234–9.

'Latest Wills', *Times* (London), (1 Dec 1964) p. 19.

LENNON, MICHAEL J., 'Sean O'Casey and His Plays', *Catholic World* (N.Y.), CXXX (Dec 1929), 295–301; CXXX (Jan 1930) 452–61.

LEVETT, JACK, 'A Great "Hurrah" for Life', *Daily Worker* (London), (30 Mar 1964) p. 2 [interview].

LEVIN, BERNARD, 'The Green Crow Folds His Wings', *Daily Mail* (London), (21 Sep 1964) p. 8 [obituary].

LEWIS, ALLAN, 'Sean O'Casey's World', *Nation* (N.Y.), CLXXXI (24 Dec 1955) 555–6 [on *Red Roses for Me*].

LEWIS, ROBERT, 'Visiting Sean O'Casey in Devon: Informal Talks with Irish Playwright', *New York Herald Tribune*, (29 July 1951) section 4, p. 2.

'Liverpool Meeting on Sean O'Casey', *Irish Democrat* (Dublin), (Jan 1967) p. 8.

'London Letter: Dr Soper', *Irish Times* (Dublin), (16 Jan 1956) p. 5. See reply by C. W. Griffin, 'Sean O'Casey' (19 Jan 1956) p. 7 [letter to the Editor].

'London Notes', *Irish Democrat* (Dublin), (Dec 1966) p. 8 [symposium on O'Casey].

LYTTLETON, E., 'Sean O'Casey's Story', *Time and Tide* (London), XIV 21 (27 May 1933) 640–1 [letter to the Editor on *I Wanna Woman*].

MACANNA, THOMAS, 'O'Casey, the Genius of Chassis', *Irish Times* (Dublin), (12 Jan 1971) p. 10.

MACAOIDH, LIAM, 'O'Casey', *Irish Times* (Dublin), (29 Aug 1961) p. 5 [letter to the Editor].

MACDONAGH, JOHN, 'Acting in Dublin', *Commonweal* (N.Y.), (19 June 1929) pp. 185–6.

MCELIGOT, GARY, 'A Last Letter from O'Casey', *Irish Independent* (Dublin), (21 Sep 1964) p. 6. Also in *Irish Times* (Dublin), (21 Sep 1964) p. 11.

MACGRIOR, D., 'Indignation and Selectivity', *Standard* (Dublin), XXVII 165 (11 Mar 1955) 11 [letter to the Editor].

MCHUGH, ROGER, 'The Legacy of Sean O'Casey', *Texas Quarterly*, VIII 1 (spring 1965) 123–37.
'Sean O'Casey and Lady Gregory', *James Joyce Quarterly* (Tulsa, Okla.), VIII 1 (fall 1970) 119–23.

MCLAUGHLIN, JOHN, 'A Tired-Out Oul' Blatherer', *America* (N.Y.), C (7 Mar 1959) 653–5.
'Political Allegory in O'Casey's *Purple Dust*', *Modern Drama* (Lawrence, Kans.), XIII 1 (May 1970) 47–53.

MAC LIAMMÓIR, MICHEÁL, 'Always the Giant', *Irish Times* (Dublin), (30 Mar 1960) p. 8.

MAGALANER, MARVIN, 'O'Casey's Autobiography', *Sewanee Review*, LXV 1 (winter 1957) 170–4. Reprinted in *Sean O'Casey*, ed. Ronald Ayling (London: Macmillan, 1969) pp. 228–31.

MAITRA, LILA, 'O'Casey's Autobiographies', *Calcutta Review*, CLI 1 (April 1959) 53–7.
'Sean O'Casey – the Man and the Dramatist', *Calcutta Review*, CLIII 1 (Oct 1959) 71–6.

MALONE, ANDREW E., 'The Decline of the Irish Drama', *Nineteenth Century and After* (London), XCVII 578 (Apr 1925) 578–88.

'Ireland Gives a New Playwright to the World', *Theatre Magazine*, XLIII (Apr 1926) 9, 58, 62.

'The Shadow of Sean O'Casey', *Bookman* (London), LXX 416 (May 1926) 104–7.

'The Coming of Age of the Irish Drama', *Dublin Review*, CLXXXI 362 (July 1927) 101–14.

'The Abbey Theatre Season', *Dublin Magazine*, II 4, n.s. (Oct–Dec 1927) 30–8.

'Ireland', *Drama Magazine*, XXI (Dec 1930) 19, 24.

'The Irish Theatre in 1933', *Dublin Magazine*, IX 3 (July–Sep 1934) 45–54.

MALONE, MAUREEN, '*Red Roses for Me*: Fact and Symbol', *Modern Drama*, IX 2 (Sep 1966) 147–52.

MARCUS, PHILLIP, 'Addendum on Joyce and O'Casey', *James Joyce Quarterly* (Tulsa, Okla.), III (fall 1965) 62–3.

'Marriage of Mr Sean O'Casey', *Times* (London), (24 Sep 1927) p. 7.

MARRIOTT, R. B., 'Sean O'Casey', *Stage and Television Today* (London), (24 Sep 1964) 8 [obituary].

MARTIN, AUGUSTINE, 'Inherited Dissent: The Dilemma of the Irish Writer', *Studies: An Irish Quarterly Review* (Dublin), LIV 213 (spring 1965) 1–20.

MEACHAEN, PATRICK, 'Two Irish Dramatists', *Library Assistant* (London), XX 341 (June 1927) 123–34 [paper read at Chiswick, before the Association of Assistant Librarians, on Yeats and O'Casey].

MERCIER, VIVIAN, 'Decline of a Playwright: The Riddle of Sean O'Casey', *Commonweal* (N.Y.), LXIV 15 (13 July 1956) 366–8. See reply by Robert Hogan (24 Aug 1956) 517, and 'Correction' by Vivian Mercier (21 Sep 1956) 612.

'O'Casey Alive', *Hudson Review* (N.Y.), XIII (winter 1960–1), 631–6.

'Mermaid O'Casey', *Plays and Players* (London), IX 12 (Sep 1962) 46 [on O'Casey Festival].

'Messages Pouring in for Sean O'Casey', *Irish Times* (Dublin), (17 Feb 1956) p. 3.

MILES, BERNARD, 'Sean O'Casey – Sources of His Greatness', *Daily Worker* (London), (18 Aug 1962) p. 3.

'Milestones: Sean O'Casey', *Time* (N.Y.), Atlantic Edition, CXXXIV 13 (25 Sep 1964) 58 [obituary].

MILI, GJON, 'O'Casey in Search of a Stage', *Irish Digest* (Dublin), LII 1 (Nov 1954) 52–4.

'Tea and Memories and Songs at a Last Fond Visit', *Life* (Chicago), LVII (9 Oct 1964) 92–3.

MITCHISON, NAOMI, 'Sean O'Casey's Story', *Time and Tide* (London), XIV 21 (27 May 1933) 641 [letter to the Editor on *I Wanna Woman*].

MOSES, ROBERT, 'A Toast to O'Casey', *New York Times Magazine* (1 Feb 1959) p. 30.

MOYA, CARMELA, 'Sean O'Casey: d'après deux livres récents', *Études Anglaises* (Paris), XX 2 (Apr–June 1967) 160–4.

'Mr Sean O'Casey', *Irish Times* (Dublin), (18 Feb 1956) p. 1.

'Mr Sean O'Casey: Controversial Dramatist of Genius', *Times* (London), (21 Sep 1964) p. 16 [obituary].

'Mr Sean O'Casey's Refusal', *Times* (London), (22 Aug 1964) p. 7 [refuses permission for use of works at World Fair in New York].

'Mrs O'Casey in Dublin', *Irish Times* (Dublin), (3 Aug 1966) p. 6.

'Mrs O'Casey Undisturbed by Sniping', *Irish Times* (Dublin), (8 Aug 1967) p. 7.

'Mrs Sean O'Casey Explains', *Times* (London), (24 Aug 1964) p. 5 [comment on O'Casey's refusal to permit the Irish Government to use recorded excerpts from his works at New York World Fair].

MULLANE, DERMOT, 'O'Casey's Funeral Passed Unnoticed', *Irish Times* (Dublin), (23 Sep 1964) p. 4.

'Sean O'Casey Dies Aged 84 After Heart Attack: A Man Who Was True to Himself', *Irish Times* (Dublin), (19 Sep 1964) p. 1.

MURPHY, ROBERT P., 'Sean O'Casey and "The Bald Primaqueera"', *James Joyce Quarterly* (Tulsa, Okla.), VIII 1 (fall 1970) 96–100.

NASON, RICHARD W., 'Shyre Batting for O'Casey: Young Actor-Producer Ignites Interest in Irish Playwright', *New York Times* (3 Mar 1957) section 2, p. 3.

NATHAN, GEORGE JEAN, 'Lament for Irish Playwrights', *American Mercury* (N.Y.), LII 208 (Apr 1941) 483–9.

'New York Buys O'Casey Papers', *Times* (London), (31 July 1969) p. 8.

'No 80 Candles for O'Casey', *Sunday Review* (Dublin), IV (20 Mar 1960) 3.

NORWOOD, GILBERT, 'The New Writers, IV: Sean O'Casey', *Canadian Forum* (Toronto), X (Apr 1930) 250–1.

'English Drama between Two Wars', *Dalhousie Review*, XXII (Jan 1943) 405–20.

'Notes and News', *Library Review* (Glasgow), XX 1 (spring 1965) 62 [obituary].

O'BROIN, SEAMUS, 'Sean O'Casey', *Standard* (Dublin), XXVII 164 (25 Feb 1955) 23 [letter to the Editor].

OBSERVER, 'Press Cuttings', *Irish Book Lover* (Dublin), XV 1 (Jan 1925) 16.

O'CASEY, SEAN, 'Pontiffs of the Theatre', *Fortnightly Review* (London), CXLVI (Oct 1936) 422–7.

'The Play of Ideas', *New Statesman and Nation* (London), XXXIX (8 Apr 1950) 397–8. Reprinted in *Blasts and Benedictions*, ed. Ronald Ayling (London: Macmillan, 1967) pp. 24–6.

'Sean O'Casey, Formerly of Dublin', *New York Herald Tribune Book Review* (12 Oct 1952) p. 12.

'Always the Plow and the Stars', *New York Times Book Review* (25 Jan 1953) section 7, pp. 1, 23. Reprinted in *The Green Crow* (New York: George Braziller, 1956; London, W. H. Allen, 1957).

'O'Casey: Playwright in Exile', *New York Times* (25 Dec 1955) section 2, pp. 3–4. Reprinted in *The Green Crow* (New York: George Braziller, 1956; London: W. H. Allen, 1957).

'Memories of a Farewell to Ireland', *New York Times* (4 Dec 1960) section 2, pp. 1, 5 [how *The Plough and the Stars* was written]. Reprinted in *Blasts and Benedictions*, ed. Ronald Ayling (London: Macmillan, 1967) pp. 95–8.

'*Cathleen Listens In*', *Tulane Drama Review*, v 4 (June 1961) 36–50 [comment by O'Casey on p. 36].

'Behind the Ban', *New York Times* (5 Jan 1964) section 2, pp. 1, 3.

'O'Casey as Letter-Writer', *Irish Times* (Dublin), (19 Sep 1962), p. 7.

'O'Casey Bans Works at World's Fair', *Irish Times* (Dublin), (22 Aug 1964) p. 11.

'O'Casey Did Not Celebrate 80th Birthday', *Irish Times* (Dublin), (31 Mar 1960) p. 9.

'O'Casey Doing Well', *Irish Times* (Dublin), (6 Mar 1956) p. 9.

'O'Casey Goes Home', *Irish Times* (Dublin), (20 Mar 1956) p. 5 [after operation].

'O'Casey Has 81st Birthday', *New York Times* (31 Mar 1961) p. 21.

'O'Casey Honoured: Lord Oxford on Most Moving Drama in 20 Years', *Daily Sketch* (London), (24 Mar 1926) p. 3.

'O'Casey May Let the Abbey Stage His Plays', *Sunday Press* (Dublin), (20 Sep 1959), p. 5 [interview].

'O'Casey on Air Again', *Irish Press* (Dublin), (23 May 1955) p. 6.

'O'Casey on Theatre Censor Body', *Irish Press* (Dublin), (2 May 1958) p. 1.

'O'Casey Plans Broadcast of Four Plays', *Irish Times* (Dublin), (28 Feb 1955) p. 9 [from Radio Eireann].

'O'Casey Progressing', *Irish Times* (Dublin), (2 Mar 1956) p. 1.

'O'Casey Records Talk for Radio Eireann', *Irish Times* (Dublin), (8 Mar 1955), p. 3.

'O'Casey Says Yes to Soviet Invitation', *Sunday Review* (Dublin), IV (10 Apr 1960) 28.

'O'Casey Service Tuesday', *New York Times* (20 Sep 1964) p. 88.

'O'Casey Speaks: More O'Casey', *Irish Times* (Dublin), (3 Mar 1962) p. 9. See replies by Gabriel Fallon (6 Mar 1962) p. 7; by Robert Hogan (10 Mar 1962) p. 7; by Gabriel Fallon (13 Mar 1962) p. 7; by Sean O'Casey and Robert Hogan (21 Mar 1962) p. 7; by

'Criticus' (26 Mar 1962) p. 7; by Ronald Ayling (25 Apr 1962) p. 9; by Gabriel Fallon and A. Sherlock (27 Apr 1962) p. 7; and by Padraic Fallon (7 May 1962) p. 7 [letters to the Editor].

'O'Casey Will Be Buried Today', *Irish Times* (Dublin), (22 Sep 1964) p. 9.

'O'Casey Will Be Cremated Tomorrow', *Irish Times* (Dublin), (21 Sep 1964) p. 1.

'O'Casey Withdraws All Plays from TV', *Irish Times* (Dublin), (19 Sep 1957) p. 1.

'O'Casey Writing New Play: Author of *Juno and the Paycock* Calls New Work "The Red Lily" ', *New York Times* (28 Jan 1927) p. 15.

'O'Casey's Court', *Irish Writing* (Cork), no. 13 (Dec 1950) 5–6.

O'CONNOR, Brother ANTONY CYRIL, 'The Successors of Synge', *Unitas*, xxvii 3 (July–Sep 1954), 444–51.

O'CONNOR, FRANK, 'O'Casey and the Ghosts', *Holiday* (Philadelphia), xix (Jan 1956) 65, 109–11.

O'CONNOR, T. P., 'Men, Women, and Memories: The Hawthornden Prize Winner', *Sunday Times* (London), (4 Apr 1926) p. 9.

O'CONNOR, ULICK, 'Dublin's Dilemma', *Theatre Arts* (N.Y.), xl 7 (July 1956) 64–5, 96.

O'FAOLAIN, SEAN, 'The Case of Sean O'Casey', *Commonweal* (N.Y.), xxii 24 (11 Oct 1935) 577–8. See reply by Terence L. Connolly, xxiii (14 Feb 1936) 442.

'The Abbey Festival', *New Statesman and Nation* (London), xvi (20 Aug 1938) 281–2.

'The Dilemma of Irish Letters', *Month* (London), ii 6 (Dec 1949) 366–79.

'Ireland after Yeats', *Bell* (Dublin), xviii 11 (summer 1953) 37–48. Reprinted in *Books Abroad*, xxvi (autumn 1953) 325–33.

O'HEGARTY, P. S., 'A Dramatist of New-Born Ireland', *North American Review* (N.Y.), ccxxiv 835 (June–Aug 1927) 315–22. Reprinted in *Sean O'Casey*, ed. Ronald Ayling (London: Macmillan, 1969) pp. 60–7.

'The Abbey Theatre', *Irish Times* (Dublin), (6 Sep 1944) p. 3.

O'MAOLÁIN, MICHÉAL, 'An Ruathar Ud Agus An Deachaigh Leis', *Feasta* (Dublin), VIII (May 1955) 2–4, 6, 24–5.

O'MAOLAIN, TOMAS, 'Pitiable O'Casey', *Standard* (Dublin), XXVII 164 (25 Feb 1955) 23 [letter to the Editor].

'OMEN', 'Mr O'Maolain Was There!', *Standard* (Dublin), XXVII 165 (11 Mar 1955) 11 [letter to the Editor].

O'NEILL-BARNA, ANNE, 'O'Casey at 80: More Rebel Than Ever', *New York Times Magazine* (27 Mar 1960) pp. 26, 90–1.

O'RIORDAN, JOHN, 'Sean O'Casey's Birthday', *Bookseller* (London), (20 Feb 1960) p. 1080 [letter to the Editor]. See reply by Timothy O'Keeffe of MacGibbon & Kee (27 Feb 1960) p. 1138.

'Exclusive Tea-Time Chat with Playwright Sean O'Casey', *Enfield Weekly Herald* (19 Apr 1963) p. 4 [interview].

'2-Hour Chat with Sean O'Casey', *Enfield Gazette and Observer* (31 May 1963) p. 7 [interview].

'Sean O'Casey', *Observer* (London), (27 Sep 1964) p. 37 [letter to the Editor].

'The Cult of Yeats', *Catholic Standard* (Dublin), II 69 (30 Oct 1964) 5 [letter to the Editor in reply to hostile criticism of Yeats and O'Casey]. See reply by R. Donnellan, II 70 (6 Nov 1964) 5; and O'Riordan's counter-reply, II 72 (20 Nov 1964) 5.

'O'Casey's Dublin Critics', *Library Review* (Glasgow), XXI 2 (summer 1967) 59–63.

'O'Casey's Plays', *Irish Times* (Dublin), (12 Oct 1967) p. 9 [letter to the Editor rebuking Tyrone Guthrie for his derogatory remarks, 'O'Casey Dated', at the International Theatre Seminar, Abbey Theatre, as reported in *Irish Times* (5 Oct 1967) p. 8]. An acrimonious correspondence followed: by Mrs Kay Quinlan (20 Oct 1967) p. 15; Peadar Mac Maghnais (27 Oct 1967) p. 11; John O'Riordan (30 Oct 1967) p. 14; Donal O'Sullivan (3 Nov 1967) p. 14; and John O'Riordan (15 Nov 1967) p. 13.

'Stage O'Casey', *Irish Times* (Dublin), (9 Oct 1968) p. 11 [letter to the Editor chiding Abbey Theatre and producers for neglecting O'Casey's later plays].

'National Theatre Omission', *Sunday Times* (London), (27 Oct 1968) p. 14 [letter to the Editor chiding Sir Laurence Olivier and the National Theatre for not performing *The Silver Tassie* instead of *Juno and the Paycock* in 1966 after O'Casey's death].

'Sean O'Casey: Colourful Quixote of the Drama', *Library Review* (Glasgow), XXII 5 (spring 1970) 235–42.

'Sean O'Casey's Legacy', *Tribune* (London), XXXIV 38 (18 Sep 1970) 11.

'An Outstanding Artist of Year', *Irish Times* (Dublin), (31 Dec 1952) p. 1.

P., V. I., 'Sean O'Casey', *Standard* (Dublin), XXVII 165 (4 Mar 1955) 12 [letter to the Editor].

PAGE, SEAN, 'The Abbey Theatre', *Dublin Magazine*, V 3–4 (autumn–winter 1966) 6–14.

' "Page 1 Awards" Made by Newspaper Guild', *New York Times* (29 Mar 1949) p. 21 [the non-fiction award went to O'Casey for his *Inishfallen, Fare Thee Well*].

PALMER, M. G., 'Writers at Odds on Art: Literary Brickbats Exchanged by A. E. and Sean O'Casey on Moderns', *New York Times* (26 Jan 1930) section 3, p. 3. See also O'Casey's letter to the Editor (20 Mar 1930).

PARKER, R. B., 'Bernard Shaw and Sean O'Casey', *Queen's Quarterly*, LXXIII (spring 1966) 13–34. Reprinted in *Shaw Seminar Papers* (Toronto), LXV (1966) 1–29.

PAUL-DUBOIS, L[OUIS], 'Le Théatre Irlandais: M. Sean O'Casey', *Revue des Deux Mondes* (Paris), XXVII (1 June 1935) 644–52.

PELEGRINI, A., 'Dalla Tragedia Irlandese e di Sean O'Casey', *Convegno*, XVII (Aug 1936) 329–42.

'Personality Cult Scorned by O'Casey: Author, in Phone Interview, Talks of Many Things – Working on "Frolic" ', *New York Times* (25 Aug 1957) section 1, p. 112.

'Personality of the Month', *Plays and Players* (London), VII 1 (Oct 1959) 5.

PHILLIPSON, Dom WULSTAN, O.S.B., 'Two Glimpses of O'Casey', *Westminster Cathedral Chronicle* (London), LIX 3 (Mar 1965) 46 [interview].

PIXLEY, EDWARD E., '*The Plough and the Stars* – The Destructive Consequences of Human Folly', *Educational Theatre Journal*, XXII 1 (Mar 1971) 75–82.

PLUNKETT, JAMES, 'The Old Spot by the River', *Irish Times* (Dublin), (20 Feb 1960) p. 6.

PRESCOTT, JOSEPH (ed.), 'Sean O'Casey Concerning James Joyce', *Massachusetts Review* (Amherst), v 2 (winter 1964) 335–6. Reprinted in Robin Skelton and David R. Clark (eds.), *Irish Renaissance: A Gathering of Essays, Memoirs, and Letters from 'The Massachusetts Review'* (Dublin: Dolmen Press, 1965).

'Profile – Sean O'Casey', *Observer* (London), (10 Mar 1946) p. 6.

PRO-QUIDNUNC, 'An Irishman's Diary: O'Casey on Connolly', *Irish Times* (Dublin), (22 Sep 1964) p. 7. See replies by Cathal O'Shannon (24 Sep 1964) p. 9; and by Thomas A. Browne (2 Oct 1964) p. 9 [letters to the Editor].

QUIDNUNC, 'An Irishman's Diary: Broadway Tribute – Consummation', *Irish Times* (Dublin), (21 Oct 1964) p. 9. See reply by Ronald Ayling (10 Nov 1964) p. 11 [letter to the Editor].

'An Irishman's Diary: O'Casey's Kisser', *Irish Times* (Dublin), (3 Mar 1956) p. 10.

'An Irishman's Diary: Sympathy', *Irish Times* (Dublin), (5 Jan 1957) p. 8 [on death of Niall O'Casey].

'An Irishman's Diary: What's in a Name?', *Irish Times* (Dublin), (12 Feb 1958) p. 6.

QUIRKE, JAMES, 'G.B.S. or O'Casey', *Irish Times* (Dublin), (28 Sep 1968) p. 9 [letter to the Editor in reply to leading article (25 Sep 1968) saying that Shaw is Ireland's most famous dramatist].

'Records Say His 70th Birthday But – "I Don't Know How Old I Am"', O'Casey Declares', *Irish Press* (Dublin), (1 Apr 1954) p. 5.

REES, LESLIE, 'Remembrance of Things Past – II: On Meeting Sean O'Casey', *Meanjin Quarterly* (Melbourne), XXIV 4 (Dec 1964) 414–20 [interview].

REGNAULT, MAURICE, 'Sean O'Casey, le poète de la rose rouge', *Lettres françaises* (Paris), no. 810 (4–10 Feb 1960) 9.

REID, ALEC, 'The Legend of the Green Crow: Observations on Recent Work by and about Sean O'Casey', *Drama Survey* (Minneapolis), III 1 (May 1963) 155–64.

'Riches Scorned', *Times Literary Supplement* (London), (31 Jan 1958) p. 61.

RITCHIE, HARRY M., 'The Influence of Melodrama on the Early Plays of Sean O'Casey', *Modern Drama*, v 2 (Sep 1962) 164–73.

ROBINSON, ERIC, '*Juno and the Paycock*: An Introduction', *Use of English* (London), XL 2 (winter 1959) 111–18.

ROGOFF, GORDON, 'Wasp against the Criticonians', *Encore* (London), III 2 (Easter 1956) 4–6, 25–6, 29.
    'Sean O'Casey's Legacy', *Commonweal* (N.Y.), LXXXI (23 Oct 1964) 128–9.

ROLLINS, RONALD G., 'Sean O'Casey's Mental Pilgrimage', *Arizona Quarterly*, XVII 3 (winter 1961) 293–302.
    'O'Casey, O'Neill, and the Expressionism in *Within the Gates*', *West Virginia University Bulletin Philological Papers*, XIII (1961) 76–81.
    'O'Casey's *The Silver Tassie*', *Explicator* (University of South Carolina), XX 8 (Apr 1962) item 62.
    'O'Casey, O'Neill and Expressionism in *The Silver Tassie*', *Bucknell Review*, X (1962) 364–9.
    'O'Casey's *Cock-a-Doodle Dandy*', *Explicator* (University of South Carolina), XXIII (Sep 1964) item 8.
    'Sean O'Casey's *The Star Turns Red*: A Political Prophecy', *Mississippi Quarterly*, XVI (1963) 67–75.
    'Form and Content in Sean O'Casey's Dublin Trilogy', *Modern Drama*, VIII 4 (Feb 1966) 419–25.
    'O'Casey and Synge: The Irish Hero as Playboy and Gunman', *Arizona Quarterly*, XXII 3 (autumn 1966) 216–22.
    'Dramatic Symbolism in Sean O'Casey's Dublin Trilogy', *West Virginia University Bulletin Philological Papers*, XV (1966) 49–56.
    'Shaw and O'Casey: John Bull and His Other Island', *Shaw Review*, X (May 1967) 60–9.
    'O'Casey's *Purple Dust*', *Explicator* (University of South Carolina), XXVI (Oct 1967) item 19.
    'Clerical Blackness in the Green Garden: Heroine As Scapegoat in *Cock-a-Doodle Dandy*', *James Joyce Quarterly* (Tulsa, Okla.), VIII 1 (fall 1970) 64–75.

'Roots', *Times Literary Supplement* (London), (26 Feb 1960) p. 129.

Ross, Don, 'O'Casey, 78, Says Hurrah to Life', *New York Herald Tribune* (16 Nov 1958) section 4, p. 1 [interview].

Roy, Gregor, 'Sean O'Casey: Genius of the Theater', *Catholic World* (N.Y.), cc (Jan. 1965) 259–60 [obituary].

Rudin, Seymour, 'Playwright to Critic: Sean O'Casey's Letters to George Jean Nathan', *Massachusetts Review* (Amherst), v 2 (winter 1964) 326–34. Reprinted in *Irish Renaissance*, ed. Robin Skelton and David R. Clark (Dublin: Dolmen Press, 1965) [a description of them, with excerpts].

'Russian Magazine's Tribute to O'Casey', *Irish Times* (Dublin), (20 Oct 1964) p. 6.

'Russians Like Sean O'Casey', *Irish Times* (Dublin), (1 Apr 1955) p. 1.

Sagarra, Juan de, 'En la Muerte de Sean O'Casey y Otras Notas', *El Noticiero Universal* (Barcelona), (2 Oct 1964) [obituary].

Saroyan, William, 'Some Frank Talk with William Saroyan', *New York Times* (4 Jan 1953) section 2, pp. 1, 3 [on lack of support for O'Casey's plays].

'Sean May End Ban on Abbey', *Sunday Review* (Dublin), iii (20 Sep 1959) 28.

'Sean O'Casey', *New York Times* (25 Sep 1964) p. 40 [editorial tribute].

'Sean O'Casey', *Irish Independent* (Dublin), (21 Sep 1964) p. 10 [editorial].

'Sean O'Casey', *New Republic* (N.Y.), cli (3 Oct 1964) 6.

'Sean O'Casey', *Irish Times* (Dublin), (21 Sep 1964) p. 7 [editorial].

'Sean O'Casey', *Publisher's Weekly* (Philadelphia), clxxxvi (28 Sep 1964) 96 [obituary].

'Sean O'Casey Dies at 84', *Daily Mail* (London), (19 Sep 1964) p. 1.

'Sean O'Casey Dies: Heart Attack in Nursing Home', *Times* (London), (19 Sep 1964) p. 8.

'Sean O'Casey Getting Along Fine', *Irish Times* (Dublin), (25 Aug 1964) p. 5.

'Sean O'Casey Has Second Operation', *Irish Times* (Dublin), (1 Mar 1956) p. 5.

'Sean O'Casey Ill on Birthday', *New York Times* (31 Mar 1962) p. 16.

'Sean O'Casey in Hospital', *Irish Times* (Dublin), (15 Feb 1956) p. 1.

'Sean O'Casey, Irish Playwright, Is Dead at 84', *New York Times* (19 Sep 1964) pp 1, 12.

'Sean O'Casey Left £1,702', *Irish Times* (Dublin), (1 Dec 1964) p. 9.

'Sean O'Casey, Playwright of Genius', *Daily Telegraph* (London), (19 Sep 1964) p. 18 [obituary].

'Sean O'Casey Recuperating', *New York Times* (15 Feb 1956) p. 3.

'Sean O'Casey R.I.P.', *National Review* (N.Y.), XVI (6 Oct 1964) 859 [obituary].

SEDGWICK, RUTH WOODBURY, 'O'Casey: Laborer – Playwright – Poet', *Stage* (N.Y.), XII (Nov 1934) 29–31.

SHCHEPILOVA, L., 'Vsegda Plug i Zvezdy [Always the Plough and the Stars]', *Teatr*, XI 11 (Nov 1967) 147–54.

SHYRE, PAUL, 'Talk with Two Titans', *New York Times* (8 Sep 1957) section 2, pp. 1, 3 [O'Casey and Gordon Craig].

SKEFFINGTON, O. SHEEHY, 'Senator Sheehy Skeffington', *Standard* (Dublin), XXVII 165 (4 Mar 1955) 11 [letter to the Editor].

'Slum Child Who Became World Famed Dramatist', *Irish Times* (Dublin), (19 Sep 1964) p. 5.

SMET, R. DE, 'Sean O'Casey et la Tragédie des "Tenements"', *Revue des Vivants*, VIII (Aug 1940) 411–26.

SMITH, BOBBY L., 'The Hat, The Whore, and The Hypocrite in O'Casey's *Bedtime Story*', *Serif: Kent State University Library Quarterly* (Kent, Ohio), IV 2 (June 1967) 3–5.

'Satire in O'Casey's *Cock-a-Doodle Dandy*', *Renascence: A Critical Journal of Letters* (Milwaukee, Wis.), XIX 2 (winter 1967) 64–73.

'Satire in *The Plough and the Stars*: A Tragedy in Four Acts', *Ball State University Forum*, X 3 (1969) 3–11.

'O'Casey's Satiric Vision', *James Joyce Quarterly* (Tulsa, Okla.), VIII 1 (fall 1970) 13–28.

Smith, Winifred, 'The Dying God in the Modern Theatre', *Review of Religion* (N.Y.), v (Mar 1941) 264–75 [largely on *The Silver Tassie*].

Snoddy, Oliver, 'Sean O'Casey as Troublemaker', *Eire–Ireland* (St Paul, Minn.), i 4 (winter 1966) 23–38.

'Son of Sean O'Casey Dies', *New York Times* (8 Jan 1957) p. 31.

'Stage Censorship Reform', *Times* (London), (2 May 1958) p. 6 [O'Casey supports a theatre censorship reform committee formed under the chairmanship of Sir Gerald Barry].

'Stage Neglects Sean O'Casey', *Times* (London), (30 Mar 1960) p. 13.

Starkie, Walter, 'The Plays of Sean O'Casey', *Nineteenth Century and After* (London), civ 618 (Aug 1928) 225–36. See also O'Casey's reply, 'The Plays of Sean O'Casey: A Reply', in the issue of Sep 1928, 399–402. Reprinted in *Blasts and Benedictions*, ed. Ronald Ayling (London: Macmillan, 1967) pp. 103–7.

Stephens, James, 'Dublin Letter', *Dial* (Chicago), lxxvii 2 (Aug 1924) 155–7.

Stewart, Andrew, J., 'The Acting of the Abbey Theatre', *Theatre Arts Monthly* (N.Y.), xvii 3 (Mar 1933) 243–45.

Sutherland, Jack, 'O'Casey, Bard of Common Folk', *Daily Worker* (London), (21 Sep 1964) p. 2 [obituary].

Sweeney, Conor, 'Réalt na h Oíche', *Comhar* (Eanáir 1961) 28–30.

Talbott, Earl G., 'For Playwright O'Casey, Long Was the Staff of Life', *New York Herald Tribune* (19 Sep 1964) pp. 1, 8.

Taubman, Howard, 'Sean O'Casey: 1880–1964', *New York Times* (27 Sep 1964) section 2, p. 3 [obituary].

Templeton, Joan, 'Sean O'Casey and Expressionism', *Modern Drama* (Lawrence, Kansas), xiv 1 (May 1971) 47–62.

Thacher, Molly Day, 'Bentley on Theater', *New Leader* (N.Y.), xxxviii (10 Jan 1955) 27 [on O'Casey's Communism].

Thersites, 'Private Views', *Irish Times* (Dublin), (5 Feb 1955) p. 6. See reply by Denis Johnston, 'Who Coddled Donizetti?' (10 Mar 1955) p. 5 [letter to the Editor].

'They Stand out from the Crowd: Sean O'Casey', *Literary Digest* (N.Y.), cxviii 14 (6 Oct 1934) 12.

CRITICISM ON SEAN O'CASEY

THOMPSON, LAURENCE, 'O'Casey in His Slippers', *Irish Digest* (Dublin), LIII 3 (May 1955) 8–10 [interview]. Condensed from *News Chronicle* (London), (3 Mar 1955) p. 6.

TINDEMANS, C., 'Requiem voor Sean O'Casey', *Streven*, XVIII (Nov 1964) 171–7.

TODD, R. MARY. 'The Two Published Versions of Sean O'Casey's *Within the Gates*', *Modern Drama*, X 4 (Feb 1968) 346–55.

'Too Shy to See His Own Play: Sean O'Casey's First Night in London', *Daily Graphic* (London), (6 Mar 1926) p. 2 [interview].

'Tragic Artist', *Irish Catholic* (Dublin), LXXVII 22 (24 Sep 1964) 3 [editorial].

TREWIN, J. C., 'O'Casey the Elizabethan', *New Theatre* (London), III 1 (June 1946) 2–3.

'Tribute to O'Casey', *Irish Times* (Dublin), (5 Oct 1964) p. 6.

'Tributes Paid to Playwright', *Irish Times* (Dublin), (19 Sep 1964) p. 5 [by Hilton Edwards, Micheál Mac Liammóir, Gabriel Fallon, Brendan Smith and Phyllis Ryan].

'Twelve British Actors Start Campus Tour', *New York Times* (30 Jan 1965) p. 17 [Theatre Group 20, including Shivaun O'Casey].

VAN DRUTEN, JOHN, 'O'Casey as Phenomenon for Dublin', *Boston Evening Transcript* (13 Feb 1926) pt 3, pp. 4, 5, 7. Reprinted from the *New York Evening Post*.

VAUGHAN, CONSTANCE, 'O'Casey Explains Himself', *Daily Sketch* (London), (24 Mar 1926) p. 7 [interview].

VILAÇA, MÁRIO, 'Sean O'Casey: eo Movimento Dramatico Irlandês', *Vertice: Revista de Cultura e Arte* (Coimbra), XI 94 (June 1951) 293–9; XI 95 (July 1951) 369–72; XI 96 (Aug 1951) 399–406; XI 97 (Sep 1951) 479–83; XI 98 (Oct 1951) 553–6.

WALSH, LOUIS J., 'The Defiance of the Abbey', *Irish Rosary* (Dublin), XXXIX 9 (Sep 1935) 650–4.

'A Catholic Theatre for Dublin', *Irish Rosary* (Dublin), XXXIX 10 (Oct 1935) 749–54.

WARDLE, IRVING, 'The Tragedy of Sean O'Casey', *Observer* (London), (20 Sep 1964) p. 27 [obituary]. See replies by John Arden and John O'Riordan (27 Sep 1964) p. 37 [letters to the Editor].

WARNER, SYLVIA TOWNSEND, 'Sean O'Casey's Story', *Time and Tide* (London), XIV 21 (27 May 1933) 640 [letter to the Editor on *I Wanna Woman*].

WASHBURN, A. M., 'Form and Effect: Mr O'Casey's *Within the Gates*', *Harvard Advocate*, CXXI (Christmas 1934) 73-6.

WEATHERBY, W. J., 'Figures in the Shadows', *Manchester Guardian* (10 Sep 1959) p. 6 [interview].
'The Sting and the Twinkle', *Manchester Guardian* (15 Aug 1962) p. 7 [interview]. Also in *Irish Times* (Dublin), (15 Aug 1962) p. 8.

WEILER, A. H., 'By Way of Report: O'Casey Autobiography Acquired', *New York Times* (13 Aug 1961) section 2, p. 7.

WEISSMAN, DAVID L., 'Writer Condemns Producers for Failure to Offer O'Casey Plays', *New York Times* (7 Dec 1952) section 2, p. 7 [letter to the Drama Editor].

WHITE, TERENCE DE VERE, 'C'est le même journal', *Irish Times* (Dublin), (7 Jan 1967) p. 8. See reply by Quidnunc, 'An Irishman's Diary' (10 Jan 1967) p. 9.

WILSON, CECIL, 'From Squalor Grew the Genius of Juno', *Daily Mail* (London), (19 Sep 1964) p. 11 [obituary].

WINNINGTON, ALAN, 'O'Casey Life Story', *Morning Star* (London), (16 May 1966) p. 2 [by Eileen O'Casey].

WOODBRIDGE, HOMER E., 'Sean O'Casey', *South Atlantic Quarterly* (Durham, N.C.), XL (Jan 1941) 50-9.

'Works by O'Casey Published in Russia', *Irish Times* (Dublin), (11 Mar 1957) p. 5.

'The World of Sean O'Casey', *Life* (Chicago), International Edition, XVII 4 (23 Aug 1954) 45-55.

WORTH, KATHARINE J., 'O'Casey's Dramatic Symbolism', *Modern Drama*, IV 3 (Dec 1961) 260-7. Reprinted in *Sean O'Casey*, ed. Ronald Ayling (London: Macmillan, 1969) pp. 183-91.

YEATS, W. B., 'Sean O'Casey's Story', *Time and Tide* (London), XIV 21 (27 May 1933) 640 [letter to the Editor on *I Wanna Woman*].

'A Defence of the Abbey Theatre', *Dublin Magazine*, 1 2 (Apr–June 1926) 8–12.

(c) Reviews of Play Productions

[For obvious reasons, this section is arranged chronologically rather than alphabetically under each play.]

THE SHADOW OF A GUNMAN

'Abbey Theatre: *The Shadow of a Gunman*', *Irish Times* (Dublin), (13 Apr 1923), p. 4.

McH., M. F., 'A Good Play. Last Piece of the Season at the Abbey. A "Gunman"', *Freeman's Journal* (Dublin), (13 Apr 1923) p. 8.

O'D., F. J. H., 'Treat at the Abbey: *The Shadow of a Gunman*', *Evening Herald* (Dublin), (13 Apr 1923) p. 2.

'New Abbey Play', *Irish Independent* (Dublin), (14 Apr 1923) p. 3.

MAC, 'Too Much Laughter at the Abbey', *Irish Statesman* (Dublin), III 2 (20 Sep 1924) 46.

'Court Theatre: *The Shadow of a Gunman* by Sean O'Casey', *Times* (London), (28 May 1927) p. 10.

'Court Theatre: *The Shadow of a Gunman*, by Sean O'Casey', *Daily Telegraph* (London), (28 May 1927) p. 12.

'Irish Players Back: Sean O'Casey's Humour and Tragedy', *Daily Mail* (London), (28 May 1927) p. 9.

P., A., 'New O'Casey Play: *The Shadow of a Gunman* at the Court Not up to Standard', *Daily Sketch* (London), (28 May 1927) p. 2.

E., M., '*The Shadow of a Gunman*: Early O'Casey Play Comes to London', *Daily Herald* (London), (28 May 1927) p. 2.

'London Theatres: *The Shadow of a Gunman*', *Scotsman* (Edinburgh), (28 May 1927) p. 11.

GRIFFITH, HUBERT, '*The Shadow of a Gunman*: Mr Sinclair's Brilliant Comedy in Another O'Casey Play', *Evening Standard* (London), (28 May 1927) p. 4.

P., W., 'Mr Sean O'Casey's First Play. And How He Slipped Away When the Curtain Fell. His Goad to Work', *Evening News* (London), (28 May 1927) p. 7.

AGATE, JAMES, 'Court: *The Shadow of a Gunman*', *Sunday Times* (London), (29 May 1927) p. 6.

H., H., 'Court: *The Shadow of a Gunman*, by Sean O'Casey', *Observer* (London), (29 May 1927) p. 15.

'The Court: *The Shadow of a Gunman*', *Stage* (London), (2 June 1927) p. 16.

BIRRELL, FRANCIS, 'Court Theatre: *The Shadow of a Gunman* by Sean O'Casey', *Nation and Athenaeum* (London), XLI 9 (4 June 1927) 304.

'*The Shadow of a Gunman* at the Court', *Illustrated London News*, CLXX (4 June 1927) 1022.

'A Troubled Ireland in *The Shadow of a Gunman*', *Illustrated Sporting and Dramatic News* (London), CXV (11 June 1927) 725.

FARJEON, HERBERT, 'The London Stage: *The Shadow of a Gunman* *Graphic and National Weekly* (London), CXVI (11 June 1927) 441.

HORSNELL, HORACE, 'Early Sean O'Casey: *The Shadow of a Gunman*. Court Theatre', *Outlook* (London), LIX (11 June 1927) 770.

GREIN, J. T., 'The World of the Theatre: *The Shadow of a Gunman*', *Illustrated London News*, CLXX (18 June 1927) 1104.

BROWN, IVOR, '*The Shadow of a Gunman* by Sean O'Casey: The Court Theatre', *Saturday Review* (London), CXLIII (18 June 1927) 938.

JENNINGS, RICHARD, '*The Shadow of a Gunman* at the Court Theatre', *Spectator* (London), CXXXVIII (18 June 1927) 1062.

CHARQUES, R. D., 'The London Stage – Various New Productions', *New York Times* (26 June 1927) section 8, p. 1.

SUTTON, G[RAHAM], '*The Shadow of a Gunman*', *Bookman* (London), LXXII (July 1927) 248.

S., W. N., 'Court: *The Shadow of a Gunman*', *Theatre World* (London), VI 30 (July 1927) 10.

D[ONAGHEY], F[REDERICK], 'Theatre', *Chicago Daily Tribune* (11 Apr 1929) p. 33 [at the Blackstone Theater].

ATKINSON, BROOKS, 'Sean O'Casey's First Drama Acted for First Time in New York: *The Shadow of a Gunman*', *New York Times* (31 Oct 1932) p. 18.

'Irish Theatre Club: *The Shadow of a Gunman* by Sean O'Casey', *Times* (London), (26 Jan 1953) p. 2.

'Sean O'Casey Play to Open', *Daily Worker* (N.Y.), (11 Dec 1953) p. 7 [by Studio 8:40].

RAYMOND, HARRY, '*The Shadow of a Gunman* by Sean O'Casey', *Daily Worker* (N.Y.), (23 Feb 1954) p. 7.

RUHLE, J., 'Schatten über der grünen Insel: Sean O'Casey's *Harfe und Gewehr* in den Kammerspielendes Deutschen Theaters', *Sonntag* (Berlin), no. 4 (1954) 19–21.

OLDEN, G. A. 'Radio Review: Plays of O'Casey', *Irish Times* (Dublin), (19 May 1955) p. 8 [Radio Eireann].

WIRTH, A. 'Warsztat rexyserki meodych', *Po Prostu* (Warsaw), no. 39 (27 Nov 1955) 4.

'Dramatic By-Ways of Edinburgh', *Times* (London), (27 Aug 1956) p. 6 [by the Irish Festival Players].

'The New Lindsey Theatre Club: A New Irish Company', *Times* (London), (10 Oct 1956) p. 3.

B[AKER], F. G., '*The Shadow of a Gunman*. By Sean O'Casey. First London Performance of This Revival by the Irish Players at the New Lindsey Theatre', *Plays and Players* (London), IV 2 (Nov 1956) 17.

'Lyric Theatre, Hammersmith: *The Shadow of a Gunman* by Sean O'Casey', *Times* (London), (15 Jan 1957) p. 9.

'London Letter: O'Casey in London', *Irish Times* (Dublin), (16 Jan 1957) p. 5.

HOBSON, HAROLD, 'Irish Drama', *Sunday Times* (London), (20 Jan 1957) p. 13.

GRAHAME, PAUL, 'The Poet and the Playboy', *Daily Worker* (London), (22 Jan 1957) p. 2.

CONRAD, DEREK, '*The Shadow of a Gunman*. By Sean O'Casey. First Performance of This Revival at Lyric Theatre, Hammersmith', *Plays and Players* (London), IV 6 (Mar 1957) 17.

PECK, SEYMOUR, 'Three with a Dream: Co-Producers and Directors of O'Casey Play Bring New Venture to Bijou', *New York Times* (16 Nov 1958) section 2, pp. 1, 3.

ATKINSON, BROOKS, 'A Prologue to Greatness: *Shadow of a Gunman* by O'Casey at Bijou', *New York Times* (21 Nov 1958) p. 26.

CHAPMAN, JOHN, 'O'Casey's *Shadow of a Gunman* Stirringly Staged at the Bijou', *New York Daily News* (21 Nov 1958) p. 72.

'O'Casey Play Divides New York Critics', *Irish Times* (Dublin), (22 Nov 1958) p. 4.

ATKINSON, BROOKS, 'Two by O'Casey: *Cock-a-Doodle Dandy* and *Shadow of a Gunman* Open within 9 Days', *New York Times* (23 Nov 1958) section 2, p. 1.

ATKINSON, BROOKS, 'Theatre Prose', *New York Times* (30 Nov 1958) section 2, p. 1.

HEWES, HENRY, 'Where Is Fancy Bred?', *Saturday Review of Literature* (N.Y.), XLI (6 Dec 1958) 37.

TYNAN, KENNETH, 'The Troubles in the Studio', *New Yorker* (N.Y.), XXXIV (6 Dec 1958) 112. Reprinted in *Curtains* (New York: Atheneum, 1961) pp. 285-8.

'N.Y. Theatre Goes Irish: O'Casey Too Much for the Actors', *Times* (London), (10 Dec 1958) p. 3.

DRIVER, TOM F., 'Studio Portrait: *The Shadow of a Gunman* by Sean O'Casey', *Christian Century* (N.Y.), LXXV (17 Dec 1958) 1463.

'*The Shadow of a Gunman*', *America* (N.Y.), C (20-27 Dec 1958) 382.

'*The Shadow of a Gunman*', *Theatre Arts* (N.Y.), XLIII (Feb 1959) 22-3.

WYATT, EUPHEMIA VAN RENSSELAER, '*The Shadow of a Gunman*', *Catholic World* (N.Y.), CLXXXVIII (Feb 1959) 417.

COLIN, SAUL, 'Plays and Players in New York: Tenement Tragedy', *Plays and Players* (London), VI 5 (Feb 1959) 24.

KERR, WALTER, '*The Shadow of a Gunman* and *Cock-a-Doodle Dandy*', *Cincinnati Daily Enquirer* (30 Nov 1959) p. 50.

PESSEMESSE, PIERRE, 'Sean O'Casey au Théâtre Quotidien de Marseille', *Lettres françaises* (Paris) no. 881 (22-28 June 1961) 9.

'Abbey Theatre's Comeback. Abbey Theatre, Dublin: *The Shadow of a Gunman*', *Times* (London), (20 Aug 1964) p. 12.

ADDISON, ALAN, 'Two O'Casey Revivals: *The Shadow of a Gunman* (Mermaid), *Morning Star* (London), (7 Apr 1967) p. 2.

BRIEN, ALAN, 'Challenge to Chaplin', *Sunday Telegraph* (London), (9 Apr 1967) p. 10.

'Two Comedies by Sean O'Casey', *Observer* (London), (9 Apr 1967) p. 25 [picture only].

HOBSON, HAROLD, 'Triumphs Unforeseen', *Sunday Times* (London), (9 Apr 1967) p. 49.

SUTHERLAND, JACK, 'Understanding O'Casey's Stature', *Morning Star* (London), (11 April 1967) p. 2.

'*Shadow of a Gunman* in Belfast', *Irish Times* (Dublin), (5 Oct 1967) p. 8 [at the Grove Theatre].

'Five European Cities Will See Abbey Players Next Year', *Irish Times* (Dublin), (15 Dec 1967) p. 1.

QUIDNUNC, 'An Irishman's Diary', *Irish Times* (Dublin), (8 Feb 1968) p. 11.

'Abbey Players to Perform in Florence', *Irish Times* (Dublin), (20 Apr 1968) p. 1. See also picture, p. 13.

KELLY, SEAMUS, 'Florence Welcomes the Abbey Players', *Irish Times*
(Dublin), (22 Apr 1968) p. 1.

KELLY, SEAMUS, '14 Curtain Calls for Abbey Players', *Irish Times*
(Dublin), (23 Apr 1968) pp. 1, 8 [at the Teatro della Pergola].

KELLY, SEAMUS, 'Italian Accolade for Abbey Players', *Irish Times*
(Dublin), (27 Apr 1968) p. 6.

KELLY, HENRY, 'Synge and O'Casey in the Abbey', *Irish Times*
(Dublin), (14 May 1968) p. 8.

CATHLEEN LISTENS IN

C[ox], J. H., '*Cathleen Listens In:* A Topical Extravaganza', *Irish
Independent* (Dublin), (2 Oct 1923) p. 6 [at the Abbey Theatre].

O'D., F. J. H., '*Cathleen Listens In*: Topical Extravaganza at the Abbey
Theatre', *Evening Herald* (Dublin), (2 Oct 1923) p. 2.

PRIOR, 'Abbey Theatre: *Cathleen Listens In*', *Irish Times* (Dublin),
(2 Oct 1923) p. 4.

McH., M. F., 'Abbey Theatre: New One-Act Phantasy Produced',
Freeman's Journal (Dublin), (2 Oct 1923) p. 4.

'The Abbey: New One-Act Phantasy Produced. A Delightful Piece',
Evening Telegraph (Dublin), (2 Oct 1923) p. 2.

M[ITCHELL], S[USAN] L., 'Dramatic Notes', *Irish Statesman* (Dublin),
1 (6 Oct 1923) 122.

'Notes and News of Dublin Productions', *Evening Telegraph* (Dublin),
(6 Oct 1923) p. 4.

'Abbey Theatre', *Irish Times* (Dublin), (4 Mar 1925) p. 9.

'Abbey Theatre', *Irish Independent* (Dublin), (4 Mar 1925) p. 8.

JUNO AND THE PAYCOCK

'Abbey Theatre: *Juno and the Paycock*', *Irish Times* (Dublin), (4 Mar
1924) p. 8.

JACQUES, 'Truth and Tragedy in a Realistic Play: Ireland's Civil
War', *Irish Independent* (Dublin), (4 Mar 1924) p. 6.

M., H. L., 'Master of Irony: Success of Mr O'Casey's New Play at
Abbey', *Freeman's Journal* (Dublin), (4 Mar 1924) p. 4.

JACQUES, 'Truth and Tragedy. Realistic Play Produced at the Abbey
Theatre', *Evening Herald* (Dublin), (4 Mar 1924) p. 2.

LAWRENCE, W. J., '*Juno and the Paycock* at the Abbey', *Irish Statesman*
(Dublin), II 1 (15 Mar 1924) 16.

GWYNN, STEPHEN, 'A Brilliant Irish Play', *Living Age* (Boston), CCCXXI (3 May 1924) 869–70.

JEWELL, EDWARD ALDEN, '*Juno and the Paycock*', *Nation* (N.Y.), CXVIII (28 May 1924) 617–19.

'Royalty Theatre: *Juno and the Paycock* by Sean O'Casey', *Times* (London), (17 Nov 1925) p. 12.

B., I., 'Dublin Fair City', *Manchester Guardian* (17 Nov 1925) p. 14.

B., G., '*Juno and the Paycock*: Harrowing Realism in Play by Former Bricklayer', *Daily Graphic* (London), (17 Nov 1925) p. 2.

P., A., 'New Irish Play: Clever Presentation of *Juno and the Paycock*', *Daily Sketch* (London), (17 Nov 1925) p. 3. Pictures, p. 13.

'London Theatres: *Juno and the Paycock*', *Scotsman* (Edinburgh), (17 Nov 1925) p. 9.

'*Juno and the Paycock*: Mr Arthur Sinclair's Delightful Acting', *Daily Mail* (London), (17 Nov 1925) p. 10.

'Royalty Theatre: *Juno and the Paycock*, by Sean O'Casey', *Daily Telegraph* (London), (17 Nov 1925) p. 12.

E., M., '*Juno and the Paycock*: Fine Irish Play Comes to London', *Daily Herald* (London), (17 Nov 1925) p. 5.

G[RIFFITH], H[UBERT], 'A Brilliant Irish Play', *Evening Standard* (London), (17 Nov 1925) p. 3.

M., A. E., 'A Page of Life from Dublin. Irish Players in *Juno and the Paycock*. An Unusual Medley', *Evening News* (London), (17 Nov 1925) p. 7.

'The Royalty: *Juno and the Paycock*', *Stage* (London), (19 Nov 1925) p. 18.

J., R., 'A New Irish Dramatist', *Spectator* (London), CXXXV (21 Nov 1925) 923–4.

BROWN, IVOR, 'Life by the Liffey: *Juno and the Paycock* by Sean O'Casey. Royalty Theatre', *Saturday Review* (London), CXL (21 Nov 1925) 594.

AGATE, JAMES, 'Royalty: *Juno and the Paycock*, a Tragedy by Sean O'Casey. Monday, November 16', *Sunday Times* (London), (22 Nov 1925) p. 6. Reprinted in *The Contemporary Theatre, 1925* (London: Chapman & Hall, 1926) pp. 114–18; in *Red Letter Nights* (London: Jonathan Cape, 1944) pp. 230–3; in *James Agate: An Anthology*, ed. Herbert Van Thal (London: Rupert Hart-Davis, 1961) pp. 76–8; and in *Sean O'Casey*, ed. Ronald Ayling (London: Macmillan, 1969) pp. 76–8.

H., H., 'Royalty: *Juno and the Paycock* by Sean O'Casey', *Observer* (London), (22 Nov 1925) p. 11.

OMICRON, 'From Alpha to Omega', *Nation and Athenaeum* (London), XXXVIII 9 (28 Nov 1925) 320–1.

MACCARTHY, DESMOND, '*Juno and the Paycock*', *New Statesman* (London), XXVI (28 Nov 1925) 207.

'*Juno and the Paycock* at the Royalty', *Illustrated London News*, CLXVII (28 Nov 1925) 1104.

ST JOHN, CHRISTOPHER, 'The Irish Bubble', *Time and Tide* (London), VI 49 (4 Dec 1925) 1195–6.

B., C. H. 'Royalty: *Juno and the Paycock*', *Theatre World and Illustrated Stage Review* (London), II 11 (Dec 1925) 65.

SHIPP, HORACE, '*Juno and the Paycock*, by Sean O'Casey (Royalty Theatre)', *English Review* (London), XLII (Jan 1926) 112–15.

WALDMAN, MILTON, '*Juno and the Paycock*, by Sean O'Casey: Royalty Theatre', *London Mercury*, XIII 76 (Feb 1926) 422–3.

ATKINSON, BROOKS, 'Irish Folk Life in a Tragedy: *Juno and the Paycock*. A Play in Three Acts by Sean O'Casey', *New York Times* (16 Mar 1926) p. 22 [at the Mayfair Theater, New York].

MANTLE, BURNS, '*Juno and the Paycock*: A Sad Irish Drama', *New York Daily News* (17 Mar 1926) p. 30.

ATKINSON, BROOKS, 'O'Casey at the Bat: *Juno and the Paycock* – His First American Production', *New York Times* (21 Mar 1926) section 8, pp. 1–2.

'The Irish Prize Play', *New York Times* (26 Mar 1926) p. 20.

B., D. W., 'Broad Comedy. Stark Realism out of Dublin: O'Casey's Play of *Juno and the Paycock*', *Boston Evening Transcript* (26 Mar 1926) p. 8.

G., G. W., 'The Theatre', *New Yorker*, II (27 Mar 1926) 25.

KRUTCH, JOSEPH WOOD, 'A Dublin Success', *Nation* (N.Y.), CXXII (31 Mar 1926) 348.

NATHAN, GEORGE JEAN, 'Judging the Shows', *Judge* (N.Y.), XC (10 Apr 1926) 15.

CARB, DAVID, '*Juno and the Paycock*', *Vogue* (N.Y.), LXVII (15 May 1926) 98, 140.

SKINNER, R. DANA, 'From Triumph to Illusion', *Independent* (N.Y.), CXVI (15 May 1926) 580.

STONE, MELVILLE E., 'A New View of *Juno*', *New York Times* (23 May 1926) section 8, p. 1.

BARRETT, LARRY, 'The New Yorker', *Bookman* (N.Y.), LVIII 3 (May 1926) 343–4.

KALONYME, LOUIS, 'Paycocks under the Moon', *Arts and Decoration* (N.Y.), XXV (May 1926) 64, 92.

BROWN, JOHN MASON, 'The Rush Hour on Broadway', *Theatre Arts Monthly* (N.Y.), X 5 (May 1926) 286–9.

HORNBLOW, ARTHUR, 'Mr Hornblow Goes to the Play', *Theatre Magazine* (N.Y.), XLIII (May 1926) 15.

ATKINSON, BROOKS, 'Again the Irish Players: *Juno and the Paycock.* A Play in Three Parts by Sean O'Casey', *New York Times* (20 Dec 1927) p. 32 [by the Irish Players at the Gallo Theater, New York].

KRUTCH, JOSEPH WOOD, 'Poet Laureate', *Nation* (N.Y.), CXXV (21 Dec 1927) 718.

BRACKETT, CHARLES, 'Humble Pie with a Drop of Vinegar', *New Yorker*, III (31 Dec 1927) 23.

DOYLE, MARY AGNES, 'Sean O'Casey Comes to Chicago', *Drama* (Chicago), XVIII 3 (Dec 1927) 68–70.

'A New York Diary', *New Republic* (N.Y.), LIII (4 Jan 1928) 191–2.

CARB, DAVID, '*Juno and the Paycock*', *Vogue* (N.Y.), LXXI 4 (15 Feb 1928) 87, 122.

BROWN, JOHN MASON, 'The Laughter of the Gods: Broadway in Review', *Theatre Arts Monthly* (N.Y.), XII 2 (Feb 1928) 91–5.

D[ONAGHEY], F[REDERICK], '*Juno and the Paycock*: Comedy in Three Acts by Sean O'Casey', *Chicago Tribune* (5 Mar 1928) p. 33 [at the Blackstone Theater, Chicago].

SELDES, GILBERT, 'The Theatre', *Dial* (Chicago), LXXXIV 3 (Mar 1928) 259–60.

'Abbey Theatre's American Tour', *Manchester Guardian Weekly*, XXV 6 (7 Aug 1931) 114.

P., H. T., 'O'Casey Gains Place at Last on Our Stage: *Juno and the Paycock* Acted by the Abbey Company to Answering Audience', *Boston Evening Transcript* (13 Apr 1932) pt 2, p. 5.

G., W. E., 'Hollis Street: *Juno and the Paycock*', *Boston Herald* (13 Apr 1932) p. 20.

ATKINSON, BROOKS, 'Tatterdemalions of Dublin in *Juno and the Paycock*', *New York Times* (20 Oct 1932) p. 24.

[OULD, HERMAN], 'No Bricks for Irish Players This Time', *Literary Digest* (N.Y.), CXIV 21 (19 Nov 1932) 17–18.

'Little Theatre: *Juno and the Paycock* by Sean O'Casey', *Times* (London), (2 Mar 1934) p. 12.

CRITICISM ON SEAN O'CASEY

C., J., 'Juno and the Paycock: Blarney, Humour and Sentiment in Revival of Charming Irish Play', Daily Sketch (London), (2 Mar 1934) p. 2.

DARLINGTON, W. A., 'Notable Irish Play Revived: Juno and the Paycock', Daily Telegraph (London), (2 Mar 1934) p. 10.

DISHER, WILLSON, 'Juno and the Paycock: Fine Acting in Revival', Daily Mail (London), (2 Mar 1934) p. 21.

'The "Paycock" Returns', Evening Standard (London), (2 Mar 1934) p. 11.

'Juno and the Paycock: First-Rate Acting by the Irish Players', Evening News (London), (2 Mar 1934) p. 3.

BROWN, IVOR, 'Little: Juno and the Paycock, by Sean O'Casey', Observer (London), (4 Mar 1934) p. 17.

'The Little: Juno and the Paycock', Stage (London), (8 Mar 1934) p. 10.

B., C., 'Juno and the Paycock. Sean O'Casey. Little', Time and Tide (London), xv 10 (10 Mar 1934) 326.

'Embassy Theatre: Juno and the Paycock by Sean O'Casey', Times (London), (27 June 1934) p. 14.

'An O'Casey Revival', New Statesman and Nation (London), vii (30 June 1934) 995.

GREGORY, RUSSELL, 'Embassy Theatre: Juno and the Paycock by Sean O'Casey', Saturday Review (London), clvii (30 June 1934) 774.

MANTLE, BURNS, 'Abbey Players Turn to O'Casey: True Picture of the Dublin Tenement Is Colorfully Acted', New York Daily News (24 Nov 1934) p. 23.

ERVINE, ST JOHN, 'At the Play', Observer (London), (27 Jan 1935) p. 15.

'Q Theatre: Juno and the Paycock by Sean O'Casey', Times (London), (13 July 1937) p. 12.

H[ART]-D[AVIS], R[UPERT], 'Juno and the Paycock by Sean O'Casey: At the Haymarket Theatre', Spectator (London), clviii (13 Aug 1937) 275.

'Juno and the Paycock at the Haymarket', New Statesman and Nation (London), xiv (14 Aug 1937) 252.

BROWN, IVOR, 'Theatre Royal, Haymarket: Juno and the Paycock by Sean O'Casey', Observer (London), (15 Aug 1937) p. 11.

MORGAN, CHARLES, 'Juno and the O'Casey', New York Times (29 Aug 1937) section 10, p. 2.

COOKMAN, A. V., 'Juno and the Paycock: By Sean O'Casey', London Mercury, xxxvi 215 (Sep 1937) 469.

ATKINSON, BROOKS, 'Sean O'Casey's *Juno and the Paycock* Acted by the Abbey Theatre Troupe', *New York Times* (7 Dec 1937) p. 32 [at the Ambassador Theatre, New York].

ATKINSON, BROOKS, 'The Play: Barry Fitzgerald and Sara Allgood Resume Their Original Parts in *Juno and the Paycock*', *New York Times* (17 Jan 1940) p. 24 [at the Mansfield Theater].

ATKINSON, BROOKS, 'Box Office Now Open: *Juno and the Paycock*', *New York Times* (21 Jan 1940) section 9, p. 1.

ATKINSON, BROOKS, '*Juno and the Paycock*', *New York Times* (28 Jan 1940) section 9, p. 1.

'Old Play in Manhatten', *Time* (N.Y.), XXXV (29 Jan 1940) 36.

NATHAN, GEORGE JEAN, 'The Best of the Irish', *Newsweek* (N.Y.), XV (29 Jan 1940) 33.

VERNON, GRENVILLE, '*Juno and the Paycock*', *Commonweal* (N.Y.), XXXI (2 Feb 1940) 327-8.

JORDAN, ELIZABETH, '*Juno and the Paycock*', *America* (N.Y.), LXII (10 Feb 1940) 502.

CONNOLLY, TERENCE L., 'No Hypersensitiveness', *America* (N.Y.), LXII (2 Mar 1940) 578 [letter to the Editor in reply to Elizabeth Jordan's review].

GASSNER, JOHN, 'Stage', *Direction* (N.Y.), III (Mar 1940) 16.

WYATT, EUPHEMIA VAN RENSSELAER, '*Juno and the Paycock*', *Catholic World* (N.Y.), CL (Mar 1940) 730-1.

GILDER, ROSAMOND, '*Juno and the Paycock*', *Theatre Arts* (N.Y.), XXIV (Mar 1940) 162, 165.

FALLON, GABRIEL, 'Sitting at the Play. The Month's Theatre: Arthur Sinclair in Sean O'Casey's *Juno and the Paycock*', *Irish Monthly* (Dublin), LXIX 818 (July 1941) 403-6 [at the Abbey Theatre].

FALLON, GABRIEL, 'The Nobility and Dignity of Juno', *Standard* (Dublin), XXIII 11 (16 Mar 1951) 5 [at the Abbey Theatre].

ARUNDEL, HONOR, 'Radio: Two Rebellions', *Daily Worker* (London), (19 Mar 1951) p. 2 [broadcast play].

'Irving Theatre: *Juno and the Paycock* by Sean O'Casey', *Times* (London), (11 Sep 1953) p. 2.

'New Lindsey Theatre: *Juno and the Paycock* by Sean O'Casey', *Times* (London), (31 Mar 1954) p. 5.

IGOE, W. J., 'London Letter', *America* (N.Y.), XCI (14 Aug 1954) 480-1.

'Sean O'Casey Play Next at Greenwich Mews', *Daily Worker* (N.Y.), (13 Jan 1955) p. 7.

ATKINSON, BROOKS, 'O'Casey's Dublin Tenements: *Juno and the Paycock* Revived Downtown', *New York Times* (24 Feb 1955) p. 20 [at the Greenwich Mews Theatre, as a community project sponsored by the Village Presbyterian Church and the Brotherhood Synagogue].

RAYMOND, HARRY, '*Juno and the Paycock* at the Mews Theatre', *Daily Worker* (N.Y.), (28 Feb 1955) p. 7.

LEVENTHAL, A. J., 'Dramatic Commentary: *Juno and the Paycock*. By Sean O'Casey. Radio Eireann', *Dublin Magazine*, XXXI 3 (July–Sep 1955) 53.

'The Gramophone: Irish Drama on Record. *Juno and the Paycock*', *Times* (London), (18 Aug 1956) p. 9.

MACLEOD, ALISON, 'Radio & TV: If Only We Could See It', *Daily Worker* (London), (1 Mar 1957) p. 2.

GARRICK, D., 'Green Room', *Plays and Players* (London), V 10 (July 1958) 23.

QUIDNUNC, 'An Irishman's Diary', *Irish Times* (Dublin), (19 Aug 1958) p. 6 [Juno as musical on Broadway soon].

'Sean O'Casey on Broadway', *Daily Worker* (London), (11 Sep 1958) p. 3.

SCHUMACH, MURRAY, 'O'Casey's Juno, Singing', *New York Times* (1 Mar 1959) section 2, p. 1 [at Winter Garden Theatre].

ATKINSON, BROOKS, 'A Musical *Juno* Arrives: Show Based on Play by O'Casey Opens', *New York Times* (10 Mar 1959) p. 41.

'Sean O'Casey Play as Musical: *Juno and the Paycock*', *Times* (London), (11 Mar 1959) p. 13.

ATKINSON, BROOKS, 'Musical *Juno*: O'Casey Play Converted into Another Medium', *New York Times* (15 Mar 1959) section 2, p. 1.

'*Juno* Posts Closing Notice', *New York Times* (17 Mar 1959) p. 42.

DRIVER, TOM F., 'O'Casey's *Juno* as Musical', *New Republic* (N.Y.), CXL 13 (30 Mar 1959) 20–1.

'O'Casey–Hansberry', *New York Times* (28 June 1959) section 2, p. 3 [*Raisin in the Sun* owes much to *Juno and the Paycock*].

L., J., 'Au Théâtre de la Renaissance: *Junon et le paon* de Sean O'Casey par la Comédie de l'Ouest', *Figaro littéraire* (Paris), (22 Apr 1961) p. 16.

BOURGET-PAILLERON, ROBERT, 'Revue dramatique. Renaissance: La Comédie de l'Ouest: Jean Goubert et Guy Parigot présentent *Junon et le paon*', *Revue des deux mondes* (Paris), (1 May 1961) pp. 154–6.

'O'Casey To Allow 2 Plays To Be Performed in Dublin', *New York Times* (6 Nov 1963) p. 35 [*Juno and the Paycock* and *The Plough and the Stars* as a preview for London].

O'CASEY, SEAN, 'Behind the Ban', *New York Times* (5 Jan 1964) section 2, pp. 1, 3 [lifting the ban on *Juno and the Paycock* and *The Plough and the Stars*].

'O'Casey Angry about Strike Call Now', *Irish Times* (Dublin), (14 Apr 1964) p. 1.

SHORTER, ERIC, 'O'Casey Old Rogues at Their Best', *Daily Telegraph* (London), (21 Apr 1964) p. 18.

'Abbey–O'Casey Reunion. Aldwych Theatre: *Juno and the Paycock*', *Times* (London), (21 Apr 1964) p. 14.

HOPE-WALLACE, PHILIP, '*Juno and the Paycock* at the Aldwych', *Guardian* (London), (21 Apr 1964) p. 9.

KELLY, SEAMUS, '*Juno* Is Received Coolly in London', *Irish Times* (Dublin), (21 Apr 1964) p. 1.

SHULMAN, MILTON, 'Begorra! Where's That Irish Sparkle?' *Evening Standard* (London), (21 Apr 1964) p. 5.

BRIEN, ALAN, 'Theatre: *Juno* at the Aldwych', *Sunday Telegraph* (London), (26 Apr 1964) p. 12.

LENOIR, JEAN-PIERRE, 'Abbey Troupe Gives *Juno* at Paris Fete', *New York Times* (6 May 1964) p. 41 [at Sarah Bernhardt Theatre].

'Abbey Reply to O'Casey: In No Position to Pronounce Judgment', *Irish Times* (Dublin), (3 July 1964) p. 1. See 'Abbey Has Been Deteriorating for Years' (4 July 1964) p. 1.

SHAW, IAIN, '*Juno* and *The Plough*', *Encore* (London), 11 (July–Aug 1964) 52–4.

'Derry Visit Subject of O'Casey's Letter to Abbey', *Irish Times* (Dublin), (3 Nov 1964) p. 11.

'O'Casey: Victim of His Own Legend. The National Theatre: *Juno and the Paycock* by Sean O'Casey', *Times* (London), (27 Apr 1966) p. 7.

LEWIS, PETER, 'O'Casey Seen for the First Time. *Juno and the Paycock*, by Sean O'Casey. National Theatre Company, Old Vic', *Daily Mail* (London), (27 Apr 1966) p. 18.

KRETZMER, HERBERT, 'English Beat the Irish. Old Vic: *Juno and the Paycock*', *Daily Express* (London), (27 April 1966) p. 4.

HOPE-WALLACE, PHILIP, '*Juno and the Paycock* at the National Theatre', *Guardian* (London), (27 Apr 1966) p. 9.

DARLINGTON, W. A., 'Joyce Redman Achieves Wonders as Juno', *Daily Telegraph* (London), (27 Apr 1966) p. 19.

SHULMAN, MILTON, '*Juno and the Paycock* at the National Theatre', *Evening Standard* (London), (27 Apr 1966) p. 4.

BARKER, FELIX, 'It's a Darlin' Thing – This Paycock', *Evening News* (London), (27 Apr 1966) p. 5.

SUTHERLAND, JACK, 'National Theatre Honours O'Casey's Memory: *Juno and the Paycock*', *Morning Star* (London), (28 Apr 1966) p. 2.

H., P., 'O'Casey Triumphs at the National Theatre', *Stage and Television Today* (London), (28 Apr 1966) p. 15.

BRYDEN, RONALD, 'Sir Laurence's Line', *Observer* (London), (1 May 1966) p. 24.

HOBSON, HAROLD, 'Theatre', *Sunday Times* (London), (1 May 1966) p. 29.

BRIEN, ALAN, 'Theatre', *Sunday Telegraph* (London), (1 May 1966) p. 12.

V., L., 'A New Tribute to O'Casey. *Juno and the Paycock*: Old Vic', *Time and Tide* (London), XLVII 18 (5–11 May 1966) 29.

JONES, MERVYN, 'O'Casey's Pessimism', *Tribune* (London), XXX 18 (6 May 1966) 14.

JONES, D. A. N., 'Designs for Dying', *New Statesman and Nation* (London), LXXI (6 May 1966) 662.

SPURLING, HILARY, 'A Darlin' Paycock: *Juno and the Paycock* (Old Vic)', *Spectator* (London), CCXVI (6 May 1966) 570.

TREWIN, J. C., 'Theatre', *Illustrated London News* (7 May 1966) p. 38.

LEONARD, HUGH, 'Olivier's O'Casey', *Plays and Players* (London), XIII 9 (June 1966) 25.

QUIDNUNC, 'An Irishman's Diary', *Irish Times* (Dublin), (21 July 1966) p. 7.

KELLY, SEAMUS, 'O'Casey's *Juno* at the Gaiety', *Irish Times* (Dublin), (2 Aug 1966) p. 8.

QUIDNUNC, 'An Irishman's Diary: At the Play', *Irish Times* (Dublin), (17 Aug 1966) p. 7.

BASTABLE, ADOLPHUS, 'Our Theatres in the Sixties', *Shavian* (London), III 6 (winter 1966–7) 20.

KELLY, SEAMUS, 'Abbey: A Gallant *Juno* Lacked the Old Magic', *Irish Times* (Dublin), (7 Oct 1969) p. 8.

COLGAN, GERALD, 'Dublin', *Plays and Players* (London), XVII 3 (Dec 1969) 54.

NANNIE'S NIGHT OUT

C[ox], J. H., 'Abbey Activities: Mr Sean O'Casey's New Play', *Irish Independent* (Dublin), (30 Sep 1924) p. 6.

'Abbey First Night: S. O'Casey's New Picture of Slum Life. Curious Humour', *Evening Telegraph* (Dublin), (30 Sep 1924) p. 2.

'New Comedy at the Abbey: *Nannie's Night Out*', *Irish Times* (Dublin), (30 Sep 1924) p. 4.

LONNDUBH, AN, 'The Worker at the Abbey: Mr O'Casey's New Play', *Voice of Labour* (Dublin), (4 Oct 1924) p. 7.

O., Y. [George Russell], '*Nannie's Night Out*', *Irish Statesman* (Dublin), III 5 (11 Oct 1924) 144–5.

BUGGY, BERTHA, 'From the Back Seats', *Irish Statesman* (Dublin), III (18 Oct 1924) 175.

THE PLOUGH AND THE STARS

'*The Plough and the Stars*: Mr Sean O'Casey's New Play', *Irish Times* (Dublin), (12 Jan 1926) p. 9 [at the Abbey Theatre, Dublin].

'*The Plough and the Stars*: Mr Sean O'Casey's New Play', *Irish Times* (Dublin), (9 Feb 1926) p. 7.

G., J. W., 'Sean O'Casey's New Play: *The Plough and the Stars*', *Irish Independent* (Dublin), (9 Feb 1926) p. 9.

'Abbey Theatre Scene: An Attempt to Stop Mr O'Casey's New Play. Fight on Stage', *Irish Times* (Dublin), (12 Feb 1926) pp. 7–8.

'Riotous Scenes in Abbey Theatre. Fights with Actors on the Stage. Women Engage in Fierce Fistic Battles. Hours of Uproar', *Irish Independent* (Dublin), (12 Feb 1926) p. 7.

'New Play Resented. Last Night's Scenes in the Abbey Theatre. 1916 Memories. Onlooker's Impressions of People's Protest', *Evening Herald* (Dublin), (12 Feb 1926) p. 1.

S[TARKIE], W[ALTER], '*The Plough and the Stars*' *Irish Statesman* (Dublin), V 23 (13 Feb 1926) 716–17.

'Cant and Facts', *Irish Times* (Dublin), (13 Feb 1926) p. 6 [leading article].

LONNDUBH, AN, '*The Plough and the Stars*: Sean O'Casey's New Play at the Abbey', *Voice of Labour* (Dublin), (13 Feb 1926) p. 4.

GWYNN, STEPHEN, 'The Dublin Play Riots: Accounts by Eye-Witnesses', *Observer* (London), (14 Feb 1926) p. 16.

MCQUEEN, JOHN, 'Letter to the Editor' *Irish Independent* (Dublin), (15 Feb 1926) p. 8.

SHEEHY-SKEFFINGTON, Mrs H[ANNAH], 'Letter to the Editor', *Irish Independent* (Dublin), (15 Feb 1926) p. 8. See O'Casey's reply (20 Feb 1926).

O'SHEA, SEAN, 'Letter to the Editor', *Irish Independent* (Dublin), (15 Feb 1926) p. 8.

PERRIN, J. H., 'Letter to the Editor', *Irish Independent* (Dublin), (15 Feb 1926) p. 8.

O'CASEY, SEAN, '*The Plough and the Stars*: A Reply to the Critics', *Irish Times* (Dublin), (19 Feb 1926) p. 6.

M., A. N., 'A Bookman's Notes: Art and the Patriot', *Manchester Guardian Weekly*, XIV 8 (19 Feb 1926) 152.

SPECTATOR, 'Politics and People', *Irish Statesman* (Dublin), V 24 (20 Feb 1926) 736–7.

O'FLAHERTY, LIAM, '*The Plough and the Stars*', *Irish Statesman* (Dublin), V 24 (20 Feb 1926) 739–40 [letter to the Editor].

CLARKE, AUSTIN, '*The Plough and the Stars*', *Irish Statesman* (Dublin), V 24 (20 Feb 1926) 740 [letter to the Editor].

'At Home and Abroad', *Illustrated London News* (London), CLXVIII (20 Feb 1926) 322.

MALONE, ANDREW E., 'Shattered Dreams', *Voice of Labour* (Dublin), n.s. VIII 8 (20 Feb 1926). 1.

'At the Abbey', *Voice of Labour* (Dublin), n.s., VIII 8 (20 Feb 1926) 4.

SHEEHY-SKEFFINGTON, Mrs H[ANNAH], '*The Plough and the Stars*: Reply to Mr O'Casey', *Irish Independent* (Dublin), (23 Feb 1926) p. 9.

O'CASEY, SEAN, 'Mr O'Casey's Play: Author's Rejoinder', *Irish Independent* (Dublin), (26 Feb 1926) p. 8 [letter to the Editor in reply to Mrs Sheehy-Skeffington's letter of 15 Feb].

O'HIGGINS, BRIGID, '*The Plough and the Stars*: As a Woman Saw It', *Irish Statesman* (Dublin), V 25 (27 Feb 1926) 770–1.

FALLON, GABRIEL, '*The Plough and the Stars*', *Irish Statesman* (Dublin), V 25 (27 Feb 1926) 768 [letter to the Editor].

DONAGHY, LYLE, '*The Plough and the Stars*', *Irish Statesman* (Dublin), V 25 (27 Feb 1926) 767–8 [letter to the Editor].

FALLON, GABRIEL, '*The Plough and the Stars*', *Irish Statesman* (Dublin), V 25 (27 Feb 1926) 768 [letter to the Editor].

'O'Casey and *The Voice*', *Voice of Labour* (Dublin), VIII 9 (27 Feb 1926) p. 5 [letter to the Editor by O'Casey and the Editor's reply].

'*The Plough and the Stars*: Criticism in a Lecture. The Author's Reply', *Irish Times* (Dublin), (2 Mar 1926) p. 5.

HIGGINS, F. R., 'The Plough and the Stars', Irish Statesman (Dublin), v 26 (6 Mar 1926) 797–8 [letter to the Editor].

SPECTATOR, 'Politics and People', Irish Statesman (Dublin), v 26 (6 Mar 1926) 794.

O'SULLIVAN, KATHLEEN, 'The Plough and the Stars', Irish Statesman (Dublin), VI 1 (13 Mar 1926) 11–12 [letter to the Editor].

A SEEKER OF TRUTH, 'The Plough and the Stars', Irish Statesman (Dublin), VI 1 (13 Mar 1926) 12 [letter to the Editor].

HAYES, J. J., 'Another by O'Casey', New York Times (21 Mar 1926) section 8, p. 2.

'Dramatic Unrest in Ireland', Living Age (Boston), CCCXXVIII (27 Mar 1926) 693–4.

'Editorial', Catholic Opinion (Dublin), XVI 3 (Mar 1926) 242–8.

BOOTH, ARTHUR, 'Lies and Libels', Dublin Opinion, v 1 (Mar 1926).

K. L., 'The Plough and the Stars: The Play of the Season', Crystal (Dublin), I 2 (Mar 1926) 47–8, 51.

'The Talk of the Town', Dublin Opinion, v 1 (Mar 1926) 6.

'Fortune Theatre: The Plough and the Stars by Sean O'Casey', Times (London), (14 May 1926) p. 4.

'Wonderful London Yesterday', Daily Graphic (London), (14 May 1926) p. 2.

AGATE, JAMES, 'Fortune: The Plough and the Stars', Sunday Times (London), (16 May 1926) p. 3. Reprinted in Red Letter Nights (London: Jonathan Cape, 1944) pp. 233–6; and in Sean O'Casey, ed. Ronald Ayling (London: Macmillan, 1969) pp. 79–81.

E., ST J., 'The Plough and the Stars, by Sean O'Casey', Observer (London), (16 May 1926) p. 4.

ATKINSON, BROOKS, 'Disillusion in Irish Drama', New York Times (16 May 1926) section 8, pp. 1–2.

'The Fortune: The Plough and the Stars', Stage (London), (20 May 1926) p. 19.

ROYDE-SMITH, N. G., 'The Drama: The Plough and the Stars by Sean O'Casey. Fortune', Outlook (London), LVII (22 May 1926) 359.

BROWN, IVOR, 'The Plough and the Stars by Sean O'Casey: The Fortune Theatre', Saturday Review (London), CXLI (22 May 1926) 614–15.

MACCARTHY, DESMOND, 'The Plough and the Stars', New Statesman (London), XXVII (29 May 1926) 170.

'Plays and Pictures', Nation and Athenaeum (London), XXXIX (29 May 1926) 207.

A., E. S., 'Mr O'Casey Again: *The Plough and the Stars* by Sean O'Casey. Fortune Theatre', *Spectator* (London), CXXXVI (29 May 1926) 904.

'London Letter: *The Plough and the Stars*', *Irish Times* (Dublin), (21 June 1926) p. 6 [to be transferred from the Fortune Theatre to the New Theatre].

SHIPP, HORACE, 'The Art of Sean O'Casey', *English Review* (London), XLII (June 1926) 851–3.

WALDMAN, MILTON, '*The Plough and the Stars* by Sean O'Casey: Fortune Theatre', *London Mercury*, XIV 81 (July 1926) 299–300.

NATHAN, GEORGE JEAN, 'The London Season', *American Mercury* (N.Y.), IX 34 (Oct 1926) 245–6.

ATKINSON, BROOKS, 'O'Casey and the Irish Players: *The Plough and the Stars*', *New York Times* (29 Nov 1927) p. 30 [at the Hudson Theatre, New York].

MANTLE, BURNS, '*The Plough and the Stars*: Irish Players Begin Their Season at the Hudson', *New York Daily News* (29 Nov 1927) p. 33.

ATKINSON, BROOKS, 'Sean O'Casey's *The Plough and the Stars* Performed by the Irish Players', *New York Times* (4 Dec 1927) section 10, p. 1.

O'F., T. J., 'O'Casey on the Gat *The Plough and the Stars* at the Hudson: a Homily on Violence', *Daily Worker* (N.Y.), (9 Dec 1927) p. 4.

BRACKETT, CHARLES, 'Art Attack', *New Yorker*, III (10 Dec 1927) 34.

SAYLER, OLIVER M., 'The Play of the Week: *The Plough and the Stars*, a Tragedy in Four Acts by Sean O'Casey. Produced by the Irish Players for George C. Taylor at the Hudson Theatre, New York', *Saturday Review of Literature* (N.Y.), IV (10 Dec 1927) 427.

NATHAN, GEORGE JEAN, 'Judging the Shows', *Judge* (N.Y.), XCII (17 Dec 1927) 18.

KRUTCH, JOSEPH WOOD, 'Poet Laureate', *Nation* (N.Y.), CXXV (21 Dec 1927) 718.

'Irish Players Amuse and Irritate', *Literary Digest* (N.Y.), XCV (24 Dec 1927) 20–1.

'A New York Diary', *New Republic* (N.Y.), LIII (4 Jan 1928) 191–2.

MAXWELL, PERRITON, '*The Plough and the Stars*', *Theatre Magazine* (N.Y.), XLVII (Feb 1928) 58.

CARB, DAVID, '*The Plough and the Stars*', *Vogue* (N.Y.), LXXI 3 (1 Feb 1928) 100.

B., F. R., 'Lights Down', *Outlook* (N.Y.), CXLVIII (1 Feb 1928) 187.

BROWN, JOHN MASON, 'The Laughter of the Gods: Broadway in Review', *Theatre Arts Monthly* (N.Y.), XII 2 (Feb 1928) 91–5.

D[ONAGHEY], F[REDERICK], '*The Plough and the Stars*', *Chicago Daily Tribune* (21 Feb 1928) p. 25 [at the Blackstone Theater].

'Duchess Theatre: *The Plough and the Stars* by Sean O'Casey', *Times* (London), (4 June 1930) p. 14.

H., H., 'Duchess: *The Plough and the Stars* by Sean O'Casey', *Observer* (London), (8 June 1930) p. 11.

OMICRON, '*The Plough and the Stars*: Duchess Theatre', *Nation and Athenaeum* (London), XLVII 11 (14 June 1930) 247–8.

P., M. E., 'The Irish Players and Sean O'Casey: *The Plough and the Stars* As It Is Acted at Providence', *Boston Evening Transcript* (11 Oct 1934) p. 11.

ATKINSON, BROOKS, 'Return of the Abbey Theatre Players in O'Casey's *The Plough and the Stars*', *New York Times* (13 Nov 1934) p. 22.

VERNON, GRENVILLE, '*The Plough and the Stars*', *Commonweal* (N.Y.), XXI (23 Nov 1934) 122.

REYNOLDS, HORACE, 'Riot in the Abbey', *American Spectator* (N.Y.), III (Dec 1934) 14.

ISAACS, EDITH J. R., 'The Abbey Players', *Theatre Arts Monthly* (N.Y.), XIX 1 (Jan 1935) 10–11.

MELVIN, EDWIN F., 'Rich Humors and Tragedy from O'Casey: His *Plough and the Stars* for First Performance in Boston', *Boston Evening Transcript* (3 June 1935) p. 10.

'Q Theatre: *The Plough and the Stars* by Sean O'Casey', *Times* (London), (27 June 1939) p. 12.

QUIDNUNC, 'An Irishman's Diary', *Irish Times* (Dublin), (10 Nov 1947) p. 5.

HOLLWAY, FRANK, '*The Plough and the Stars*: Sean O'Casey. Nothing Derogatory', *Tyneside Phoenix* (Newcastle upon Tyne), VIII (summer 1949) 5–6.

RUBIN, B., 'Good Production of O'Casey's *The Plough and the Stars*', *Daily Worker* (N.Y.), (6 Feb 1950) p. 7.

O'CASEY, SEAN, 'O'Casey Reports: Irish Author Discusses His Own Play', *New York Times* (12 Mar 1950) section 2, p. 2 [letter to the Hudson Guild Players on their production of the play].

CLURMAN, HAROLD, 'Theatre', *Nation* (N.Y.), CLXXVI (25 Apr 1953) 353–4 [at the Cherry Lane Theater, Greenwich Village].

HEWES, HENRY, 'Broadway Postscript: *The Plough and the Stars*', *Saturday Review of Literature* (N.Y.), XXXVI (6 June 1953) 25.

'New Lindsey Theatre: *The Plough and the Stars* by Sean O'Casey', *Times* (London), (28 May 1954) p. 2.

IGOE, W. J., 'A Handful of Dubliners: *The Plough and the Stars*', *Catholic Herald* (London), (11 June 1954) p. 5.

IGOE, W. J., 'London Letter', *America* (N.Y.), XCI (14 Aug 1954) 480–1.

CARROLL, NIALL, 'New Actor in Old Robe', *Irish Press* (Dublin), (14 Mar 1955) p. 6 [by the Abbey Theatre at the International Festival, in the Sarah Bernhardt Theatre in Paris].

CARROLL, NIALL, 'O'Casey Didn't Get Mad at Me', *Irish Press* (Dublin), (25 Apr 1955) p. 4.

'Abbey Players in Paris', *Irish Times* (Dublin), (17 May 1955) p. 5.

'Abbey Won Paris with a "Plough"', *Irish Press* (Dublin), (20 May 1955) p. 7.

TRIOLET, ELSA, 'De Dublin à Pékin: Introduction au IIe Festival International d'Art Dramatique de la Ville de Paris', *Lettres françaises* (Paris) no. 570 (26 May–2 June 1955) 1, 7.

S., R., 'Hilarious and Tragic O'Casey: *The Plough and the Stars* (Tower Theatre)', *Daily Worker* (London), (2 Mar 1959) p. 3.

TAUBMAN, HOWARD, 'Easter Rising: O'Casey's *The Plough and the Stars* Opens', *New York Times* (7 Dec 1960) p. 56 [at the Phoenix Theater].

BALLIETT, WHITNEY, 'Groucho in Dublin', *New Yorker*, XXXVI (17 Dec 1960) 96–8.

CLURMAN, HAROLD, 'Theatre', *Nation* (N.Y.), CXCI (24 Dec 1960) 510–11.

'*The Plough and the Stars*', *Theatre Arts* (N.Y.), XLV (Feb 1961) 11.

SULLIVAN, A. M., 'The Off-Broadway Phoenix Theater', *Catholic World* (N.Y.), CXCII (Feb 1961) 320.

LECLERC, GUY, 'Au Théâtre Montparnasse: *La Charrue et les étoiles*', *L'Humanité* (Paris), (4 May 1962) p. 2.

LEMARCHAND, J., '*La Charrue et les étoiles* de Sean O'Casey au Théâtre Montparnasse', *Figaro littéraire* (Paris), (12 May 1962) p. 20.

OLIVIER, CLAUDE, '*La Charrue et les étoiles* de Sean O'Casey au Montparnasse-Gaston Baty', *Lettres françaises* (Paris), no. 927 (17–23 May 1962) 8.

CAMP, ANDRÉ, 'La Quinzaine Dramatique: *La Charrue et les étoiles*, de Sean O'Casey, par la Comédie de Saint-Étienne', *Avant-Scène* (Paris), no. 267 (15 June 1962) 40–2.

SAUREL, RENÉE, 'Un dramaturge incomparable', *Temps Modernes* (Paris), XVII 193 (June 1962) 1938–44 [on the French version of the play, as done by the Comédie de Saint-Etienne].

'Pleasant End to Theatre Season', *Times* (London), (28 June 1962) p. 10 [at the Théâtre Montparnasse-Gaston Baty in Paris].

'Mere Sketch of *The Plough*. Uphill Struggle: Mermaid Theatre', *Times* (London), (26 Sep 1962) p. 8.

LEVIN, BERNARD, 'Well, the Things We've Seen Here: *The Plough and the Stars*, by Sean O'Casey. Mermaid Theatre', *Daily Mail* (London), (26 Sep 1962) p. 3.

KRETZMER, HERBERT, 'Irish Heresy Becomes Museum Piece', *Daily Express* (London), (26 Sep 1962) p. 9.

DARLINGTON, W. A., 'Richness of O'Casey Lost in Space', *Daily Telegraph* (London), (26 Sep 1962) p. 14.

FAY, GERARD, '*The Plough and the Stars* at the Mermaid', *Guardian* (London), (26 Sep 1962) p. 9.

SHULMAN, MILTON, 'A Fitting Climax to the O'Casey Festival', *Evening Standard* (London), (26 Sep 1962) p. 14.

BARKER, FELIX, 'Shadow of "The Trouble"', *Evening News* (London), (26 Sep 1962) p. 5.

M., M., 'The Harsh Truth: *The Plough and the Stars* (Mermaid)', *Daily Worker* (London), (27 Sep 1962) p. 2.

H., P., 'Mermaid Reaches Zenith of O'Casey Festival', *Stage and Television Today* (London), (27 Sep 1962) p. 13.

TYNAN, KENNETH, 'Theatre: On the Trail of the True Self', *Observer* (London), (30 Sep 1962) p. 25.

LAMBERT, J. W., 'London Theatre', *Sunday Times* (London), (30 Sep. 1962) p. 41.

CHURCHILL, ANDREW, '*The Plough and the Stars*: Sean O'Casey (Mermaid)', *Time and Tide* (London), XLIII 40 (4–11 Oct 1962) 28.

GELLERT, ROGER, 'Sportive Peer', *New Statesman* (London), LXIV (5 Oct 1962) 464.

GASCOIGNE, BAMBER, 'Organised Blarney: *The Plough and the Stars*. (Mermaid)', *Spectator* (London), CCIX (5 Oct 1962) 513.

TREWIN, J. C. 'Men of the Hour', *Illustrated London News*, CCXLI (6 Oct 1962) 530.

BRIEN, ALAN, 'O'Casey for Today', *Sunday Telegraph* (London), (7 Oct 1962) p. 10.

GOLDSWORTHY, E., 'Gascoigne on O'Casey', *Spectator* (London), CCIX (12 Oct 1962) 555 [letter to the Editor].

S., F., 'Mermaid: *The Plough and the Stars*', *Theatre World* (London), LVIII 454 (Nov 1962) 6.

ESSLIN, MARTIN, '*The Plough and the Stars*', *Plays and Players* (London), x 3 (Dec 1962) 58.

'O'Casey to Allow 2 Plays to be Performed in Dublin', *New York Times* (6 Nov 1963) p. 35 [*Juno and the Paycock* and *The Plough and the Stars* as a preview for World Theatre Season in London].

O'CASEY, SEAN, 'Behind the Ban', *New York Times* (5 Jan 1964) section 2, pp. 1, 3 [lifting ban on *Juno and the Paycock* and *The Plough and the Stars*].

'O'Casey Play in Rehearsal at Abbey', *Irish Times* (Dublin), (29 Jan 1964) p. 5.

'The O'Casey Truce', *Irish Times* (Dublin), (29 Jan 1964) p. 7 [leader].

'O'Casey Play Opens at the Abbey Theatre', *Irish Times* (Dublin), (12 Feb 1964) p. 9.

K., '*The Plough and the Stars* Returns to the Abbey', *Irish Times* (Dublin), (12 Feb 1964) p. 9.

'Abbey Scores with Second O'Casey Play', *Irish Times* (Dublin), (28 Apr 1964) p. 1.

'Abbey Make Amends. Aldwych Theatre: *The Plough and the Stars*', *Times* (London), (28 Apr 1964) p. 15.

SHORTER, ERIC, ' "Plough and Stars" Is Not Moving Enough', *Daily Telegraph* (London), (28 Apr 1964) p. 18.

LEVIN, BERNARD, 'This Time, a Better Deal for the "Heroes" ', *Daily Mail* (London), (28 Apr 1964) p. 14.

MORTIMER, JOHN, 'O'Casey Triumphs in This Test of a Great Play', *Evening Standard* (London), (28 Apr 1964) p. 4.

BAKER, BERT, 'More to O'Casey Than Comedy: *The Plough and the Stars* (World Theatre Season, Aldwych)', *Daily Worker* (London), (29 Apr 1964) p. 2.

GASCOIGNE, BAMBER, 'Living Through the Troubles', *Observer* (London), (3 May 1964) p. 25.

HOBSON, HAROLD, 'Who'd Be a Patriot?', *Sunday Times* (London), (3 May 1964) p. 33.

BRIEN, ALAN, 'Theatre: It's Hard to Listen', *Sunday Telegraph* (London), (3 May 1964) p. 14.

'Abbey Reply to O'Casey: In No Position to Pronounce Judgment',

Irish Times (Dublin), (3 July 1964) p. 1. See 'Abbey Has Been Deteriorating for Years' (4 July 1964) p. 1.

SHAW, IAIN, '*Juno and The Plough*', *Encore* (London), II (July–Aug 1964) 52–4.

'O.U.D.S. True to O'Casey. Oxford Playhouse: *The Plough and the Stars*', *Times* (London), (12 May 1965) p. 15.

KELLY, SEAMUS, '*The Plough and the Stars* at the Abbey', *Irish Times* (Dublin), (16 Aug 1966) p. 6.

KELLY, HENRY, '*The Plough and the Stars*', *Irish Times* (Dublin), (14 Feb 1968) p. 10 [by 66 Theatre Company, Dun Laoghaire].

QUIDNUNC, 'An Irishman's Diary: The Scene Changes', *Irish Times* (Dublin), (6 Apr 1968) p. 11.

THE SILVER TASSIE

'Mr O'Casey's New Play. Why It Was Rejected. Mr Yeats on the Dramatist's Job. The War and the Stage', *Observer* (London), (3 June 1928) p. 19 [correspondence on the play by O'Casey, Yeats, Lennox Robinson and Walter Starkie]. Reprinted in *Irish Statesman* (Dublin), x 14 (9 June 1928) 268–72. Yeats's letter also reprinted in *The Letters of W. B. Yeats*, ed. A. Wade (London: Rupert Hart-Davis, 1954) pp. 740–2.

'O'Casey's New Play Rejected: Severe Criticism by Abbey Directors', *Irish Times* (Dublin), (4 June 1928) p. 8 [correspondence].

'Ploughing the Star', *Manchester Guardian* (4 June 1928) p. 8 [leader]. See O'Casey's reply (12 June 1928) p. 22 [letter to the Editor].

'Our London Letter: *The Silver Tassie*', *Irish Independent* (Dublin), (5 June 1928) p. 6.

'Mr Sean O'Casey Angry: Abbey Rejects His New Play', *Irish Independent* (Dublin), (5 June 1928) p. 9.

'Mr O'Casey Replies to His Critics: Strong Comment on Treatment of His Play. "The Big Four"', *Irish Times* (Dublin), (9 June 1928) p. 7 [correspondence].

O'CASEY, SEAN, 'The Rejected Play: O'Casey and the Big Four', *Irish Independent* (Dublin), (9 June 1928) p. 10 [letter to the Editor].

WEBB, ARTHUR, 'Abbey Rejects Sean O'Casey's New Play', *New York Times* (10 June 1928) section 3, p. 1.

T., M. A., 'O'Casey and the Critics', *Sunday Independent* (Dublin), (10 June 1928) p. 2.

O'CASEY, SEAN, 'Mr O'Casey's "Last Word"', *Irish Times* (Dublin), (21 June 1928) p. 4 [letter to the Editor].

O'CASEY, SEAN, 'Tying Things Together: Mr O'Casey's Rejected Play', *Irish Independent* (Dublin), (21 June 1928) p. 9 [letter to the Editor].

B., G. W., '*The Silver Tassie*: Interview with Mr Sean O'Casey', *Observer* (London), (6 Oct 1929) p. 13.

MORGAN, CHARLES, 'Apollo Theatre: *The Silver Tassie*, a Tragi-Comedy by Sean O'Casey' *Times* (London), (12 Oct 1929) p. 8. Reprinted in *The English Dramatic Critics: An Anthology 1660–1932*, ed. James Agate (London: Arthur Barker, 1932; New York: Hill & Wang, n.d. [1958]) pp. 347–9; and in *Sean O'Casey*, ed. Ronald Ayling (London: Macmillan, 1969) pp. 88–90.

D[ARLINGTON], W. A., 'Sean O'Casey's New Play. An Author Worth a Message. Originality and Purpose. *The Silver Tassie*', *Daily Telegraph* (London), (12 Oct 1929) p. 8.

'London Theatres: *The Silver Tassie*', *Scotsman* (Edinburgh), (12 Oct 1929) p. 14.

PARSONS, ALAN, 'Mr S. O'Casey's War Play. Girl and V.C. in a Poignant Scene. Mr Bernard Shaw's Praise', *Daily Mail* (London), (12 Oct 1929) p. 21.

E., M., 'Irishman's War Play. Mr Sean O'Casey Tries an Experiment. Not a Success. Chanting Soldiers at the Front', *Daily Herald* (London), (12 Oct 1929) p. 5.

GRIFFITH, HUBERT, 'Sean O'Casey's New Play. War Disillusionment and a Tragic Irish Aftermath. A Scenic Triumph. "Behind the Lines" as rendered by Mr Augustus John', *Evening Standard* (London), (12 Oct 1929) p. 8.

B., J. G., 'Mr Sean O'Casey's War Play: *The Silver Tassie* an Ambitious Work', *Evening News* (London), (12 Oct 1929) p. 7.

AGATE, JAMES, 'Apollo: *The Silver Tassie*', *Observer* (London), (13 Oct 1929), p. 6.

ERVINE, ST JOHN, 'Mr Sean O'Casey's Passion Play. Apollo: *The Silver Tassie*', *Observer* (London), (13 Oct 1929) p. 15.

'The Apollo: *The Silver Tassie*' *Stage* (London), (17 Oct 1929) p. 18.

ST JOHN, CHRISTOPHER, 'Another Irish Victory', *Time and Tide* (London), x 42 (18 Oct 1929) 1254.

B., I., '*The Silver Tassie*: Mr O'Casey's New Play', *Manchester Guardian Weekly*, XXI 16 (18 Oct 1929) 318.

BROWN, IVOR, '*The Silver Tassie* by Sean O'Casey: Apollo Theatre', *Saturday Review* (London), CXLVIII (19 Oct 1929) 446–7.

B.-W., J., 'The Silver Tassie', New Statesman (London), XXXIV (19 Oct 1929) 52–3.

JENNINGS, RICHARD, 'The Silver Tassie, by Sean O'Casey: At the Apollo Theatre', Spectator (London), CXLIII (19 Oct 1929) 523.

'The Silver Tassie at the Apollo', Illustrated London News, CLXXV (19 Oct 1929) 696.

O'F[AOLAIN], S[EAN], 'The Silver Tassie Staged', Irish Statesman (Dublin), XIII 7 (19 Oct 1929) 134–5.

ATKINSON, BROOKS, 'O'Casey's War Drama: The Silver Tassie', New York Times (25 Oct 1929) p. 26.

SHAW, GEORGE BERNARD, 'Letter to the Producer of The Silver Tassie', Times (London), (26 Oct 1929) p. 14. Reprinted in Sean O'Casey, ed. Ronald Ayling (London: Macmillan, 1969) p. 91.

NORGATE, MATTHEW, 'Mr O'Casey's Experiment. Apollo Theatre: The Silver Tassie', Nation and Athenaeum (London), XLVI (26 Oct 1929) 138–9.

MORGAN, CHARLES, 'As London Sees O'Casey', New York Times (3 Nov 1929) section 9, p. 4.

ATKINSON, BROOKS, 'Making or Breaking O'Casey', New York Times (10 Nov 1929) section 10, p. 1.

BARTON, RALPH, 'Theatre', Life (Chicago), XCIV (15 Nov 1929) 24.

YOUNG, STARK, 'The Silver Tassie, by Sean O'Casey', New Republic (N.Y.), LXI (27 Nov 1929) 17–18 [at the Irish Theater, New York].

SHIPP, HORACE, 'The Silver Tassie', English Review (London), XLIX (Nov 1929) 639.

H., T., 'Apollo: The Silver Tassie', Theatre World (London), X 58 (Nov 1929) 14.

GWYNN, STEPHEN, 'Ebb and Flow: Mr O'Casey's Play', Fortnightly Review (London), CXXVI, n.s. (2 Dec 1929) 851–3.

MACDONELL, A. G., 'The Silver Tassie by Sean O'Casey: Apollo Theatre', London Mercury, XXI 122 (Dec 1929) 166–7.

R[EILLY], J[OSEPH] J., 'The Silver Tassie', Catholic World (N.Y.), CXXX (Dec 1929) 334–5.

'The World and the Theatre: The Silver Tassie', Theatre Arts Monthly (N.Y.), XIV 1 (Jan 1930) 6–10.

S., J. E., 'Suspense', New Statesman (London), XXXV (10 May 1930) 148–9.

MACCARTHY, DESMOND, 'Very Much on the Spot', New Statesman (London), XXXV (17 May 1930) 130 [Charles Laughton's performance in the play].

LEVY, BENN, 'Mr Morgan Shudders at the Theatre', *Theatre Arts Monthly* (N.Y.), xv 8 (Aug 1931) 648–52.

BOTTOMLEY, GORDON, 'To the Editor', *Theatre Arts Monthly* (N.Y.), xv 10 (Oct 1931) 790–2.

'Mr Sean O'Casey and the Abbey Theatre', *Times* (London), (26 June 1935) p. 14 [to be produced by the Abbey Theatre].

'Dublin Drama Feud Ends: Abbey Theatre to Let O'Casey Produce *Silver Tassie*', *New York Times* (26 June 1935) p. 17.

O'CASEY, SEAN, 'Mr O'Casey Dissents', *New York Times* (11 Aug 1935) section 9, p. 1.

B., M., 'O'Casey Obscenity: Play That May Shock Christians', *Evening Herald* (Dublin), (13 Aug 1935) p. 6 [at the Abbey].

P., J. A., 'O'Casey Play at the Abbey: Packed House for *The Silver Tassie*', *Irish Independent* (Dublin), (13 Aug 1935) p. 8.

'*The Silver Tassie*: Abbey Players Produce O'Casey Play', *Irish Press* (Dublin), (13 Aug 1935) p. 2. See O'Casey's reply (20 Aug 1935) p. 6; and counter-reply (20 Aug 1935) p. 6.

'An Outrage on Our Faith', *Standard* (Dublin), VIII 15 (16 Aug 1935) 8.

ULAD, CU, 'The Abbey Theatre', *Irish Independent* (Dublin), (21 Aug 1935) p. 10 [letter to the Editor].

'*The Silver Tassie* at Abbey Theatre', *Catholic Herald* (London), (24 Aug 1935) p. 5. See reply by Robert Speaight, 'In Defence of Sean O'Casey' (30 Aug 1935) p. 13.

'Galway Critics of the Abbey', *Irish Independent* (Dublin), (28 Aug 1935) p. 9.

STARKIE, WALTER, 'Dr Starkie's Reply to Galway's Critics', *Irish Independent* (Dublin), (29 Aug 1935) p. 7 [letter to the Editor].

MACNAMARA, BRINSLEY, 'Abbey Production of O'Casey Play: Revelations by a Director of the Theatre', *Irish Independent* (Dublin), (29 Aug 1935) p. 7.

MACNAMARA, BRINSLEY, 'An Abbey Play: Views of Three Directors', *Irish Times* (Dublin), (29 Aug 1935) p. 7.

'Cleanse the Theatre', *Standard* (Dublin), VIII 17 (30 Aug 1935) 8.

'Abbey Directors Reply to Mr MacNamara', *Evening Herald* (Dublin), (3 Sep 1935) p. 4.

'The Abbey Theatre', *Irish Times* (Dublin), (3 Sep 1935) p. 6 [leading article].

MURPHY, J., 'The Abbey Theatre', *Irish Times* (Dublin), (3 Sep 1935) p. 6 [letter to the Editor].

COSTELLOE, J., 'The Silver Tassie: Reply to Mr Brinsley MacNamara by His Fellow Directors', Irish Press (Dublin), (3 Sep 1935) p. 2 [letter to the Editor].

MURPHY, J., 'Abbey Theatre Productions', Irish Press (Dublin), (3 Sep 1935) p. 6 [letter to the Editor].

'Unchristian and Pagan: The Silver Tassie. Voice of Galway Protests', Irish Catholic (Dublin), XLVIII 36 (7 Sep 1935) 2.

COSTELLOE, JOHN, 'To the Editor', Irish Catholic (Dublin), XLVIII 36 (7 Sep 1935) 2.

O'CASEY, SEAN, 'Mr O'Casey and the Abbey Theatre: "Defensive Words" on The Silver Tassie', Irish Press (Dublin), (11 Sep 1935) p. 8 [letter to the Editor].

SMITH, HUGH, 'Dublin Is Harassed Again', New York Times (22 Sep 1935) section 10, p. 3.

F[UNKE], L[EWIS], 'O'Casey's Silver Tassie: A Criticism of War and Effect on Youth. Given in Carnegie Hall', New York Times (22 July 1949) p. 16.

ATKINSON, BROOKS, 'The Silver Tassie: Interplayers' Revival Is Signal Service', New York Times (4 Sep 1949) section 2, p. 1.

CLURMAN, HAROLD, 'Theatre: Off Broadway', New Republic (N.Y.), CXXI 12 (19 Sep 1949) 21–2.

PHELAN, KAPPO, 'A Note on O'Casey', Commonweal (N.Y.), L (7 Oct 1949) 631–2.

K., 'The Silver Tassie at the Queen's', Irish Times (Dublin), (25 Sep 1951) p. 6.

M., I., 'Abbey Players' First Night at the Queen's Theatre', Irish Independent (Dublin), (25 Sep 1951) p. 7.

C., N., 'First Abbey Play in New Home', Irish Press (Dublin), (25 Sep 1951) p. 9.

'O'Casey Drama of Soccer Star', Evening Herald (Dublin), (25 Sep 1951) p. 4.

FALLON, GABRIEL, 'The Fatal Rejection', Standard (Dublin), XXIII 39 (28 Sep 1951) 5.

KENNEDY, MAURICE, 'Shadow of a Playwright', Sunday Press (Dublin), (30 Sep 1951) p. 9.

'The Silver Tassie: A Broadcast Full of Atmosphere', Times (London), (9 Apr 1957) p. 3.

SMITH, R. D., 'The Silver Tassie', Radio Times (London), CLXXI (7 Apr 1966) 58 [B.B.C. Third Programme].

RUNDALL, JEREMY, 'Ballet in Sound', Sunday Times (London),

(17 Apr 1966) p. 32. See reply by John O'Riordan, 'Sentimental?' (24 Apr 1966) p. 15 [letter to the editor].

AYLING, RONALD, 'Stage History of *The Silver Tassie*', Programme note to Nottingham Playhouse production, 5 Apr 1967.

ADDISON, ALAN, 'Two O'Casey Revivals: *The Silver Tassie* (Nottingham Playhouse)', *Morning Star* (London), (7 Apr 1967) p. 2.

HASTINGS, RONALD, 'O'Casey after 40 Years', *Daily Telegraph* (London), (6 Sep 1969) p. 15 [at the Aldwych].

SUTHERLAND, JACK, 'Sean O'Casey and *The Silver Tassie*', *Morning Star* (London), (9 Sep 1969) p. 2.

'*The Silver Tassie*', *Irish Times* (Dublin), (10 Sep 1969) p. 11 [leader].

LEWIS, PETER, 'O! What a Lovely O'Casey', *Daily Mail* (London), (11 Sep 1969) p. 14.

KRETZMER, HERBERT, 'A Brave Cry Against War. *The Silver Tassie*: Aldwych', *Daily Express* (London), (11 Sep 1969) p. 18.

BRAHMS, CARYL, 'Aldwych Theatre: *The Silver Tassie*', *Guardian* (London), (11 Sep 1969) p. 8.

WARDLE, IRVING, 'Welcome Revival. Aldwych Theatre: *The Silver Tassie*', *Times* (London), (11 Sep 1969) p. 15.

BARBER, JOHN, 'Non-Irish Cast Shine in O'Casey', *Daily Telegraph* (London), (11 Sep 1969) p. 21.

NATHAN, DAVID, 'Dusting Off the Beauty of O'Casey', *Sun* (London), (11 Sep 1969) p. 9.

SHULMAN, MILTON, 'At the Theatre', *Evening Standard* (London), (11 Sep 1969) p. 19.

BARKER, FELIX, 'The O'Casey Genius Comes Across – In Flashes. *The Silver Tassie*: Royal Shakespeare Company, Aldwych', *Evening News* (London), (11 Sep 1969) p. 2.

YOUNG, B. A., 'Aldwych: *The Silver Tassie*', *Financial Times* (London), (12 Sep 1969) p. 3.

SUTHERLAND, JACK, 'Memorable O'Casey Revival: *The Silver Tassie* (Aldwych)', *Morning Star* (London), (12 Sep 1969) p. 2.

WARDLE, IRVING, 'A Neglected Masterpiece', *Times* (London), (13 Sep 1969) Saturday Review Section, p. iii.

MARCUS, FRANK, 'No Tarnish on the Tassie', *Sunday Telegraph* (London), (14 Sep 1969) p. 14.

LAMBERT, J. W., 'O'Casey Says Yes', *Sunday Times* (London), (14 Sep 1969) p. 58.

BRYDEN, RONALD, 'O'Casey and His Raw Torso', *Observer* (London), (14 Sep 1969) p. 26.

KINGSTON, JEREMY, 'At the Theatre', *Punch* (London), CCLVII (17 Sep 1969) 469–70.

BLAKE, DOUGLAS, '*The Silver Tassie*: Forty Years On', *Stage and Television Today* (London), (18 Sep 1969) p. 15.

NIGHTINGALE, BENEDICT, 'Without Apology', *New Statesman* (London), LXXVIII (19 Sep 1969) 389–90.

SPURLING, HILARY, 'Nut-and-Apple Case', *Spectator* (London), (20 Sep 1969) p. 381.

JONES, D. A. N., 'Known Warriors', *Listener* (London), (25 Sep 1969) p. 431.

TRUSSLER, SIMON, 'Theatre', *Tribune* (London), (26 Sep 1969) p. 15.

TREWIN, J. C., 'O'Casey Speaks Again', *Illustrated London News* (27 Sep 1969) p. 35.

TREWIN, J. C., 'The New Plays: *The Silver Tassie* (Aldwych)', *Lady* (London), CLXX (2 Oct 1969) 500.

O'BRIEN, KATE, 'Long Distance', *Irish Times* (Dublin), (6 Oct 1969) p. 10.

'Punch Choice: *The Silver Tassie*', *Punch* (London), CCLVII (22 Oct 1969) vii.

LEONARD, HUGH, 'Aldwych: *The Silver Tassie*', *Plays and Players* (London), XVII (Nov 1969) 20–3.

WITHIN THE GATES

STEWART, M. C., 'Mr Sean O'Casey's New Play', *Times* (London), (2 Dec 1933) p. 8 [letter to the Editor].

ERVINE, ST JOHN, 'At the Play: Mr O'Casey's Apocalypse', *Observer* (London), (7 Jan 1934) p. 15.

'Dramatis Personae', *Observer* (London), (4 Feb 1934) p. 13.

B[ECKLES], G[ORDON], 'A Challenge to Sean O'Casey', *Daily Express* (London), (8 Feb 1934) p. 3.

'Royalty Theatre: *Within the Gates* by Sean O'Casey', *Times* (London), (8 Feb 1934) p. 12.

DARLINGTON, W. A., 'Sean O'Casey's New Play. Prose Poem on the Stage: *Within the Gates*', *Daily Telegraph* (London), (8 Feb 1934) p. 8.

C., J., 'Last Night's First Nights: Sordid Parade. Sean O'Casey's Biting Satire of Modern Life', *Daily Sketch* (London), (8 Feb 1934) p. 13.

M., P. L., 'O'Casey Mocks World in Hyde Park. Odd Experiment in Symbolism. Royalty Theatre: *Within the Gates*', *Daily Herald* (London), (8 Feb 1934) p. 11.

'London Theatres: *Within the Gates*', *Scotsman* (Edinburgh), (8 Feb 1934) p. 8.

DISHER, WILLSON, 'A New Sort of Play. Sean O'Casey's Genius. Raw Life', *Daily Mail* (London), (8 Feb 1934) p. 17.

B., I., '*Within the Gates*: Sean O'Casey's New Play', *Manchester Guardian* (8 Feb 1934) p. 12.

BAUGHAN, E. A., 'Sean O'Casey Epic of Pessimism: Play That Will Distress Many', *News Chronicle* (London), (8 Feb 1934) p. 11.

P., P., 'Mr Sean O'Casey Loses His Way', *Evening Standard* (London), (8 Feb 1934) p. 9.

B., J. G., 'An Irish Man's General Grouse: Sean O'Casey's Play on a London Park Theme', *Evening News* (London), (8 Feb 1934) p. 9.

'New Play by O'Casey Produced in London: *Within the Gates*', *New York Times* (8 Feb 1934) p. 14.

AGATE, JAMES, 'Royalty: *Within the Gates*. A Play, by Sean O'Casey', *Observer* (London), (11 Feb 1934) p. 6.

AGATE, JAMES, 'The Dramatic World: Beyond the Agates. A Difficult Play. Royalty: *Within the Gates*', *Sunday Times* (London), (11 Feb 1934) p. 6.

BROWN, IVOR, 'Royalty: *Within the Gates* by Sean O'Casey', *Observer* (London), (11 Feb 1934) p. 15.

'The Royalty: *Within the Gates*', *Stage* (London), (15 Feb 1934), p. 10.

VERSCHOYLE, DEREK, '*Within the Gates* by Sean O'Casey: At the Royalty Theatre', *Spectator* (London), CLII (16 Feb 1934) 235.

BOSANQUET, THEODORA, '*Within the Gates*. Sean O'Casey. Royalty Theatre', *Time and Tide* (London), XV 7 (17 Feb 1934) 222.

MACCARTHY, DESMOND, 'Hyde Park', *New Statesman and Nation* (London), VII (17 Feb 1934) 226–7. Reprinted in *Drama* (London and New York: Putnam, 1940) pp. 349–54.

'*Within the Gates* at the Royalty', *Illustrated London News*, CLXXXIV (17 Feb 1934) 264.

GALITZINE, Prince NICOLAS, 'The Theatre', *Saturday Review* (London), CLVII (24 Feb 1934) 219.

MORGAN, CHARLES, '*Within the Gates*: Further Thoughts on Sean O'Casey's Recently Shown Play', *New York Times* (25 Feb 1934) section 9, p. 3.

GREIN, J. T., 'The World of the Theatre', *Illustrated London News*, CLXXXIV (3 Mar 1934) 320.

REYNOLDS, HORACE, 'Sean O'Casey's Symbolic Drama: *Within the Gates*', *Saturday Review of Literature* (N.Y.), X (3 Mar 1934) 519.

HUGHES, ELINOR, 'The Irish Drama Contributes Sean O'Casey's *Within the Gates*', *Boston Herald* (25 Mar 1934) p. 9.

'Broadway To See New O'Casey Play: *Within the Gates* Will Be Produced by Bushar and Tuerk Next Season', *New York Times* (26 Mar 1934) p. 18.

GREIN, J. T., 'The World of the Theatre', *Illustrated London News*, CLXXXIV (31 Mar 1934) 498.

D., F. J., 'Royalty: *Within the Gates*', *Theatre World* (London), XXI 110 (Mar 1934) 120.

CODMAN, FLORENCE, 'Sean O'Casey', *Nation* (N.Y.), CXXXVIII (25 Apr 1934) 476-7.

DUKES, ASHLEY, 'The English Scene', *Theatre Arts Monthly* (N.Y.), XVIII 4 (Apr 1934) 258-9.

'Irish Playwright, Sean O'Casey, Here: Author of *Within the Gates* Comes to Be Present at Play's Rehearsal', *New York Times* (18 Sep 1934) p. 23.

O'CASEY, SEAN, 'From *Within the Gates*', *New York Times* (21 Oct 1934) section 9, pp. 1, 3.

ATKINSON, BROOKS, 'The Play: Fantasy of the Seasons in Hyde Park in Sean O'Casey's *Within the Gates*', *New York Times* (23 Oct 1934) p. 23 [at the National Theatre, New York].

BROWN, JOHN MASON, 'Without Mr O'Casey's Gates', *New York Evening Post* (23 Oct 1934). Reprinted in *Two on the Aisle* (New York: W. W. Norton, 1938) pp. 126-30.

MANTLE, BURNS, '*Within the Gates* Thru a Pink Haze', *New York Daily News* (23 Oct 1934) p. 41.

ALEXANDER, LEON, 'Sean O'Casey Tilts a Dull Lance Against Puritanism in Play *Within the Gates*', *Daily Worker* (N.Y.), (27 Oct 1934) p. 5.

'Not Good Enough for Ireland', *Literary Digest* (N.Y.), CXVIII 17 (27 Oct 1934) 26.

ATKINSON, BROOKS, '*Within the Gates*: Sean O'Casey's Fantasy of Hyde Park – Drama of Life as They Lead It Out-of-Doors', *New York Times* (28 Oct 1934) section 9, p. 1.

'Stage: Sean O'Casey Brings His *Within the Gates* to N.Y.', *Newsweek* (N.Y.), IV (3 Nov 1934) 27.

BENCHLEY, ROBERT, 'A Big Week for Everybody', *New Yorker*, X (3 Nov 1934) 29-30.

'New Plays in Manhattan: *Within the Gates*', *Time* (N.Y.), XXIV (5 Nov 1934) 30.

KRUTCH, JOSEPH WOOD, 'Mr O'Casey's Charade', *Nation* (N.Y.), CXXXIX (7 Nov 1934) 546.

YOUNG, STARK, 'Theatre Gates: *Within the Gates* by Sean O'Casey, National Theatre', *New Republic* (N.Y.), LXXX (7 Nov 1934) 369.

VERNON, GRENVILLE, 'The Play and Screen: *Within the Gates*', *Commonweal* (N.Y.), XXI (9 Nov 1934) 66.

BLANKFORT, MICHAEL, 'The Theatre', *New Masses* (N.Y.), (13 Nov 1934) 28.

JORDAN, ELIZABETH, 'Sean O'Casey's Crawling World', *America* (N.Y.), LII (24 Nov 1934) 160–1.

MANNES, MARYA, '*Vogue*'s Spotlight', *Vogue* (N.Y.), LXXXIV 12 (15 Dec 1934) 51, 72.

WYATT, EUPHEMIA VAN RENSSELAER, '*Within the Gates*', *Catholic World* (N.Y.), CXL (Dec 1934) 338–40.

FADIMAN, CLIFTON, '*Within the Gates*', *Stage* (N.Y.), XII (Dec 1934) 13.

SEDGWICK, RUTH WOODBURY, '*Within the Gates*: An Appreciation', *Stage* (N.Y.), XII (Dec 1934) 18–19.

BLAKE, BEN, '*Within the Gates*', *New Theatre* (N.Y.), I (Dec 1934) 19.

ISAACS, EDITH J. R., 'Playhouse Gates: Broadway in Review', *Theatre Arts Monthly* (N.Y.), XVIII 12 (Dec 1934) 894–9. Reprinted in *Theatre Arts Anthology* (New York, 1950).

FARMA, WILLIAM J., 'The New York Stage: Concerning Elmer Rice, and Sean O'Casey's New Play', *Players Magazine* (Racine, Wis.), XI (Dec 1934) 10.

NATHAN, GEORGE JEAN, '*Within the Gates*', *American Spectator* (N.Y.), III (Dec 1934) 12.

C., A. V. 'The Theatre', *Time and Time* (London), XVI 1 (5 Jan 1935) 20.

REYNOLDS, HORACE, 'Sean O'Casey and *Within the Gates*', *Boston Evening Transcript* (5 Jan 1935) pt 2, pp. 4–5.

'Telegrams in Brief', *Times* (London), (17 Jan 1935) p. 11 [production of play banned in Boston].

CONNOLLY, TERENCE L., 'Critics, Interviews, and Sean O'Casey', *America* (N.Y.), LII (19 Jan 1935) 357–8.

ATKINSON, BROOKS, 'Thundering in the Index: In Banning *Within the Gates* Boston Withdraws from Universe Again – Religion of O'Casey's Play', *New York Times* (27 Jan 1935) section 8, pp. 1, 3.

NATHAN, GEORGE JEAN, 'The Theatre: *Within the Gates*', *Vanity Fair* (N.Y.), XLIII (Jan 1935) 31–2.

MELVILLE, NINA, 'Within the Gates', Modern Quarterly (Baltimore), VIII (Jan 1935) 695.

CRAVEN, THOMAS, 'Within the Gates', Stage (N.Y.), XII (Jan 1935) 15.

THE END OF THE BEGINNING

'Abbey Theatre: New Play by Sean O'Casey', Irish Times (Dublin), (9 Feb 1937), p. 8.

S., D. 'The Abbey: New Play by Sean O'Casey', Irish Independent (Dublin), (9 Feb 1937), p. 10.

'Sean O'Casey Play. First Production at the Abbey Theatre', Evening Herald (Dublin), (9 Feb 1937), p. 5.

'Q Theatre: A Triple Bill: A Pound on Demand by Sean O'Casey. Pariah by August Strindberg. The End of the Beginning by Sean O'Casey', Times (London), (17 Oct 1939) p. 6.

BARKER, DUDLEY, 'Study of the Criminal Mind', Evening Standard (London), (17 Oct 1939) p. 10.

'The Q: One-Act Plays: The End of the Beginning', Stage (London), (19 Oct 1939) p. 8.

BROWN, IVOR, 'Q: The End of the Beginning', Observer (London), (22 Oct 1939) p. 11.

'Unity Theatre: Sean O'Casey's Short Plays', Times (London), (23 May 1953) p. 8.

TREWIN, J. C., 'Five Plays', Observer (London), (24 May 1953) p. 11.

'The Unity: Three in a Row', Stage (London), (28 May 1953) p. 9.

DOUGLAS, DONALD, 'O'Casey Smashes His Targets', Daily Worker (London), (29 May 1953) p. 2.

HARLE, EVE, 'Irish Life on London Stage', Challenge (London), XVIII 23 (6 June 1953) 2.

QUIDNUNC, 'An Irishman's Diary: O'Casey, Too', Irish Times (Dublin), (12 Jan 1967) p. 7 [at the Carouge, Geneva].

A POUND ON DEMAND

'Q Theatre: A Triple Bill: A Pound on Demand by Sean O'Casey. Pariah by August Strindberg. The End of the Beginning by Sean O'Casey', Times (London), (17 Oct 1939) p. 6.

BARKER, DUDLEY, 'Study of the Criminal Mind', Evening Standard (London), (17 Oct 1939) p. 10.

'The Q: One-Act Plays: A Pound on Demand', Stage (London), (19 Oct 1939) p. 8.

BROWN, IVOR, 'Q: *A Pound on Demand* by Sean O'Casey', *Observer* (London), (22 Oct 1939) p. 11.

'Irishmen and Christians', *Newsweek* (N.Y.), XXVIII (30 Dec 1946) 71 [by the American Repertory Theater].

KRUTCH, JOSEPH WOOD, 'Drama', *Nation* (N.Y.), CLXIV (4 Jan 1947) 26.

YOUNG, STARK, 'Welcome Repertory', *New Republic* (N.Y.), CXVI (6 Jan 1947) 42.

ATKINSON, BROOKS, 'Triple Play', *New York Times* (16 Apr 1959) p. 28 [at the Playhouse].

ATKINSON, BROOKS, 'Triple Play', *New York Times* (26 Apr 1959) section 2, p. 1.

'Broadway Plans', *New York Times* (11 May 1959) p. 30 ['Triple Play' to close].

'Triple Play', *Theatre Arts* (N.Y.), XLIII (June 1959) 9.

BRIEN, ALAN, 'Challenge to Chaplin', *Sunday Telegraph* (London), (9 Apr 1967) p. 10 [at the Mermaid].

'Fifteen Plays for Galway Festival', *Irish Times* (Dublin), (18 Mar 1968) p. 10.

THE STAR TURNS RED

NATHAN, GEORGE JEAN, 'O'Casey Turns Red', *Newsweek* (N.Y.), XIII (26 June 1939) 25 [synopsis of the play].

'Unity Theatre: *The Star Turns Red*', *Times* (London), (14 Mar 1940) p. 6.

D., A., 'Mr Sean O'Casey's New Play: *The Star Turns Red*', *Manchester Guardian* (14 Mar 1940) p. 8 [at the Unity Theatre on Tuesday, 12 March 1940].

'Authors Should Not Go To First Nights – Says Sean O'Casey', *News Chronicle* (London), (14 Mar 1940) p. 7.

'Red Star', *News Review* (London), IX 11 (14 Mar 1940) 32.

MOORE, L. E., '*The Star Turns Red*. Sean O'Casey. Unity', *Time and Tide* (London), XXI 11 (16 Mar 1940) 286–7.

SPENDER, STEPHEN, 'A Morality Play with No Morals: *The Star Turns Red*, at the Unity', *New Statesman and Nation* (London), XIX (16 Mar 1940) 363–4. See O'Casey's reply (30 Mar 1940) 432–3.

AGATE, JAMES, 'A Masterpiece. Unity: *The Star Turns Red* – A Play by Sean O'Casey', *Sunday Times* (London), (17 Mar 1940) p. 3.

BENNETT, ERIC, 'Fun, Moon and Stars', *Sunday Chronicle* (Manchester), (17 Mar 1940) p. 13.

BROWN, IVOR, 'Unity: *The Star Turns Red*, by Sean O'Casey', *Observer* (London), (17 Mar 1940) p. 11.

P., H. D. C., 'We Are Amused: Art As Propaganda', *Weekly Review* (London), xxx, 26 (21 Mar 1940) 466–7.

'Amusements: Unity', *Cavalcade* (London), II 107 (23 Mar 1940) 16.

BROWN, IVOR, 'The Bright and the Light', *Illustrated London News*, CXCVI (6 Apr 1940) 464.

'*The Star Turns Red*', *Theatre World* (London), XXXIII 183 (Apr 1940) 95.

DUKES, ASHLEY, 'Social Basis: The English Scene', *Theatre Arts* (N.Y.), XXIV 6 (June 1940) 409–14.

LYND, SHEILA, 'This Is a Play for Our Time: *The Star Turns Red* (Unity Theatre)', *Daily Worker* (London), (26 July 1946) p. 2.

ALLEN, JOHN, 'An O'Casey Landmark', *New Theatre* (London), III 3 (Aug 1946) 15.

GANZL, SERGE, 'Le Théâtre: *L'Étoile devient rouge* de Sean O'Casey, au Festival d'Aubervilliers (Été 1962)', *Europe* (Paris), année 40, nos. 401–2 (Sep–Oct 1962) 191–4.

CAPELLE, J.-L., '*L'Étoile devient rouge*', *France nouvelle* (Paris), (24–30 Oct 1962) p. 33.

'Minor O'Casey Play Performed in Paris', *New York Times* (25 Oct 1962) p. 47.

LECLERC, GUY, 'Le Théâtre d'Aubervilliers à Paris avec *L'Étoile devient rouge* de Sean O'Casey', *L'Humanité* (Paris), (26 Oct 1962) p. 2.

'*The Star Turns Red* in Paris', *Times* (London), (31 Oct 1962) p. 8.

L., J., '*L'Étoile devient rouge*. Au Théâtre Récamier', *Figaro littéraire* (Paris), (3 Nov 1962) p. 20.

GISSELBRECHT, ANDRÉ, 'Réflexions sur la critique théâtrale (A propos de *L'Étoile devient rouge*)', *L'Humanité* (Paris), (3 Nov 1962) p. 2.

SAUREL, RENÉE, 'De l'Esthétisme à la réalité: *L'Étoile devient rouge*, de Sean O'Casey au Théâtre Récamier', *Temps modernes* (Paris), année 18, no. 199 (Dec 1962) 1137–8.

TRILLING, OSSIA, 'East Berlin Arts Festival Let-Down', *Stage and Television Today* (London), (13 Feb 1969) p. 21.

RED ROSES FOR ME

'Olympia Theatre: *Red Roses for Me*', *Irish Times* (Dublin), (16 Mar 1943) p. 3.

S., D., 'New O'Casey Play', *Irish Independent* (Dublin), (16 Mar 1943) p. 2.

'*Red Roses for Me*', *Evening Herald* (Dublin), (16 Mar 1943) p. 2.

FALLON, GABRIEL, 'Red, Red Roses', *Standard* (Dublin), xv 13 (26 Mar 1943) 3.

'*Red Roses for Me:* Olympia Theatre, Dublin', *Theatre Arts* (N.Y.), xxviii 10 (Oct 1943) 586.

KELLEHER, JOHN V., 'O'Casey in Boston', *New Republic* (N.Y.), cx (20 Mar 1944) 380 [at the Tributary Theatre].

'Embassy Theatre: *Red Roses for Me* by Sean O'Casey', *Times* (London), (27 Feb 1946) p. 6.

D., A., 'O'Casey Play with All-Irish Cast: *Red Roses for Me*. Embassy Theatre', *News Chronicle* (London), (27 Feb 1946) p. 3.

DARLINGTON, W. A., 'Sean O'Casey's Fine Play: Realism with Symbolism', *Daily Telegraph* (London), (27 Feb 1946) p. 5.

GRANT, ELSPETH, 'Sean O'Casey Gets Away with It', *Daily Sketch* (London), (27 Feb 1946) p. 3.

HALE, LIONEL, 'At the Play – O'Casey on the Right Road Back', *Daily Mail* (London), (27 Feb 1946) p. 3.

WILLIAMS, STEPHEN, 'A New Sean O'Casey Play', *Evening News* (London), (27 Feb 1946) p. 2.

'The Embassy: *Red Roses for Me*', *Stage* (London), (28 Feb 1946) p. 4.

AGATE, JAMES, 'A Poet's Play: *Red Roses for Me*. Embassy', *Sunday Times* (London), (3 Mar 1946) p. 2.

T., J. C., '*Red Roses for Me*', *Observer* (London), (3 Mar 1946) p. 2.

REDFERN, JAMES, '*Red Roses for Me* at the Embassy Theatre', *Spectator* (London), clxxvi (8 Mar 1946) 244.

POTTER, STEPHEN, '*Red Roses for Me* at the Embassy', *New Statesman and Nation* (London), xxxi (9 Mar 1946) 173.

HOPE-WALLACE, PHILIP, '*Red Roses for Me*. Sean O'Casey. Embassy', *Time and Tide* (London), xxvii 10 (9 Mar 1946) 224.

DARLINGTON, W. A., 'O'Casey Scores a Hit', *New York Times* (10 Mar 1946) section 2, p. 2.

TREWIN, J. C., 'Roses for Sean O'Casey', *John O'London's Weekly*, liv (22 Mar 1946) 254.

HOPE-WALLACE, PHILIP, 'Theatre', *Time and Tide* (London), xxvii 13 (30 Mar 1946) 296.

AICKMAN, ROBERT FORDYCE, 'Mr O'Casey and the Striker. *Red Roses for Me*: Embassy, Swiss Cottage', *Nineteenth Century and After* (London), cxxxix 830 (Apr 1946) 172–5.

M., H. G., 'Red Roses for Me', Theatre World (London), XLII 255 (Ap 1946) 7–8.

'New Theatre: Red Roses for Me by Sean O'Casey', Times (London), (29 May 1946) p. 6.

W., T., 'Theatre', Irish Press (Dublin), (3 June 1946) p. 4.

STOKES, SEWELL, 'New Plays at Last! The English Spotlight: Red Roses for Me', Theatre Arts (N.Y.), XXX 6 (June 1946) 355–6.

FALLON, GABRIEL, 'All Professionals Now', Standard (Dublin), XVIII 27 (5 July 1946) 5. See reply by O'Casey, XVIII 30 (26 July 1946) 5; and counter-reply by Fallon, XVIII 30 (26 July 1946) 5 [letters to the Editor].

W., A., 'Red Roses for Me', Theatre World (London), XLII 258 (July 1946) 7 [at the Lyric Theatre, Hammersmith, to which it was transferred from the Embassy Theatre on 9 April 1946].

FALLON, GABRIEL, 'Calling Mr O'Casey', Standard (Dublin), XVIII 32 (9 Aug 1946) 5. See O'Casey's reply, 'And Sean O'Casey Wrote', XVIII 32 (9 Aug 1946) 5 [letter to the Editor].

McHUGH, ROGER, 'Dublin Theatre', Bell (Dublin), XII 6 (Sep 1946) 520–3.

MACLEOD, ALISON, 'Radio and TV: Drama High and Low', Daily Worker (London), (2 Nov 1953) p. 2 [B.B.C.].

CALTA, LOUIS, 'O'Casey Play Set for October Bow: Red Roses for Me, Slightly Autobiographical, To Be Produced by Pollock', New York Times (29 Mar 1955) p. 33.

NORTON, ELLIOT, 'Red Roses for Me', Boston Post (14 Dec 1955) p. 5.

NORTON, ELLIOT, 'Second Thoughts of a First-Nighter. Irish Drama Is Good But Actors Not Right: Red Roses for Me', Boston Sunday Post (18 Dec 1955) Dramatic Page.

LEWIS, ALLAN, 'Sean O'Casey's World', Nation (N.Y.), CLXXXI (24 Dec 1955) 555–6.

'After 21 Years, Broadway to See a New O'Casey Play', Daily Worker (N.Y.), (26 Dec 1955) p. 8.

ATKINSON, BROOKS, 'Sean O'Casey', New York Times (29 Dec 1955) p. 15 [at the Booth Theater, New York].

CHAPMAN, JOHN, 'Red Roses for Me Pure O'Casey, Lilting, Beautiful, and a Bit Dull', New York Daily News (29 Dec 1955) p. 43.

COLEMAN, ROBERT, 'Red Roses for Me', New York Daily Mirror (29 Dec 1955).

WATTS, RICHARD, 'Sean O'Casey's Red Roses for Me', New York Post (29 Dec 1955) p. 12.

KERR, WALTER, 'Red Roses for Me', New York Herald Tribune (29 Dec 1955) p. 11.

'O'Casey's Red Roses Opens in New York', Irish Times (Dublin), (30 Dec 1955) p. 7.

'O'Casey's Play in New York', Times (London), (30 Dec 1955) p. 3.

McCLAIN, JOHN, 'O'Casey's Play Follows a Tortuous Course', New York Theatre Critics' Review, XVI (31 Dec 1955) 183.

COLEMAN, ROBERT, 'Red Roses for Me', New York Theatre Critics' Review, XVI (31 Dec 1955) 184.

HAWKINS, WILLIAM, 'Red Roses for Me a Rare and Major Event', New York Theatre Critics' Review, XVI (31 Dec 1955) 184.

RAYMOND, HARRY, 'O'Casey's Red Roses for Me a Song of Human Brotherhood', Daily Worker (N.Y.), (3 Jan 1956) p. 7.

ATKINSON, BROOKS, 'Red Roses for Me: O'Casey's Beautiful Ode to the Glory of Life', New York Times (8 Jan 1956) section 2, p. 1.

'New Play in Manhattan', Time (N.Y.), LXVII (9 Jan 1956) 41.

'Huzzas for O'Casey: Red Roses for Me: Produced by Gordon W. Pollock. Directed by John O'Shaughnessy', Newsweek (N.Y.), XLVII (9 Jan 1956) 44–5.

GIBBS, WOLCOTT, 'Red Roses for Me', New Yorker, XXXI 48 (14 Jan 1956) 58–64.

HEWES, HENRY, 'Sean O'Casey's One-Shilling Opera', Saturday Review of Literature (N.Y.), XXXIX (14 Jan 1956) 20.

CLURMAN, HAROLD, 'Red Roses for Me', Nation (N.Y.), CLXXXII (14 Jan 1956) 39–40. Reprinted in Lies Like Truth (New York: Macmillan, 1958) pp. 122–4.

SHIPLEY, JOSEPH T., 'Red Roses for Me. By Sean O'Casey. Presented by Gordon W. Pollock. At the Booth Theatre', New Leader (N.Y.), XXXIX (16 Jan 1956) 27.

LEWIS, THEOPHILUS, 'Theatre: Red Roses for Me', America (N.Y.), XCIV (21 Jan 1956) 459–60.

BENTLEY, ERIC, 'The Politics of Sean O'Casey', New Republic (N.Y.), CXXXIV (30 Jan 1956) 21. Reprinted in What Is Theatre? (London: Dennis Dobson, 1957) pp. 107–11; (New York: Atheneum 1968) pp. 265–8.

WYATT, EUPHEMIA VAN RENSSELAER, 'Red Roses for Me', Catholic World (N.Y.), CLXXXII (Feb 1956) 387–8.

GASSNER, JOHN, 'Red Roses for Me', Educational Theatre Journal (Ann Arbor, Mich.), VIII (Mar 1956) 37–8.

'*Red Roses for Me.* December 28, 1955. Booth Theatre', *Theatre Arts* (N.Y.), XL 3 (Mar 1956) 15.

SKOUMAL, ALOYS, 'Irské drama znovu v Realistickém divadle: Sean O'Casey', *Divadlo* (Prague), VIII 12 (Dec 1957) 1007–12.

VERDOT, GUY, 'Paris Fait Connaissance avec l'Irlandais O'Casey', *Figaro littéraire* (Paris), no. 772 (4 Feb 1961) 3 [at the Théâtre national populaire].

'Théâtre Populaire Performs O'Casey', *New York Times* (11 Feb 1961) p. 26.

'*Roses Rouges pour moi*, de Sean O'Casey', *Lettres françaises* (Paris), (16–22 Feb 1961).

LEMARCHAND, JACQUES, '*Roses Rouges pour moi* de Sean O'Casey, au Théâtre national populaire', *Figaro littéraire* (Paris), no. 774 (18 Feb 1961) 16.

'*Roses Rouges pour moi*, de Sean O'Casey (T.N.P.)', *L'Avant-Scène* (Paris), no. 238 (1 Mar 1961) 36.

BOURGET-PAILLERON, ROBERT, 'Théâtre National Populaire: *Roses Rouges pour moi*, quatre actes de Sean O'Casey, texte français de Michel Habart', *Revue de Deux Mondes* (Paris), (1 Mar 1961) 155–6.

'O'Casey in Epic Style: Vilar Produces *Red Roses for Me*', *Times* (London), (25 Apr 1961) p. 20.

TAUBMAN, HOWARD, 'Sean O'Casey: *Red Roses for Me* Is Revived Downtown', *New York Times* (18 Nov 1961) p. 41 [at Greenwich Mews Theatre].

OLIVER, EDITH, 'Off Broadway: Presses Flowers', *New Yorker* (N.Y.), XXXVII (9 Dec 1961) 162–4.

'Irish Worker's Mission. Mermaid Theatre: *Red Roses for Me*', *Times* (London), (5 Sep 1962) p. 13.

LEWIS, PETER, 'On the Boil and All's Well in the O'Caseyland', *Daily Mail* (London), (5 Sep 1962) p. 3.

HOPE-WALLACE, PHILIP, '*Red Roses for Me* at the Mermaid', *Guardian* (London), (5 Sep 1962) p. 7.

KRETZMER, HERBERT, 'Just a Golden Stream of Irish Words', *Daily Express* (London), (5 Sep 1962) p. 4.

PACEY, ANN, 'Red Roses Get No Bouquet', *Daily Herald* (London), (5 Sep 1962) p. 3.

DARLINGTON, W. A., 'O'Casey Play Problems Unsolved', *Daily Telegraph* (London), (5 Sep 1962) p. 14.

SHULMAN, MILTON, 'O'Casey Brought to Shining Life', *Evening Standard* (London), (5 Sep 1962) p. 4.

CRITICISM ON SEAN O'CASEY

FRAME, COLIN, 'Poetry Out of the Grime', *Evening News* (London), (5 Sep 1962) p. 5.

CASHIN, FERGUS, 'O'Casey Bouquet', *Daily Sketch* (London), (6 Sep 1962) p. 4.

M., M., 'Bright Shilling: *Red Roses for Me* (Mermaid)', *Daily Worker* (London), (6 Sep 1962) p. 2.

M., R. B., 'Garlands of Beautiful Words', *Stage and Television Today* (London), (6 Sep 1962) p. 13.

HOBSON, HAROLD, 'Responsibility of War', *Sunday Times* (London), (9 Sep 1962) p. 33.

BRIEN, ALAN, 'Mermaid Score', *Sunday Telegraph* (London), (9 Sep 1962) p. 8.

TYNAN, KENNETH, 'Theatre. Second Lap: *Red Roses for Me* (Mermaid)', *Observer* (London), (9 Sep 1962) p. 22.

GELLERT, ROGER, 'Cold Fry', *New Statesman* (London), LXIV (14 Sep 1962) 334.

GASCOIGNE, BAMBER, 'Meccano Drama: *Red Roses for Me* (Mermaid)', *Spectator* (London), CCIX (14 Sep 1962) 364.

B., D. F., 'Mermaid: *Red Roses for Me*', *Theatre World* (London), LVIII 453 (Oct 1962) 8.

TAYLOR, JOHN RUSSELL, '*Red Roses for Me*', *Plays and Players* (London), X 2 (Nov 1962) 66–7.

KERNDL, R., '*Rote Rosen für mich*: Die optimistische Tragödie des Iren Sean O'Casey auf der Bühne des Deutschen Theaters', *Neues Deutschland* (Berlin), (10 May 1963) p. 4.

KELLY, SEAMUS, '*Red Roses for Me* at the Abbey', *Irish Times* (Dublin), (1 Aug 1967) p. 8.

F., J. J., 'Abbey First Night: Many Echoes in *Red Roses*', *Evening Herald* (Dublin), (1 Aug 1967) p. 4.

'*Red Roses* at Abbey Falls Flat', *Irish Independent* (Dublin), (2 Aug 1967) p. 10.

PAGE, SEAN, 'What Happened to O'Casey?' *Sunday Press* (Dublin), (6 Aug 1967) p. 19. See reply by John O'Riordan, 'The Croak of a Critical Corncrake' (24 Sep 1967) p. 12 [letter to the Editor].

COUGHLAN, AILEEN, 'All-Ireland Drama Festival', *Irish Times* (Dublin), (30 Apr 1968) p. 10.

COUGHLAN, AILEEN, 'Athlone Festival: O'Casey', *Irish Times* (Dublin), (6 May 1968) p. 10.

COUGHLAN, AILEEN, 'Amateur Drama', *Irish Times* (Dublin), (31 May 1968) p. 10.

PURPLE DUST

AGATE, JAMES, 'A New Challenge', *Sunday Times* (London), (19 Apr 1942) p. 2 [to be produced by Alec Clunes at the Arts Theatre]. See replies by O'Casey, 'A New Challenge', (26 Apr 1942) p. 4; and 'Mr Agate: A Curt Reply', (10 May 1942) p. 2 [letters to the Editor].

HUGHES, ELINOR, '*Purple Dust*: A Comedy in Three Acts by Sean O'Casey', *Boston Herald* (7 Dec 1944) p. 23 [at N.E. Mutual Hall by the Boston Tributary Theater].

'London Letter', *Irish Times* (Dublin), (28 Aug 1945) p. 3 [to open at Liverpool Playhouse].

'London Letter: O'Casey Play', *Irish Independent* (Dublin), (25 Mar 1953) p. 6 [to open at Theatre Royal, Glasgow].

'Mr Sean O'Casey's *Purple Dust*: An Anglo-Irish Comedy New to London', *Times* (London), (30 Mar 1953) p. 9 [forthcoming production].

'Advice from Sean O'Casey', *Daily Worker* (London), (1 Apr 1953) p. 3.

S., N., 'Mr Sean O'Casey's Play: *Purple Dust*', *Manchester Guardian* (29 Apr 1953) p. 4.

'Croydon Players: *Purple Dust* by Sean O'Casey', *Times* (London), (3 Nov 1954) p. 6.

THESPIS, 'Plays and Films', *English* (London), x (spring 1955) 139–40.

ATKINSON, BROOKS, 'The O'Casey', *New York Times* (28 Dec 1956) p. 15 [at the Cherry Lane Theatre, Greenwich Village].

CHAPMAN, JOHN, '*Purple Dust*', *New York Daily News* (28 Dec 1956) p. 39.

RAYMOND, HARRY, 'O'Casey's *Purple Dust* in Glowing Production', *Daily Worker* (N.Y.), (2 Jan 1957) p. 6.

BEAUFORT, JOHN, 'O'Casey Off-Broadway: *Purple Dust*', *Christian Science Monitor* (Boston), (5 Jan 1957) p. 10.

KERR, WALTER, 'O'Casey, Molière: A Jig and a Minuet', *New York Herald Tribune* (6 Jan 1957) section 4, pp. 1, 2.

'O'Casey at Play: *Purple Dust*. Produced by Paul Shyre, Noel Behan, Lewis Manilow, Howard Gottfried. Directed by Philip Burton', *Newsweek* (N.Y.), XLIX (12 Jan 1957) 67.

HATCH, ROBERT, 'Theatre and Films', *Nation* (N.Y.), CLXXXIV (19 Jan 1957) 65–6.

HEWES, HENRY, '*Purple Dust*', *Saturday Review of Literature* (N.Y.), XL (19 Jan 1957) 48.

SHIPLEY, JOSEPH T., '*Purple Dust*. By Sean O'Casey. At the Cherry Lane Theater', *New Leader* (N.Y.), XL (21 Jan 1957) 28.

'*Purple Dust*', *New York Times Magazine* (24 Feb 1957) p. 24 [picture].

WYATT, EUPHEMIA VAN RENSSELAER, '*Purple Dust*', *Catholic World* (N.Y.), CLXXXIV (Mar 1957) 469–70.

COLIN, SAUL, 'Plays and Players in New York', *Plays and Players* (London), IV 7 (Apr 1957) 17.

'Cast's Support for Mr O'Casey: Demands Well Met in Wayward Comedy', *Times* (London), (19 Mar 1960) p. 8 [at the Tower Theatre].

'O'Casey Festival Is Set for London. Mermaid Theatre To Offer 3 of Irish Playwright's Works', *New York Times* (15 Aug 1962) p. 37 [*Purple Dust*, *Red Roses for Me* and *The Plough and the Stars*].

'Bright and Dusty Bits in O'Caseyland. Mermaid Theatre: *Purple Dust*', *Times* (London), (16 Aug 1962) p. 5.

WORSLEY, T. G., 'The Mermaid: *Purple Dust*', *Financial Times* (London), (16 Aug 1962) p. 16.

SHORTER, ERIC, 'Snook Cocked at English: Mermaid Miss Full O'Casey', *Daily Telegraph* (London), (16 Aug 1962) p. 12.

NATHAN, DAVID, 'First Night: Sad Time for Sean O'Casey', *Daily Herald* (London), (16 Aug 1962) p. 3.

LEVIN, BERNARD, 'It's an Uncontrolled Shambles: And As For the Irish Accents!' *Daily Mail* (London), (16 Aug 1962) p. 3.

KRETZMER, HERBERT, 'A Bitter Joke Behind the Laughter', *Daily Express* (London), (16 Aug 1962) p. 8.

HOPE-WALLACE, PHILIP, '*Purple Dust*', *Guardian* (London), (16 Aug 1962) p. 5.

SHULMAN, MILTON, 'The English Can't Be Irish', *Evening Standard* (London), (16 Aug 1962) p. 4.

CASHIN, FERGUS, 'A Dust-up over Nothing', *Daily Sketch* (London), (17 Aug 1962) p. 8.

M., M., 'A Flying Start for O'Casey Season: *Purple Dust* (Mermaid)', *Daily Worker* (London), (17 Aug 1962) p. 2.

BRIEN, ALAN, 'Graves and Guffaws', *Sunday Telegraph* (London), (19 Aug 1962) p. 8.

HOBSON, HAROLD, 'Doom Without a Profit', *Sunday Times* (London), (19 Aug 1962) p. 25.

TYNAN, KENNETH, 'Theatre: *Purple Dust* (Mermaid)', *Observer* (London), (19 Aug 1962) p. 18.

KEOWN, ERIC, 'At the Play: Sean O'Casey's *Purple Dust*', *Punch* (London), CCXLIII (22 Aug 1962) 280–1.

H., P., 'Making Sport of the Irish and Mincemeat of the English', *Stage and Television Today* (London), (23 Aug 1962) p. 25.

GELLERT, ROGER, 'Dumb Show', *New Statesman* (London), LXIV (24 Aug 1962) 237.

RUTHERFORD, MALCOLM, '*Purple Dust* (Mermaid)', *Spectator* (London), CCIX (24 Aug 1962) 272.

TREWIN, J. C., 'On with the Dance', *Illustrated London News*, CCXLI (1 Sep 1962) 338.

B., D. F., 'Mermaid: *Purple Dust*' *Theatre World* (London), LVIII 452 (Sep 1962) 32.

WINNINGTON, ALAN, 'Ensemble's O'Casey: *Purple Dust* (Berliner Ensemble, Berlin)', *Daily Worker* (London), (1 Mar 1966) p. 2.

CANDIDA, 'An Irishwoman's Diary', *Irish Times* (Dublin), (19 June 1967) p. 9 [by the Berliner Ensemble].

OAK LEAVES AND LAVENDER

'The Lyric Theatre, Hammersmith: *Oak Leaves and Lavender* by Sean O'Casey', *Times* (London), (14 May 1947) p. 6.

MOSLEY, LEONARD, 'The Praise of O'Casey. *Oak Leaves and Lavender*. Lyric, Hammersmith', *Daily Express* (London), (14 May 1947) p. 3.

'O'Casey's New Play', *Irish Press* (Dublin), (14 May 1947) p. 4.

'London Greets New O'Casey Play', *Irish Independent* (Dublin), (14 May 1947) p. 6.

BISHOP, GEORGE W., 'Sean O'Casey's New Play: Ghosts and War', *Daily Telegraph* (London), (14 May 1947) p. 5.

GRANT, ELSPETH, 'Last Night's First Night: Strange Play with Good Actors', *Daily Graphic* (London), (14 May 1947) p. 2.

HALE, LIONEL, 'Last Night's Play: Mr O'Casey's Revenge on Cromwell', *Daily Mail* (London), (14 May 1947) p. 3.

M., P. L., 'Patchy Play by O'Casey. Lyric, Hammersmith: *Oak Leaves and Lavender*', *Daily Herald* (London), (14 May 1947) p. 3.

WILLIAMS, STEPHEN, 'Where Land Girls Sing', *Evening News* (London), (14 May 1947) p. 2.

'London Letter: *Oak Leaves and Lavender*', *Irish Times* (Dublin), (14 May 1947) p. 5.

'Lyric, Hammersmith: *Oak Leaves and Lavender*', *Stage* (London), (15 May 1947) p. 4.

BROWN, IVOR, 'Slump and Sean', *Observer* (London), (18 May 1947) p. 2.

HOBSON, HAROLD, '*Oak Leaves and Lavender*: Lyric, Hammersmith', *Sunday Times* (London), (18 May 1947) p. 2.

HOPE-WALLACE, PHILIP, '*Oak Leaves and Lavender*: Sean O'Casey. Lyric, Hammersmith', *Time and Tide* (London), XXVIII 19 (24 May 1947) 542.

S., F., '*Oak Leaves and Lavender*', *Theatre World* (London), XLIII 269 (June 1947) 9–10.

'London Letter: New O'Casey Play', *Irish Independent* (Dublin), (6 Dec 1949) p. 6.

COCK-A-DOODLE DANDY

K., 'Play To Arouse Anger and Pity', *Irish Times* (Dublin), (14 Dec 1949) p. 7 [at the People's Theatre, Newcastle upon Tyne].

O'CASEY, SEAN, '*Cock-a-Doodle Dandy*', *Irish Times* (Dublin), (30 Dec 1949) p. 5 [letter to the Editor].

O'CASEY, SEAN, '*Cock-a-Doodle Dandy*', *Irish Times* (Dublin), (13 Jan 1940) p. 5 [letter to the Editor].

HOLLWAY, FRANK, '*Cock-a-Doodle Dandy*: Sean O'Casey', *Tyneside Phoenix* (Newcastle-upon-Tyne), X (spring 1950) 9–10 [at the People's Theatre, Newcastle upon Tyne, on 10 December 1949].

ATKINSON, BROOKS, 'O'Casey at Yale: *Cock-a-Doodle Dandy* on School Stage', *New York Times* (4 Nov 1955) p. 26.

HEWES, HENRY, 'Broadway Postscript', *Saturday Review of Literature* (N.Y.), XXXVIII (19 Nov 1955) 37.

QUIDNUNC, 'An Irishman's Diary', *Irish Times* (Dublin), (19 Aug 1958) p. 6.

'O'Casey Play Acclaimed in Toronto', *Evening Mail* (Dublin), (2 Oct 1958) p. 6 [at the Playhouse].

'Catholics Angered by O'Casey', *Evening Herald* (Dublin) (2 Oct 1958) p. 7.

'Trouble over O'Casey Play in Toronto', *Irish Times* (Dublin), (7 Oct 1958) p. 9.

'O'Casey Play Is Guarded', *Evening Herald* (Dublin), (7 Oct 1958), p. 1.

'Shouters at Play Chided by O'Casey: Dramatist Scores Manners of Couples Who Interrupted His Drama in Toronto', *New York Times* (7 Oct 1958) p. 40.

NORDELL, ROD, 'Cock-a-Doodle Casey', *New Leader* (N.Y.), LXI (3 Nov 1958) 20-2.

O'CASEY, SEAN, 'O'Casey's Credo: His First Concern Is To Make a Play Live', *New York Times* (9 Nov 1958) section 2, pp. 1, 3. Reprinted in *Playwrights on Playwrighting*, ed. Toby Cole (New York: Hill & Wang, 1960) pp. 247–9.

ATKINSON, BROOKS, 'O'Casey's Defense of Joy: *Cock-a-Doodle Dandy* Has Premiere Here', *New York Times* (13 Nov 1958) p. 39 [at Carnegie Hall Playhouse, New York].

McHARRY, CHARLES, 'O'Casey an Angry Old Man in Latest Drama', *New York Daily News* (13 Nov 1958) p. 75.

MALCOLM, DONALD, 'Off Broadway: Import News', *New Yorker*, XXXIV 40 (22 Nov 1958) 100–2.

ATKINSON, BROOKS, 'Two by O'Casey: *Cock-a-Doodle Dandy* and *Shadow of a Gunman* Open Within 9 Days', *New York Times* (23 Nov 1958) section 2, p. 1.

'New Play in Manhattan', *Time* (N.Y.), LXXII (24 Nov 1958) 90.

'Another from O'Casey: *Cock-a-Doodle Dandy*. By Sean O'Casey', *Newsweek* (N.Y.), LII (24 Nov 1958) 78.

CLURMAN, HAROLD, 'Theatre', *Nation* (N.Y.), CLXXXVII (29 Nov 1958) 416.

HEWES, HENRY, 'Where Is Fancy Bred?', *Saturday Review of Literature* (N.Y.), XLI (6 Dec 1958) 37.

'N.Y. Theatre Goes Irish: O'Casey Too Much for the Actors', *Times* (London), (10 Dec 1958) p. 3.

'*Cock-a-Doodle Dandy*', *Theatre Arts* (N.Y.), XLIII (Jan 1959) 64.

COLIN, SAUL, 'Plays and Players in New York: Fighting Superstition', *Plays and Players* (London), VI 5 (Feb 1959) 24.

FUNKE, LEWIS, 'O'Casey Awaits Opening of Play: Looks Forward to London *Cock-a-Doodle Dandy*', *New York Times* (2 Sep 1959) p. 35.

HOPE-WALLACE, PHILIP, 'The Edinburgh Festival', *Time and Tide* (London), XL 36 (5 Sep 1959) 956.

'Fine Acting in O'Casey Play', *Times* (London), (8 Sep 1959) p. 14 [at the Lyceum, Edinburgh].

MAVOR, RONALD, 'Sean O'Casey's Hymn to Life: Fine and Beautiful Play', *Scotsman* (Edinburgh), (8 Sep 1959) p. 11.

DARLINGTON, W. A., 'Sean O'Casey Cracks at the Kill-Joys: Lively Satire', *Daily Telegraph* (London) (8 Sep 1959) p. 10.

WILSON, CECIL, 'The Young Heart of Old Sean: *Cock-a-Doodle Dandy*, by Sean O'Casey. Lyceum, Edinburgh', *Daily Mail* (London), (8 Sep 1959) p. 5.

LEVIN, BERNARD, 'The Devil and Mr O'Casey', *Daily Express* (London), (8 Sep 1959) p. 13.

DARLINGTON, W. A., '*Cock-a-Doodle Dandy* Given Moving Showing at Edinburgh', *New York Times* (8 Sep 1959) p. 43.

A., E., 'O'Casey's Farce and Fantasy', *Stage and Television Today* (London), (10 Sep 1959) p. 18.

A., H., 'Edinburgh Festival: O'Casey's Message Is – Life', *Daily Worker* (London), (10 Sep 1959) p. 3.

BRIEN, ALAN, 'Edinburgh Theatre: *Cock-a-Doodle Dandy* (Lyceum)', *Spectator* (London), CCIII (11 Sep 1959) 331–2.

HOBSON, HAROLD, 'Visions and Judgments. *Cock-a-Doodle Dandy*. Lyceum, Edinburgh', *Sunday Times* (London), (13 Sep 1959) p. 25.

PRYCE-JONES, ALAN, 'Genius and Wind', *Observer* (London), (13 Sep 1959) p. 23.

'Youth Theatre Prospects', *Times* (London), (14 Sep 1959) p. 5.

'O'Casey Play in London: *Cock-a-Doodle Dandy*', *Times* (London), (18 Sep 1959) p. 13.

CARTHEW, ANTHONY, 'Showpiece: Irishman Who Hates His Home', *Daily Herald* (London), (18 Sep 1959) p. 3.

DARLINGTON, W. A., 'First Night: Royal Court Goes Irish. Enjoyable O'Casey', *Daily Telegraph* (London), (18 Sep 1959) p. 12.

LEVIN, BERNARD, 'O'Casey Gives the Angels and Devils Plenty to Crow About. *Cock-a-Doodle Dandy*: Royal Court', *Daily Express* (London), (18 Sep 1959) p. 4.

TANFIELD, PAUL, 'C-U-C-K-O-O!', *Daily Mail* (London), (18 Sep 1959) p. 16.

SHULMAN, MILTON, 'The O'Casey Flashes Are Still Enough', *Evening Standard* (London), (18 Sep 1959) p. 14.

HOBSON, HAROLD, 'The Dublin Singing', *Sunday Times* (London), (20 Sep 1959) p. 25.

MYSON, MYKE, 'Theatre: O'Casey Has the Voice of Youth', *Daily Worker* (London), (21 Sep 1959) p. 2.

'Triumph of Living Is Celebrated in *Cock-a-Doodle Dandy*', *Stage and Television Today* (London), (24 Sep 1959) p. 17.

JONES, MERVYN, 'Two More from the Irish', *Tribune* (London), (25 Sep 1959) p. 11.

HOPE-WALLACE, PHILIP, '*Cock-a-Doodle Dandy*: O'Casey. Royal Court', *Time and Tide* (London), XL 39 (26 Sep 1959) 1038.

ALVAREZ, A., 'The Arts and Entertainment', *New Statesman* (London), LVIII (26 Sep 1959) 388.

B[AKER], F. G., 'Cock-a-Doodle Dandy', Plays and Players (London), VII I (Oct 1959) 15.

'Cock-a-Doodle Dandy', Theatre World (London), LV 417 (Oct 1959) 7 [pictures].

KERR, WALTER, 'The Shadow of a Gunman and Cock-a-Doodle Dandy', Cincinnati Daily Enquirer (30 Nov 1959) p. 50.

HOBSON, HAROLD, 'Doom Without a Profit', Sunday Times (London), (19 Aug 1962) p. 25 [at the Mermaid].

BARNES, CLIVE, 'The Theatre: Cock-a-Doodle Dandy – APA Stages O'Casey Play at the Lyceum', New York Times (21 Jan 1969) p. 40.

BRUCE, ALAN N., 'Theater: O'Casey, Yeats, Mrozek, and the "Fantasticks" Team Again', Christian Science Monitor (Boston), London Edition (29 Jan 1969) p. 6.

'A Rooster for Phoenix', Time (N.Y.), XCIII (31 Jan 1969) 54.

GILL, BRENDAN, 'The Devil's Advocate', New Yorker, XLIV (1 Feb 1969) 44.

HEWES, HENRY, 'The Theatre: Spirit Power', Saturday Review (N.Y.), (8 Feb 1969) 41.

CLURMAN, HAROLD, 'Theatre', Nation (N.Y.), CCVIII (Feb 1969) 187–9.

'Theater: On Broadway – Cock-a-Doodle Dandy', Time (N.Y.), XCIII 8 (21 Feb 1969) 3.

'Cock-a-Doodle Dandy', America (N.Y.), CXX (22 Feb 1969) 232.

WEST, ANTHONY, 'Cock-a-Doodle Dandy', Vogue (Boulder, Col.), CLIII (1 Mar 1969) 112.

SAVERY, RONALD, 'New York Theatre', Stage and Television Today (London), (6 Mar 1969) 9.

TRILLING, OSSIA, 'Berlin Festival Twenty Years Old', Stage and Television Today (London), (6 Nov 1969) p. 14.

HALL OF HEALING

ATKINSON, BROOKS, 'Three New One-Act Plays by Sean O'Casey Put on by an Off-Broadway Group of Actors', New York Times (8 May 1952) p. 35 [at the New York Yugoslav–American Hall].

'Unity Theatre: Sean O'Casey's Short Plays', Times (London), (23 May 1953) p. 8.

TREWIN, J. C., 'Five Plays', Observer (London), (24 May 1953) p. 11.

'The Unity: Three in a Row', Stage (London), (28 May 1953) 9.

DOUGLAS, DONALD, 'O'Casey Smashes His Targets', Daily Worker (London), (29 May 1953) p. 2.

SHARE, BERNARD, 'O'Casey and Lorca at the Abbey', *Irish Times* (Dublin), (1 Mar 1966) p. 6.

C., C., 'O'Casey Play Is Staged for First Time', *Irish Press* (Dublin), (1 Mar 1966) p. 7.

F., J. J., 'Abbey: Fine Acting in Two Plays', *Evening Herald* (Dublin), (1 Mar 1966) p. 6.

RUSHE, DESMOND, 'Splendid Double Bill at Abbey', *Irish Independent* (Dublin), (2 Mar 1966) p. 6.

BEDTIME STORY

ATKINSON, BROOKS, 'Three New One-Act Plays by Sean O'Casey Put on by an Off-Broadway Group of Actors', *New York Times* (8 May 1952) p. 35 [at the New York Yugoslav–American Hall].

'He Called O'Casey "Unsavoury": Ex-Fun Fair Man Puts Foot in It', *Daily Worker* (London), (20 Feb 1954) p. 3 [at Chingford Unity Theatre].

ATKINSON, BROOKS, 'Triple Play', *New York Times* (16 Apr 1959) p. 28 [at the Playhouse].

ATKINSON, BROOKS, 'Triple Play', *New York Times* (26 Apr 1959) section 2, p. 1.

'Broadway Plans', *New York Times* (11 May 1959) p. 30 ['Triple Play' to close].

'Triple Play', *Theatre Arts* (N.Y.), XLIII (June 1959) 9.

CAPELLE, J.-L., 'O'Casey et Strindberg', *France Nouvelle* (Paris), (24 Aug 1960) p. 21.

QUIDNUNC, 'An Irishman's Diary: O'Casey, Too', *Irish Times* (Dublin), (12 Jan 1967) p. 7 [at the Carouge, Geneva].

ROSENFIELD, RAY, 'Some Plays Puzzle MacLiammoir. Belfast Festival Choice', *Irish Times* (Dublin), (24 Mar 1969) p. 10 [at the Irish Universities Drama Association Festival at Queen's University, Belfast]. See reply by John O'Riordan, 'MacLiammoir and O'Casey' (29 Mar 1969) p. 15 [letter to the Editor].

TIME TO GO

ATKINSON, BROOKS, 'Three New One-Act Plays by Sean O'Casey Put on by an Off-Broadway Group of Actors', *New York Times* (8 May 1952) p. 35 [at the New York Yugoslav–American Hall].

'Unity Theatre: Sean O'Casey's Short Plays', *Times* (London), (23 May 1953) p. 8.

TREWIN, J. C., 'Five Plays', *Observer* (London), (24 May 1953) p. 11.

'The Unity: Three in a Row', *Stage* (London), (28 May 1953) p. 9.

DOUGLAS, DONALD, 'O'Casey Smashes His Targets', *Daily Worker* (London), (29 May 1953) p. 2.

ATKINSON, BROOKS, 'O'Casey and Carroll Plays on ANTA Bill', *New York Times* (23 Mar 1960) p. 33 [at the Theatre de Lys].

THE BISHOP'S BONFIRE

'A New O'Casey Play', *Manchester Guardian* (29 Dec 1954) p. 4 [details of forthcoming production announced].

'Mr Sean O'Casey's New Play: *A* [*sic*] *Bishop's Bonfire*' *Times* (London), (12 Jan 1955) p. 7 [forthcoming production in Dublin].

FALLON, GABRIEL, 'O'Casey Will Give Us a Badly Needed Tonic', *Evening Press* (Dublin), (29 Jan 1955) p. 5.

'Sean O'Casey Again', *Standard* (Dublin), XXVII 163 (18 Feb 1955) 1.

'Dublin Première of O'Casey's Latest Play', *Evening Mail* (Dublin), (24 Feb 1955) p. 6.

'Sean O'Casey's Play: Art – For Whose Sake?' *Standard* (Dublin), XXVII 164 (25 Feb 1955) 1.

FALLON, GABRIEL, 'What Will Mr Guthrie Do to O'Casey?' *Evening Press* (Dublin), (26 Feb 1955) p. 5.

'A Letter from Sean O'Casey', *Times Pictorial* (Dublin), XXXI (26 Feb 1955) 1.

'Will O'Casey's *Bonfire* Cause Another Blaze?', *Times Pictorial* (Dublin), XXXI (26 Feb 1955) 11.

O'CASEY, EILEEN, 'Mrs O'Casey on Her Husband's Latest Play', *Sunday Independent* (Dublin), (27 Feb 1955) p. 7.

WHITE, JACK, 'An O'Casey First Night', *Observer* (London), (27 Feb 1955) p. 10.

'Mrs. O'Casey Arrives for *Bonfire* First Night', *Sunday Press* (Dublin), (27 Feb 1955) p. 1.

'O'Casey on His New Play', *Times* (London), (28 Feb 1955) p. 3.

'Tanfield's Diary: Shy Mr O'Casey Will Not See His World Première', *Daily Mail* (London), (28 Feb 1955) p. 4.

'Return of the Native', *Evening Herald* (Dublin), (28 Feb 1955) p. 4 [editorial].

'1,200 Queued for Gallery', *Irish Times* (Dublin), (1 Mar 1955) p. 1.

'By-Line', *Irish Times* (Dublin), (1 Mar 1955) p. 1 [cartoon].

'*The Bishop's Bonfire*: Dublin's Mixed Reception for New O'Casey Play', *Times* (London), (1 Mar 1955) p. 8 [at the Gaiety Theatre, Dublin].

BARBER, JOHN, 'O'Casey Turns up with a Shocker', *Daily Express* (London), (1 Mar 1955) p. 3.

CASHIN, FERGUS, 'O'Casey Goes to Town Again ... And It's a Blaze of Cheeky Fun', *Daily Mirror* (London), (1 Mar 1955) p. 4.

FALLON, GABRIEL, 'The "Bonfire" Never Did Really Blaze at All', *Evening Press* (Dublin), (1 Mar 1955) p. 4.

FRANK, ELIZABETH, 'Boos, Hisses for O'Casey's Play: Wife in Tears', *News Chronicle* (London), (1 Mar 1955) p. 1.

F., J. J., 'Sean O'Casey Out of Touch', *Evening Herald* (Dublin), (1 Mar 1955) p. 6.

F., R. M., '*Bonfire* – Kindled on Comedy, Quenched by Melodrama', *Evening Mail* (Dublin), (1 Mar 1955) p. 3.

'Cheers and Boos for Sean O'Casey', *Irish Press* (Dublin), (1 Mar 1955) p. 1.

'K' [Seamus Kelly], '*The Bishop's Bonfire* in Gaiety Theatre', *Irish Times* (Dublin), (1 Mar 1955) p. 4.

M., I., 'O'Casey's Première at the Gaiety', *Irish Independent* (Dublin), (1 Mar 1955) p. 7.

'Mr Sean O'Casey's New Play: *The Bishop's Bonfire* at the Gaiety Theatre, Dublin', *Times* (London), (1 Mar 1955) p. 6.

CARROLL, NIALL, 'O'Casey, Mostly Sound and Fury', *Irish Press* (Dublin), (1 Mar 1955) p. 3.

DARLINGTON, W. A., 'First Nights: Anti-Clerical Bias in O'Casey Play. *The Bishop's Bonfire*', *Daily Telegraph* (London), (1 Mar 1955) p. 8.

'Thousands Queue for O'Casey', *Daily Worker* (London), (1 Mar 1955) p. 1.

'What the Critics Say About O'Casey's New Play', *Evening Herald* (Dublin), (1 Mar 1955) p. 6.

WILSON, CECIL, 'O'Casey Explodes a Stick of Dramatic Dynamite', *Daily Mail* (London), (1 Mar 1955) p. 8.

'What the Irish Critics Think', *Evening Herald* (Dublin), (1 Mar 1955) p. 6.

'New O'Casey Play Is Booed in Dublin', *New York Times* (1 Mar 1955) p. 22.

FAY, GERARD, '*The Bishop's Bonfire*', *Manchester Guardian* (2 Mar 1955) p. 5.

K., 'British Critics Found Journey Worth While', *Irish Times* (Dublin), (2 Mar 1955) p. 4.

'Dublin Sees Best O'Casey: Gets Première – After 20 Years', *Daily Worker* (London), (2 Mar 1955) p. 3.

CAREY, EDW., 'Self-Respect', *Standard* (Dublin), XXVII 165 (4 Mar 1955) 12 [letter to the Editor].

BYRNE, SEAMUS, 'The Shadow of an O'Casey', *Standard* (Dublin), XXVII 165 (4 Mar 1955) 8.

'Sean O'Casey's Play: The "Gods" Can't be Fooled!" *Standard* (Dublin), XXVII 165 (4 Mar 1955) 1.

O'FLAHERTY, DESMOND, 'Pat on the Back for Pat Murphy', *Standard* (Dublin), XXVII 165 (4 Mar 1955) 11 [letter to the Editor].

WHITE, JACK, ' *The Bishop's Bonfire* by Sean O'Casey. (Gaiety Theatre, Dublin)', *Spectator* (London), CXCIV (4 Mar 1955) 256.

FALLON, GABRIEL, 'Why Sean O'Casey Has Failed This Time', *Evening Press* (Dublin), (5 Mar 1955) p. 7.

FINEGAN, J. J., 'Dublin's Advice to O'Casey', *Evening Herald* (Dublin), (5 Mar 1955) p. 6.

'Mrs O'Casey and Shivaun Fly Home', *Irish Press* (Dublin), (5 Mar 1955) p. 1 [after attending the première of the play].

'Melodrama Defended', *Evening Herald* (Dublin), (5 Mar 1955) p. 6 [interview].

O'DONNELL, DONAT, 'No Bishop, No Bonfire', *New Statesman and Nation* (London), XLIX (5 Mar 1955) 320.

'O'Casey's Return', *Daily Worker* (London), (5 Mar 1955) p. 3.

GRAY, KEN, 'O'Casey Draws the Critics Across the Sea', *Times Pictorial* (Dublin), XXXI (5 Mar 1955) 11.

O'CONNOR, ULICK, 'A Dublin Première. *The Bishop's Bonfire*: Sean O'Casey. Gaiety, Dublin', *Time and Tide* (London), XXXVI 10 (5 Mar 1955) 296.

HOBSON, HAROLD, 'Dublin Double: *The Bishop's Bonfire*. Gaiety Theatre, Dublin', *Sunday Times* (London), (6 Mar 1955) p. 11.

TYNAN, KENNETH, 'Irish Stew', *Observer* (London), (6 Mar 1955) p. 11. Reprinted in *Curtains* (London: Longmans; New York: Atheneum, 1961) pp. 83–5.

'Critics Hail New Play by Sean O'Casey', *Chicago Sunday Tribune* (6 Mar 1955) pt 7, section 2, p. 5.

DARLINGTON, W. A., 'O'Casey Play: Opening Night in Dublin', *New York Times* (6 Mar 1955) section 2, p. 3.

'O'Casey's New Play', *Sunday Independent* (Dublin), (6 Mar 1955) p. 12.

CARROLL, NIALL, 'Only Great Are Hissed', *Irish Press* (Dublin), (7 Mar 1955) p. 4.

REID, RITA, '*The Bishop's Bonfire*', *Evening Press* (Dublin), (7 Mar 1955) p. 5 [letter to the Editor].

QUIDNUNC, 'An Irishman's Diary', *Irish Times* (Dublin), (8 Mar 1955) p. 6.

O'DOHERTY, VINCENT, 'O'Casey: *Standard* Attitude Criticised', *Irish Press* (Dublin), (8 Mar 1955) p. 6 [letter to the Editor].

CARMODY, PATRICK, '*The Bishop's Bonfire*', *Evening Mail* (Dublin), (9 Mar 1955) p. 7 [letter to the Editor].

CARMODY, PATRICK, 'That Bonfire', *Evening Press* (Dublin), (9 Mar 1955) p. 6.

O'SEARBHAIN, SEAN, 'Was There Really a Bonfire?', *Irish Press* (Dublin), (9 Mar 1955) p. 4.

KEOWN, ERIC, 'At the Play: *The Bishop's Bonfire* (Gaiety, Dublin)', *Punch* (London), CCXXVIII (9 Mar 1955) 327–8.

'Visitors to Russia, Sean O'Casey Plays Criticised', *Irish Press* (Dublin), (9 Mar 1955) p. 1.

'Students Criticize Newspaper', *Irish Times* (Dublin), (10 Mar 1955) p. 7.

Playgoer, 'Admonition from Outside', *Irish Times* (Dublin), (10 Mar 1955) p. 5 [letter to the Editor].

O'DONOVAN, JOHN, "Admiring Bow" in the Direction of Devon', *Evening Herald* (Dublin), (11 Mar 1955) p. 7 [letter to the Editor].

O'DONOVAN, JOHN, '*The Bishop's Bonfire*', *Evening Press* (Dublin), (11 Mar 1955) p. 4 [letter to the Editor].

'The O'Casey Controversy Rages On: Mr Hobson Snipes for *The Sunday Times*', *Standard* (Dublin), XXVII 165 (11 Mar 1955) 1, 12.

'Bishop Refers to O'Casey Play', *Irish Times* (Dublin), (11 Mar 1955) p. 4.

FALLON, GABRIEL, 'May Heaven Preserve Us from These London Critics!' *Evening Press* (Dublin), (12 Mar 1955) p. 5.

'Theatre News', *Sphere* (London), CCXX (12 Mar 1955) 424.

HOBSON, HAROLD, 'O'Casey's *Bishop's Bonfire*', *Christian Science Monitor* (Boston), (12 Mar 1955) p. 6.

THERSITES, 'Private Views', *Irish Times* (Dublin), (12 Mar 1955) p. 6.

'Big Audiences for Play', *Irish Times* (Dublin), (12 Mar 1955) p. 9.

'X', 'Sean O'Casey', *Leader* (Dublin), LV 5 (12 Mar 1955) 17–18.

GRAY, KEN, 'Plenty of Sparks – But No Big Blaze', *Times Pictorial* (Dublin), XXXI (12 Mar 1955) 11.

BURROWS, GEORGE H., 'Sean O', *Times Pictorial* (Dublin), XXXI (12 Mar 1955) 12, 19.

'O'Casey Visit Off', *Sunday Press* (Dublin), (13 Mar 1955) p. 5.

BARRETT, JAMES, 'Sean O'Casey', *Sunday Times* (London), (13 Mar 1955) p. 2 [letter to the Editor].

MACNAMARA, D., 'Sean O'Casey', *Sunday Times* (London), (13 Mar 1955) p. 2 [letter to the Editor].

'New Play in Dublin', *Time* (N.Y.), LXV (14 Mar 1955) 74.

O'CASEY, SEAN, '*Bishop's Bonfire*', *Irish Press* (Dublin), (15 Mar 1955) p. 8 [letter to the Editor].

O'DONOVAN, JOHN, '*The Bonfire*', *Evening Press* (Dublin), (15 Mar 1955) p. 4 [letter to the Editor].

NOLAN, CARMEL M., '*The Bonfire*', *Evening Press* (Dublin), (15 Mar 1955) p. 4 [letter to the Editor].

O'FLAHERTY, DESMOND, 'A "Playgoer" and "The Bonfire"', *Standard* (Dublin), XXVII 166 (18 Mar 1955) 11 [letter to the Editor].

O'MAOLÁIN, MICHÉAL, '*The Bonfire*', *Irish Press* (Dublin), (19 Mar 1955) p. 2.

GRAY, KEN, 'Why Not a Festival of Drama?', *Times Pictorial* (Dublin), XXXI (19 Mar 1955) 11.

O'CASEY, SEAN, 'Sean O'Casey and Dublin', *Sunday Times* (London), (20 Mar 1955) p. 2 [letter to the Editor].

HOBSON, HAROLD, 'Sean O'Casey and Dublin', *Sunday Times* (London), (20 Mar 1955) p. 2 [letter to the Editor].

O'CASEY, SEAN, '*The Bishop's Bonfire*', *Irish Times* (Dublin), (23 Mar 1955) p. 5 [letter to the Editor].

FALLON, GABRIEL, '*The Bonfire*', *Evening Press* (Dublin), (23 Mar 1955) p. 6 [letter to the Editor].

BARRINGTON, MAEVE, 'Bookings', *Irish Press* (Dublin), (24 Mar 1955) p. 6 [letter to the Editor].

O'CASEY, SEAN, 'O'Casey and the Dublin Critics', *Irish Press* (Dublin), (24 Mar 1955) p. 6 [letter to the Editor].

HOLLANDER, JAMES, 'Mr O'Casey's Wrath', *Irish Press* (Dublin), (24 Mar 1955) p. 6 [letter to the Editor].

'If Critics Did Their Duty', *Standard* (Dublin), XXVII 167 (25 Mar 1955) 6.

'People and Principles', *Standard* (Dublin), XXVII 167 (25 Mar 1955) 6 [editorial].

'Mr O'Donovan and *The Bishop's Bonfire*', *Standard* (Dublin), XXVII 167 (25 Mar 1955) 11 [letters to the Editor].

'Lecturer's Comments on New O'Casey Play', *Irish Independent* (Dublin), (26 Mar 1955) p. 12.

FALLON, GABRIEL, 'An Open Letter to Sean O'Casey', *Irish Press* (Dublin), (30 Mar 1955) p. 4.

'O'Casey's Return to Irish Stage', *Daily Worker* (N.Y.), (30 Mar 1955) p. 7.

SWEENEY, GERALD, 'Mr O'Donovan and *The Bonfire*' *Standard* (Dublin), XXVII 168 (1 Apr 1955) 11 [letter to the Editor].

O'CASEY, SEAN, '*The Bishop's Bonfire*', *Irish Press* (Dublin), (5 Apr 1955) p. 8 [letter to the Editor].

BEHAN, MARIE, 'O'Casey "Rude and Revolting"', *Irish Press* (Dublin), (5 Apr 1955) p. 8 [letter to the Editor].

'No *Bonfire* Yet for London', *Irish Press* (Dublin), (6 Apr 1955) p. 5.

'U.S. Pressmen Comment on O'Casey Play: Why Was It Produced?', *Standard* (Dublin), XXVII 169 (8 Apr 1955) 3.

'X', 'Sean O'Casey: A Postscript', *Leader* (Dublin), LV 7 (9 Apr 1955) 7–8.

O'CASEY, SEAN, '*The Bonfire*', *Irish Press* (Dublin), (12 Apr 1955) p. 9 [letter to the Editor].

'*Bonfire*', *Standard* (Dublin), XXVII 170 (15 Apr 1955) 8.

KEATING, M. J., 'The American View', *Irish Times* (Dublin), (16 Apr 1955) p. 9.

MACWILLIAMS, BOURKE, '*The Bishop's Bonfire* by Sean O'Casey: First Performance at the Gaiety Theatre, Dublin', *Plays and Players* (London), II 7 (Apr 1955) 14. See O'Casey's reply, 'Sean O'Casey Complains', (May 1955) 23; and MacWilliams's counter-reply, 'Reply to Sean O'Casey', (June 1955) 21.

'Between the Acts', *Irish Tatler and Sketch* (Dublin), LXIV 7 (Apr 1955) 66.

'No Plans To Bring Play To London', *Irish Times* (Dublin), (2 May 1955) p. 9.

LEVENTHAL, A. J., '*The Bishop's Bonfire* by Sean O'Casey. Cyril Cusack Productions. Gaiety Theatre', *Dublin Magazine*, XXXI 2 (Apr–June 1955) 28–9.

ADAMS, PHOEBE LOU, 'Reader's Choice', *Atlantic Monthly* (Boston), CXCVI (Oct 1955) 96.

DIBB, FRANK, '*The Bishop's Bonfire*', *Plays and Players* (London), VI 3 (Dec 1958) 31 [at the Highbury Little Theatre, Sutton Coldfield, on 14 October 1958].

PRO-QUIDNUNC, 'An Irishman's Diary', *Irish Times* (Dublin), (14 June 1961) p. 8.

'An O'Casey Occasion', *Irish Times* (Dublin), (1 July 1961) p. 9.

'The Londoner's Diary: No Smooth Talk', *Evening Standard* (London), (22 July 1961) p. 6.

FERGUSON, T. S., ' "A Sad Play Within the Tune of a Polka": Ireland's Troubles', *Sunday Telegraph* (London), (23 July 1961) p. 8.

'Sean O'Casey Whirls His Blackthorn. Mermaid Theatre: *The Bishop's Bonfire*', *Times* (London), (27 July 1961) p. 5.

NATHAN, DAVID, 'There Aren't Enough Sparks in O'Casey's Irish Fire', *Daily Herald* (London), (27 July 1961) p. 3.

MULLER, ROBERT, 'The Bonfire That Fails to Burn: *The Bishop's Bonfire*, by Sean O'Casey. Mermaid Theatre', *Daily Mail* (London), (27 July 1961) p. 3.

'O'Casey at the Mermaid', *Irish Times* (Dublin), (27 July 1961) p. 7.

'No Seat for Crosby at O'Casey Play', *Irish Press* (Dublin), (27 July 1961) p. 3.

BARNES, CLIVE, 'Few Sparks from Sean O'Casey's *Bonfire. The Bishop's Bonfire. The Mermaid*', *Daily Express* (London), (27 July 1961) p. 4.

DARLINGTON, W. A., 'First Night: O'Casey's Lurid Eire. Mixed Play of Jarring Moods', *Daily Telegraph* (London), (27 July 1961) p. 14.

SHULMAN, MILTON, 'O'Casey in His Seventies: Unquenchable As Ever', *Evening Standard* (London), (27 July 1961) p. 4.

BARKER, FELIX, 'Not One Murmur at the Mermaid', *Evening News* (London), (27 July 1961) p. 4.

'O'Casey's *Bishop's Bonfire* Opens in London', *New York Times* (27 July 1961) p. 22.

'*The Bishop's Bonfire*', *Irish Times* (Dublin), (28 July 1961) p. 7.

HOBSON, HAROLD, '*The Bishop's Bonfire*: Mermaid', *Sunday Times* (London), (30 July 1961) p. 27.

BRIEN, ALAN, 'Beware of the Dogma', *Sunday Telegraph* (London), (30 July 1961) p. 8.

TYNAN, KENNETH, 'At the Theatre: A Second Look at O'Casey and Osborne', *Observer* (London), (30 July 1961) p. 20.

M., R. B., 'O'Casey Spirit Gives Truth and Value', *Stage and Television Today* (London), (3 Aug 1961) p. 7.

FINDLATER, RICHARD, 'The Life Force Is Still Burning', *Time and Tide* (London), XLII 31 (3 Aug 1961) 1273.

GELLERT, ROGER, 'Wring Its Neck', *New Statesman* (London), LXII (4 Aug 1961) 164.

GASCOIGNE, BAMBER, 'The Symbol of the Carpet: *The Bishop's Bonfire*. (Mermaid)', *Spectator* (London), CCVII (11 Aug 1961) 204.

TREWIN, J. C., 'A Word in the Ear', *Illustrated London News*, CCXXXIX (12 Aug 1961) 266.

ROBERTS, PETER, '*The Bishop's Bonfire*. By Sean O'Casey', *Plays and Players* (London), VIII 12 (Sep 1961) 13.

M., H. G., 'Mermaid: *The Bishop's Bonfire*', *Theatre World* (London), LVII 440 (Sep 1961) 4 [pictures p. 39].

DUNLOP, FRANK, 'Preparing the Bonfire', *Plays and Players* (London), VIII 12 (Sep 1961) 7, 19.

THE DRUMS OF FATHER NED

'Tostal Council to Proceed with Plays: No Inaugural Mass', *Irish Times* (Dublin), (10 Jan 1958) p. 1.

'Objectionable Plays: Unions to Send Protest to Tostal Council', *Irish Independent* (Dublin), (12 Feb 1958) p. 10.

'Play Withdrawn by Mr Sean O'Casey', *Times* (London), (12 Feb 1958) p. 3 [from the Dublin Festival].

'Dublin Not To See Play by O'Casey', *Irish Times* (Dublin), (12 Feb 1958) p. 1.

'O'Casey Cancels Play: Withdraws *Drums of Father Ned* from Dublin Fete', *New York Times* (12 Feb 1958) p. 33.

'O'Casey Refuses to Alter Play', *Irish Times* (Dublin), (13 Feb 1958) p. 1.

QUIDNUNC [Patrick Campbell], 'An Irishman's Diary', *Irish Times* (Dublin), (15 Feb 1958) p. 8.

'Final Curtain?' *Irish Times* (Dublin), (15 Feb 1958) p. 7 [leading article].

McCLELLAND, ALAN, 'Got Raw Deal', *Sunday Press* (Dublin), (16 Feb 1958) p. 1.

CARROLL, NIALL, 'That O'Casey Play', *Irish Press* (Dublin), (24 Feb 1958) p. 6. See O'Casey's reply, 'O'Casey Makes Challenge', (1 Mar 1958) p. 6; Carroll's counter-reply, 'Reply to O'Casey' (3 Mar 1958) p. 6; and O'Casey's counter-counter-reply, 'O'Casey Play', (12 Mar 1958) p. 6.

O'CASEY, SEAN, 'The Theatre Festival', *Irish Times* (Dublin), (11 Mar 1958) p. 5 [letter to the Editor].

'O'Casey Bans His Plays from Irish Theatres', *New York Times* (20 Mar 1958) p. 34.

HOGAN, ROBERT, 'Riches Scorned', *Times Literary Supplement* (London), (21 Mar 1958) p. 153 [letter to the Editor].

'Sean O'Casey – Salesman: Playwright under Pressure', *Plays and Players* (London), v 6 (Mar 1958) 22.

HOGAN, ROBERT, 'O'Casey and the Archbishop', *New Republic* (N.Y.), CXXXVIII (19 May 1958) 29–30.

O'CASEY, SEAN, '*The Drums of Father Ned*', *Enquiry* (Nottingham), I 2 (June 1958) 37–9.

O'CASEY, SEAN, 'Abbey Can't Have My Plays', *Sunday Press* (Dublin), (27 July 1958) p. 1 [interview].

'O'Casey Bans Performance of His Plays in Dublin', *Irish Times* (Dublin), (28 July 1958) p. 1.

'O'Casey Ban on Plays in Dublin', *Irish Press* (Dublin), (28 July 1958) p. 5.

'By-Line', *Irish Times* (Dublin), (29 July 1958) p. 1 [cartoon].

'Radio Eireann Ban by O'Casey', *Irish Times* (Dublin), (29 July 1958) p. 7.

FALLON, GABRIEL, 'He's Wrong-Shipped This Time', *Evening Press* (Dublin), (2 Aug 1958) p. 7.

QUIDNUNC, 'An Irishman's Dairy', *Irish Times* (Dublin), (19 Aug 1958) p. 6.

HEWES, HENRY, 'The Green Crow Flies Again', *Saturday Review of Literature* (N.Y.), XLII (9 May 1959) 22 [at the Little Theatre, Lafayette, Indiana, on 25 April 1959].

'Abbey Managing Director Sees O'Casey', *Irish Times* (Dublin), (21 Sep 1959) p. 4.

WRIGHT, A., 'Pasternak and Joyce', *Irish Times* (Dublin), (22 July 1960) p. 7 [letter to the Editor].

CRAIG, H. A. L., 'Red Roses for O'Casey', *New Statesman and Nation* (London), LX (19 Nov 1960) 782 [at Hornchurch, Essex].

ROBERTS, PETER, '*The Drums of Father Ned*. By Sean O'Casey. First Performance in Europe at the Queen's Theatre, Hornchurch, on November 8, 1960', *Plays and Players* (London), VIII 4 (Jan 1961) 11.

'O'Casey Bans Festival Production', *Irish Times* (Dublin), (24 Aug 1961) p. 6.

'O'Casey', *Irish Times* (Dublin), (25 Aug 1961) p. 7 [leader]. See replies by Gabriel Fallon (26 Aug 1961) p. 7; by Katherine MacCormack (29 Aug 1961) p. 5; by Brendan Behan (29 Aug 1961) p. 5; by Liam

MacAoidh (29 Aug 1961) p. 5; by J. O. G. MacNamara, (31 Aug 1961) p. 7; and by Anthony Mangan (4 Sep 1961) p. 7 [letters to the Editor].

PESSEMESSE, PIERRE, 'Au Théâtre Quotidien de Marseille: *Les Tambours du Père Ned* de Sean O'Casey', *Lettres françaises* (Paris), no. 916 (1–7 Mar 1962) 9.

'O'Casey Played with Spirit. Tower Theatre: *The Drums of Father Ned*', *Times* (London), (22 May 1965) p. 12 [by the Tavistock Repertory Company at the Tower Theatre, London].

BYRNE, P. F., '*Father Ned* Comes to Dublin', *Evening Herald* (Dublin), (4 June 1966) p. 8 [to open on 6 June 1966 at the Olympia Theatre, Dublin].

KELLY, SEAMUS, 'O'Casey Play at the Olympia', *Irish Times* (Dublin), (7 June 1966) p. 6.

O'D., T., ' "Drums" Beat in the Olympia', *Irish Press* (Dublin), (7 June 1966) p. 4.

B., P. F., 'Excellent Acting and Direction in O'Casey Play', *Evening Herald* (Dublin), (7 June 1966) p. 8.

FIGURO IN THE NIGHT

'O'Casey Satire on Censorship', *Sunday Press* (Dublin), (9 Aug 1959) p. 6.

TAUBMAN, HOWARD, 'ANTA Stages 2 New Plays by O'Casey', *New York Times* (31 Oct 1962) p. 33 [at the Theatre de Lys].

'O'Casey Gave Daughter One-Act Play for Young People', *Irish Times* (Dublin), (4 Jan 1965) p. 1.

'Twelve British Actors Star Campus Tour', *New York Times* (30 Jan 1965) p. 17 [one of the bills consists of *Figuro*].

'O'Casey Figaro [sic]', *Stage and Television Today* (London), (26 Nov 1970) p. 18 [to be presented at the Peacock Theatre, Dublin]. See 'O'Casey' by John O'Riordan (31 Dec 1970) p. 14 [letter to the Editor].

THE MOON SHINES ON KYLENAMOE

'Sean O'Casey Gives Play to Telefis', *Sunday Press* (Dublin), (24 June 1962) p. 4 [interview].

TAUBMAN, HOWARD, 'ANTA Stages 2 New Plays by O'Casey', *New York Times* (31 Oct 1962) p. 33 [at the Theatre de Lys].

BEHIND THE GREEN CURTAINS
'O'Casey Satire on Censorship', *Sunday Press* (Dublin), (9 Aug 1959) p. 6.

(d) Reviews of Staged Autobiographies
[This section is arranged chronologically.]

ATKINSON, BROOKS, 'O'Casey Reading', *New York Times* (19 Mar 1956) p. 27 [*I Knock at the Door* at the Kaufman Auditorium].

HEWES, HENRY, 'O'Casey Unbound', *Saturday Review of Literature* (N.Y.), XXXIX (7 Apr 1956) 22.

ATKINSON, BROOKS, 'Autobiography of O'Casey: *Pictures in the Hallway* Given as a Reading', *New York Times* (28 May 1956) p. 23.

HEWES, HENRY, 'Broadway Postscripts: *Pictures in the Hallway*', *Saturday Review of Literature* (N.Y.), XXXIX (16 June 1956) 32.

O'CASEY, SEAN, 'Sidelights on Some "Pictures"', *New York Times* (16 Sep 1956) section 2, pp. 1, 3.

FUNKE, LEWIS, 'Self-Portrait: O'Casey's *Pictures in the Hallway* Returns', *New York Times* (17 Sep 1956) p. 23.

ATKINSON, BROOKS, 'O'Casey Reading: *Pictures in the Hallway* Shows How Prose Can Be Theatricalized', *New York Times* (23 Sep 1956) section 2, p. 1.

WYATT, EUPHEMIA VAN RENSSELAER, '*Pictures in the Hallway*', *Catholic World* (N.Y.), CLXXXIV (Nov 1956) 146.

GASSNER, JOHN, 'Broadway in Review', *Educational Theatre Journal* (Ann Arbor, Mich.), VIII (Dec 1956) 325-6 [*Pictures in the Hallway*].

SHYRE, PAUL, 'O'Casey's Pictures Come to Life', *Theatre Arts* (N.Y.), XLI (Mar 1957) 31-2.

GELB, ARTHUR, 'O'Casey As A Boy', *New York Times* (30 Sep 1957) p. 27 [*I Knock at the Door* at the Belasco Theatre, New York].

'Group Gives Stage Readings of O'Casey', *Irish Times* (Dublin), (1 Oct 1957) p. 4.

HEWES, HENRY, 'Broadway Postscript', *Saturday Review of Literature* (N.Y.), XL (12 Oct 1957) 30.

'Recitation in Manhattan', *Time* (N.Y.), LXX 16 (14 Oct 1957) 50.

CLURMAN, HAROLD 'Theatre', *Nation* (N.Y.), CLXXXV (19 Oct 1957) 272.

DRIVER, Tom F., 'Chamber Drama', *Christian Century* (Chicago), LXXIV (30 Oct 1957) 1288-9.

CRITICISM ON SEAN O'CASEY

WYATT, EUPHEMIA VAN RENSSELAER, 'I Knock at the Door', *Catholic World* (N.Y.), CLXXXVI (Dec 1957) 227.

GASSNER, JOHN, 'Broadway in Review', *Educational Theatre Journal* (Ann Arbor, Mich.), IX (Dec 1957) 315–16.

'I Knock at the Door', *Theatre Arts* (N.Y.), XLI (Dec 1957) 25.

'Crux over O'Casey Recordings', *Irish Times* (Dublin), (30 July 1958) p. 5 ["Sean O'Casey's Pictures in the Hallway" recording by Connoisseur Records Ltd.]. See reply by Gerard P. Sheehy, "O'Casey Records" (9 Aug 1958) p. 7 [letter to the Editor].

ATKINSON, BROOKS, 'Pictures in the Hallway. Phoenix in Revival of O'Casey Work', *New York Times* (28 Dec 1959) p. 19.

ATKINSON, BROOKS, 'The O'Casey', *New York Times* (3 Jan 1960) section 2, p. 1.

GELB, ARTHUR, 'Campaigner in the Cause of Sean O'Casey', *New York Times* (25 Sep 1960) section 2, pp. 1, 3 [*Drums under the Windows* to open at Cherry Lane Theatre on 13 October 1960].

TAUBMAN, HOWARD, 'Cascade of Words from Sean O'Casey: Shyre's *Drums under the Windows* Staged', *New York Times* (14 Oct 1960) p. 26.

BALLIETT, WHITNEY, 'Off Broadway: Turtle Soup', *New Yorker*, XXXVI (22 Oct 1960) 90–3.

DRIVER, TOM F., 'Incorrigible Romantic', *Christian Century* (Chicago), LXXVII (9 Nov 1960) 1320–1.

'Mr O'Casey and His Young Self. Mermaid Theatre: *Pictures in the Hallway*', *Times* (London), (1 Oct 1962) p. 17.

SHEPARD, RICHARD F., 'O'Casey Play: *I Knock at the Door* Opens at de Lys', *New York Times* (26 Nov 1964) p. 53.

OLIVER, EDITH, 'Off Broadway: On the One Hand, on the Other', *New Yorker*, XL (5 Dec 1964) 88–90.

OLIVER, EDITH, 'Off Broadway: *Pictures in the Hallway*', *New Yorker*, XL (26 Dec 1964) 52–3.

QUIDNUNC, 'An Irishman's Diary: Lantern Shines', *Irish Times* (Dublin), (20 July 1967) p. 9 [on *Pictures*].

'At the Reception', *Irish Times* (Dublin), (1 Mar 1968) p. 9 [picture of *I Knock*].

PRO-QUIDNUNC, 'An Irishman's Diary: Knocking Twice', *Irish Times* (9 Mar 1968) p. 11 [on *I Knock*].

KELLY, HENRY, 'Gaiety: Early Years of O'Casey', *Irish Times* (Dublin), (13 Mar 1968) p. 8 [on *I Knock*]. See replies by Philomena

Cunningham and J. J. O'Leary (16 Mar 1968) p. 9 [letters to the Editor].

'David Kelly in the Rôle of Sean O'Casey', *Irish Times* (Dublin), (15 Mar 1968) p. 11 [picture].

KELLY, SEAMUS, 'All the Makings of a Good Show', *Irish Times* (Dublin), (18 July 1968) p. 8 [*Drums under the Windows*, adapted by Patrick Funge and David Krause, produced by P. Funge at the Lantern Theatre, Dublin, on 17 July 1968].

LOWRY, BETTY, 'Two New Irish Plays [*Big Maggie* at the Grove, and *Pictures in the Hallway* at the Lyric]', *Belfast Telegraph* (5 Apr 1969) p. 4.

RAFFERTY, GERALD, 'O'Casey on the Threshold', *Belfast Telegraph* (9 Apr 1969) p. 8.

'*Pictures in the Hallway* at the Lyric', *Irish Times* (Dublin), (10 Apr 1969).

HILL, IAN, 'Belfast Lyric Players: *Pictures in the Hallway*', *Guardian* (London), (10 Apr 1969) p. 10.

'The Lyric Theatre Players Make Most of O'Casey *Pictures*', *Irish News* (Belfast), (10 Apr 1969) p. 5.

STEWART, JOHN D., 'Sean Would Have Been Annoyed', *Sunday News* (Belfast), (13 Apr 1969) p. 6.

MCCREESH, GERARD, 'An Evening with Sean O'Casey', *Sunday Press* (Dublin), (13 Apr 1969).

GUSSOW, MEL, 'Theater: Sean O'Casey. Shyre's Adaptation of "Hallway" at Forum', *New York Times* (1 May 1971).

(e) Reviews of Films

[This section is arranged chronologically.]

SIMPSON, CELIA, 'The Cinema: *Juno and the Paycock*', *Spectator* (London), CXLIV (8 Mar 1930) 363.

'Filmed O'Casey: *The Plough and the Stars*', *Literary Digest* (N.Y.), CXXII (19 Sep 1936) 21–2.

CUNNINGHAM, JAMES P., '*The Plough and the Stars*', *Commonweal* (N.Y.), XXV (8 Jan 1937) 304.

'Irish Tragedy: RKO Presents Faithful Film Version of *The Plough and the Stars*', *Literary Digest* (N.Y.), CXXIII (16 Jan 1937) 23.

R., M. B., '*The Plough and the Stars*', *Scholastic* (Pittsburgh), XXIX (23 Jan 1937) 14, 31.

'Screen: England Stamps Out Ireland's Easter Week Revolt', *Newsweek* (N.Y.), IX (23 Jan 1937) 30.

NUGENT, FRANK S., 'The RKO-Radio Version of *The Plough and the Stars*, by Sean O'Casey, Opens at the Music Hall', *New York Times* (29 Jan 1937) p. 15.

'The New Pictures: *The Plough and the Stars* (RKO)', *Time* (N.Y.), XXIX 5 (1 Feb 1937) 45.

VAN DOREN, MARK, 'Films: *The Plough and the Star* (RKO-Radio)', *Nation* (N.Y.), CXLIV 7 (13 Feb 1937) 194. Partially reprinted in *Private Reader* (New York: Henry Holt, 1942) pp. 351–2.

'Pictures Now Showing: *The Plough and the Stars*', *Stage* (N.Y.), XIV (Feb 1937) 18.

REYNOLDS, HORACE, 'Hollywood Unfurls: *The Plough and the Stars*', *Stage* (N.Y.), XIV (Feb 1937) 54.

'Sean O'Casey Film for Television', *Times* (London), (18 Oct 1955) p. 3 [on O'Casey's life, for the National Broadcasting Company of America].

GOULD, JACK, 'TV: Sean O'Casey Is Interviewed. Irish Playwright Seen on N.B.C. Program', *New York Times* (23 Jan 1956) p. 49.

VAN HORNE, HARRIET, 'Camera Dulls Glow of Elder Wise Men', *New York Herald Telegram and Sun* (24 Jan 1956).

'B.B.C. Television: *Juno and the Paycock* by Sean O'Casey', *Times* (London), (18 Mar 1957) p. 12.

MACLEOD, ALISON, 'You Were Right about *Juno*', *Daily Worker* (London), (19 Mar 1957) p. 2.

'*The Shadow of a Gunman*: Independent Television by Sean O'Casey', *Times* (London), (12 July 1957) p. 5.

SHANLEY, JOHN P., 'Film of O'Casey Deleted', *New York Times* (14 Mar 1960) p. 51 [from 'Ed Sullivan Show' after protests to producer].

'TV Show Drops O'Casey Interview', *Irish Times* (Dublin), (15 Mar 1960) p. 11. See reply by Gabriel Fallon, 'Sean O'Casey' (18 Mar 1960) p. 9; and 'O'Casey Cut in TV Film Condemned' (21 Mar 1960) p. 4.

'Television Catches Play's Impact', *Times* (London), (15 Feb 1961) p. 4 [on *The Plough and the Stars*].

'O'Casey Play for T.E.', *Sunday Review* (Dublin), VI (24 June 1962) 3 [on *The Moon Shines on Kylenamœ*].

'O'Casey One-Act Play To Be Televised', *Irish Times* (Dublin), (25 June 1962) p. 1.

LENNON, PETER, 'French Irishry', *Guardian* (London), (30 Apr 1963) p. 9 [French TV filming *The Plough and the Stars*].

'Film of Young Cassidy', *Times* (London), (13 Sep 1963) p. 13.

'To Appear in Film Based on Early Years of O'Casey', *Irish Times* (Dublin), (16 May 1964) p. 11.

CURTISS, THOMAS QUINN, 'O'Casey, at 84, Is Pleased by Movie on His Life: But "Young Cassidy" Puzzles the Playwright, Too', *New York Times* (21 Aug 1964) p. 16.

' "Young Cassidy" Employees' Wages Stolen', *Irish Times* (Dublin), (22 Aug 1964) p. 5.

WATTS, STEPHEN, 'O'Casey In a Movie "Mirror" ', *New York Times* (27 Sep 1964) section 2, pp. 11, 13 ['Young Cassidy'].

QUIDNUNC, 'An Irishman's Diary: Young Cassidy', *Irish Times* (Dublin), (3 Nov 1964) p. 9.

HIBBIN, NINA, 'O'Casey's Own Genius Needed', *Daily Worker* (London), (27 Feb 1965) p. 3.

LOCKHART, FREDA BRUCE, 'Young Cassidy', *Catholic Herald* (Dublin), (5 Mar 1965) p. 7. See reply by John O'Riordan (12 Mar 1965) p. 5 [letter to the Editor].

DENT, ALAN, 'O'Casey – Cassidy', *Illustrated London News*, CCXLVI (13 Mar 1965) 30.

CROWTHER, BOSLEY, 'Sean O'Casey's Early Years: Rod Taylor Is Starred in "Young Cassidy" ', *New York Times* (23 Mar 1965) p. 35.

CROWTHER, BOSLEY, 'Wearin' of the Green', *New York Times* (28 Mar 1965) section 2, pp. 1, 24.

ATKINSON, BROOKS, 'Movie of Sean O'Casey's Early Years Captures Writer's Romantic Spirit', *New York Times* (6 Apr 1965) p. 36.

GOULD, JACK, 'The World of O'Casey Glows on WNDT', *New York Times* (15 July 1965) p. 59 [part of TV series 'The Creative Person'].

GRAY, KEN, 'Television: A Memorable "Plough" ', *Irish Times* (Dublin), (22 Sep 1966) p. 10.

TAYLOR, DON, 'The Exile', *Radio Times* (London), CLXXVIII (1 Feb 1968) 27 [B.B.C.-1 TV on 6 February 1968 at 10.25–11.25 p.m., 'Omnibus' series].

'ATTICUS' [Philip Oakes], 'New Line on O'Casey', *Sunday Times* (London), (4 Feb 1968) p. 13 [Press preamble on 'The Exile'].

'Briefing: Sean O'Casey. Omnibus Presents "The Exile" ', *Observer* (London), (4 Feb 1968) p. 22.

RAYNOR, HENRY, 'Television: Permissiveness, Drugs, and De-bauchery', *Times* (London), (7 Feb 1968) p. 6.

D.–L., S., 'Excellent "Omnibus" on Sean O'Casey', *Daily Telegraph* (London), (7 Feb 1968) p. 17.

REYNOLDS, STANLEY, 'Television', *Guardian* (London), (7 Feb 1968) p. 6.

GRAY, KEN, 'Television', *Irish Times* (Dublin), (15 Feb 1968) p. 14.

(f) Unpublished Material

ALLT, G. D. P., 'The Anglo-Irish Literary Movement in Relation to Its Antecedents', Ph.D. dissertation, St Catherine's College, Cambridge University, 1952.

AYLING, RONALD, 'The Dramatic Artistry of Sean O'Casey: A Study of Theme and Form in the Plays Written for the Abbey Theatre, 1922–1928', Ph.D. dissertation, University of Bristol, 1968.

BERNARDBEHAN, Brother MERRILL, 'Anglo-Irish Literature', M.A. dissertation, University of Montreal, 1939.

BUCKLEY, IAN, 'An Analysis of the Plays of Sean O'Casey', M.A. dissertation, University of Kent at Canterbury, 1970.

BUTLER, HENRY J., 'The Abbey Theatre and the Principal Writers Connected Therewith', MS. 2263 at the National Library of Ireland, Dublin (Aug 1925).

CASWELL, ROBERT W., 'Sean O'Casey as a Poetic Dramatist', Ph.D. dissertation, Trinity College, Dublin, 1960.

COLE, A. S., 'Stagecraft in the Modern Dublin Theatre', Ph.D. dissertation, Trinity College, Dublin, 1953.

COOPER, MABEL, 'The Irish Theatre: Its History and Its Dramatists', M.A. dissertation, University of Manitoba, 1931.

COSTON, HERBERT HULL, 'The Idea of Courage in the Works of Sean O'Casey', Ph.D. dissertation, Columbia University, 1960. Abstract in *Dissertation Abstracts*, XXI (1960) 619–20.

DANIEL, WALTER C., 'O'Casey and the Comic', Ph.D. dissertation, Bowling Green University, 1963. Abstract in *Dissertation Abstracts*, XXV (1964) 6621–2.

ESSLINGER, PATRICIA MOORE, 'The Dublin *Materia Poetica* of Sean O'Casey', Ph.D. dissertation, Tulane University, 1960. Abstract in *Dissertation Abstracts*, XXI (1961) 2291.

FIRTH, JOHN MIRKIL, 'O'Casey and Autobiography', Ph.D. dissertation, University of Virginia, 1965. Abstract in *Dissertation Abstracts*, XXVI (1966) 6039.

GARRISON, EMERY CLAYTON, 'The Structure of Sean O'Casey's Plays', Ph.D. dissertation, Stanford University, 1956. Abstract in *Dissertation Abstracts*, XVII (1957) 186.

HOGAN, ROBERT, 'Sean O'Casey's Experiments in Dramatic Form', Ph.D. dissertation, University of Missouri, 1956.

HOLLOWAY, JOSEPH, 'Impressions of a Dublin Playgoer', MSS. at the National Library of Ireland, Dublin: MS. 1877 (Apr–June 1923); MS. 1881 (Sep–Dec 1923); MS. 1884 (Jan–Mar 1924); MS. 1885 (Apr–June 1924); MS. 1886 (Apr–June 1924); MS. 1888 (July–Sep 1924); MS. 1889 (Oct–Dec 1924); MS. 1892 (Jan–Mar 1925); MS. 1898 (Oct–Dec 1925); MS. 1899 (Jan–Mar 1926); MS. 1900 (Jan–Mar 1926).

HOWSE, HANS FREDERICK, 'The Plays of Sean O'Casey', M.A. dissertation, University of Liverpool, 1951.

KRAUSE, DAVID, 'Prometheus of Dublin', Ph.D. dissertation, New York University, 1956.

KREGOSKY, JOANNE IRENE, 'O'Casey's Autobiographies and Their Relationship to His Drama', M.A. dissertation, University of Alberta, 1968.

LANDOW, URSULA TRASK, 'O'Casey and His Critics as Seen through the Nathan Correspondence', M.A. dissertation, Cornell University, 1961.

LARSON, GERALD A., 'The Dramaturgy of Sean O'Casey', Ph.D. dissertation, University of Utah, 1957. Abstract in *Dissertation Abstracts*, XVIII (1958) 1147–8.

LOCKLIN, MAE, 'Sean O'Casey: A Critical Study', M.A. dissertation, Queen's University, Kingston, Ontario, 1932.

McGUIRE, JAMES BRADY, 'Realism in Irish Drama', Ph.D. dissertation, Trinity College Dublin, 1954.

MAITRA, LILA, 'Sean O'Casey: A Critical Review', Ph.D. dissertation, University of Calcutta, 1960.

MALONE, M. G., 'The Plays of Sean O'Casey in Relation to Their Political and Social Background', M.A. dissertation, King's College, University of London, 1964.

MAROLDO, WILLIAM JOHN, 'Sean O'Casey and the Art of Autobiography: Form and Content in the Irish Books', Ph.D. dissertation, Columbia University, 1964. Abstract is *Dissertation Abstracts*, XXVI (1965) 1649–50.

MASSEY, J., 'The Development of the Theme in the Plays of Sean O'Casey, with a Study of Some Technical Devices Common to His Plays', M.A. dissertation, Birkbeck College, University of London, 1955.

Moya, Carmela, 'L'Univers de Sean O'Casey', Ph.D. dissertation, Paris University, 1969.

Nordell, Hans Roderick, 'The Dramatic Practice and Theory of Sean O'Casey', B.Litt. dissertation, Trinity College Dublin, 1951.

O'Neill, Michael J., 'The Diaries of a Dublin Playgoer as a Mirror of the Irish Literary Revival', Ph.D. dissertation, National University, Dublin, 1952.

O'Riley, Margaret Catherine, 'The Dramaturgy of Sean O'Casey', Ph.D. dissertation, University of Wisconsin, 1955. Abstract in *Dissertation Abstracts*, XVI (1956) 340.

Palter, Lewis, 'The Comedy in the Plays of Sean O'Casey', Ph.D. dissertation, Northwestern University, 1965. Abstract in *Dissertation Abstracts*, XXVI (1965) 3537.

Peteler, Patricia M., 'The Social and Symbolic Drama of the English-Language Theatre, 1929–1949', Ph.D. dissertation, University of Utah, 1961.

Ritchie, Harry M., 'Form and Content in the Plays of Sean O'Casey', D.F.A. dissertation, Yale University, 1960.

Rollins, Ronald Gene, 'Sean O'Casey: The Man with Two Faces', Ph.D. dissertation, University of Cincinnati, 1960. Abstract in *Dissertation Abstracts*, XXI (1961) 2721.

Saddlemyer, E. A., 'A Study of the Dramatic Theory Developed by the Founders of the Irish Literary Theatre and the Attempt to Apply This Theory in the Abbey Theatre, with Particular Reference to the Achievements of the Major Figures during the First Two Decades of the Movement', Ph.D. dissertation, Bedford College, University of London, 1961.

Smith, Bobby L., 'Satire in the Drama of Sean O'Casey', Ph.D. dissertation, University of Oklahoma, 1965. Abstract in *Dissertation Abstracts*, XXVI (1965) 1655.

Smyth, Dorothy Pearl, 'The Playwrights of the Irish Literary Renaissance', M.A. dissertation, Acadia University, 1936.

Suss, Irving David, 'The Decline and Fall of Irish Drama', Ph.D. dissertation, Columbia University, 1951.

Templeton, Alice Joan, 'Expressionism in British and American Drama', Ph.D. dissertation, University of Oregon, 1966. Abstract in *Dissertation Abstracts*, XXVII (1966).

Thomas, Noel K., 'The Major Plays of Sean O'Casey Considered in the Light of Their Theatrical Production and Critical Reception', Ph.D. dissertation, University of Birmingham, 1963.

WILLIAMSON, WARD, 'An Analytical History of American Criticism of the Works of Sean O'Casey, 1924–1958', Ph.D. dissertation, State University of Iowa, 1962. Abstract in *Dissertation Abstracts*, XXIII (1962) 1713.

WORTH, KATHARINE J., 'Symbolism in Modern English Drama', Ph.D. dissertation, University of London, 1953.

Index of Works

In these indexes the figures in parentheses after page numbers indicate the number of references.

Index of Authors

A., E., 121
A., E. S., 93
A., H., 121
A., J. D., 13
Abirached, Robert, 47
Adamov, Arthur, 47
Adams, Phoebe Lou, 129
Addison, Alan, 80, 103
Adelman, Irving, 3
A. E. (George Russell), 8
Agate, James, 10 (2), 23, 39, 78, 82, 92, 99 (2), 105 (2), 109, 111, 116
Aickman, Robert Fordyce, 111
Alexander, Leon, 106
Alldridge, John, 47
Allen, John, 14, 23, 110
Allen, Ralph, 47
Allison, Alexander W., 23
Allsop, Kenneth, 19
Allt, G. D. P., 139
Alsop, Joseph, Jr, 47
Alvarez, A., 121
Anderson, Maxwell, 23, 47
Arden, John, 20, 76
Armstrong, William A., 3, 23, 47
Arns, Karl, 46
Arundel, Honor, 86
Atkinson, Brooks, 3, 7, 10, 11, 13 (2), 15, 16, 17, 18 (2), 19, 20, 24, 28, 36, 48, 78, 79 (3), 83 (2), 84 (2), 86 (4), 87 (3), 92, 93 (2), 94, 100 (2), 102, 106 (2), 107, 109 (2), 112, 113, 116, 119, 120 (2), 122, 123 (4), 124, 134 (3), 135 (2), 138
'Atticus' (Philip Oakes), 138
Ayling, Ronald, 3, 19, 20, 23, 24, 26, 27 (2), 28, 29, 30 (3), 35 (2), 36, 37, 38 (4), 39, 40 (2), 44, 48–9, 51, 56, 58, 59, 60, 62, 67 (2), 70, 74, 76, 82, 92, 99, 100, 103, 139

B., A., 46
B., C., 85
B., C. H., 83
B., D. F., 115, 118
B., D. W., 83
B., F. R., 94
B., F. W., 8
B., G., 82
B., G. W., 20, 99
B., I., 9 (2), 82, 99, 105
B., J. G., 99, 105
B., M., 101

B., P. F., 133
B.-W., J., 100
Bachmann, C. H., 49
Baggett, Patricia, 49
Bain, Bruce, 15
Baker, Bert, 97
Baker, F. G., 79, 122
Balashov, Peter, 24
Balliett, Whitney, 95, 135
Ballou, Jenny, 13
Banks, Paul, 9
Barber, John, 103, 125
Barker, Dudley, 108 (2)
Barker, Felix, 89, 96, 103, 130
Barnes, Clive, 122, 130
Barnet, Sylvan, 24
Barrett, James, 128
Barrett, Larry, 84
Barrington, Maeve, 128
Barrows, Herbert, 24
Barton, Ralph, 100
Barzun, Jacques, 49
Bastable, Adolphus, 89
Baughan, E. A., 105
Beaufort, John, 116
Beckerman, Bernard, 25
Beckett, Samuel, 10, 50
Beckles, Gordon, 104
Behan, Brendan, 50, 132
Behan, Marie, 129
Bellak, George, 50
Benchley, Robert, 106
Bennett, Eric, 109
Benstock, Bernard, 50
Bentley, Eric, 12, 16, 25, 50, 113
Bergh, Mary, 38
Bergholz, Harry, 25, 50
Berman, Morton, 24
Bernardbehan, Brother Merrill, 139
Birrell, Francis, 78
Bishop, George W., 25, 50, 118
Black, Hester M., 3, 25
Blake, Ben, 107
Blake, Douglas, 104
Blankfort, Michael, 107
Blanshard, Paul, 25
Blau, Herbert, 25
Block, Haskell M., 25
Blythe, Ernest, 25, 29
Boas, Cicely, 17
Boas, Guy, 25, 50

INDEX OF AUTHORS

INDEX OF AUTHORS